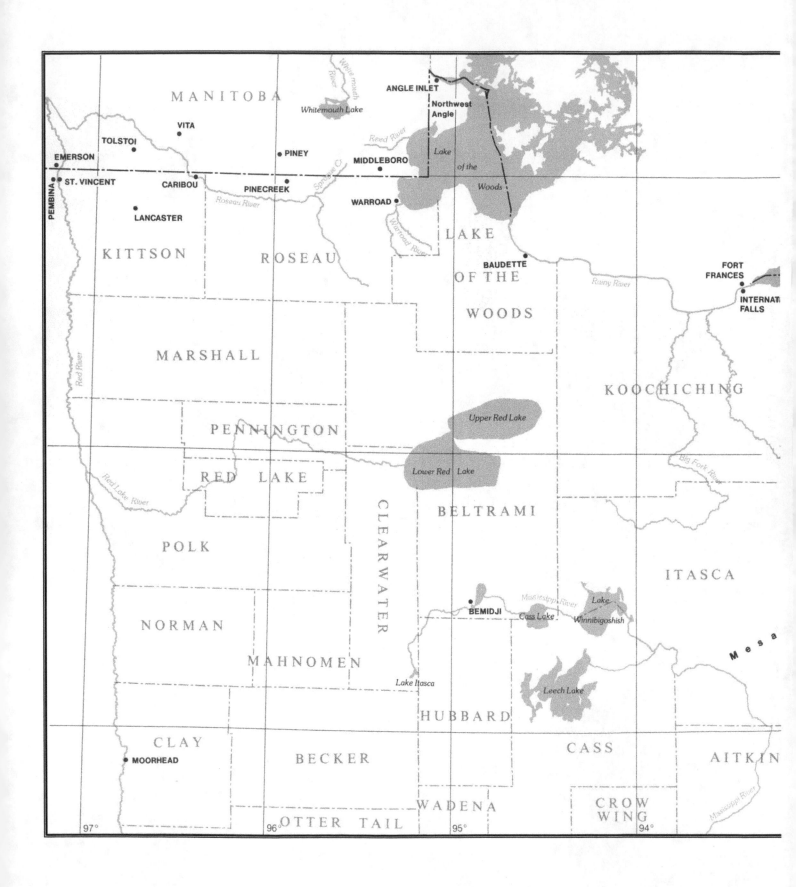

THE MINNESOTA - CANADA BOUNDARY

ONTARIO

49°

Senavine River

Dog River

Lac des Mille Lacs

Baril
Lake

Windigoostiguan
Lake

Pickerel Lake

Rainy Lake

NATIONAL

Kabetogama Lake

Namakan River

Sturgeon
Lake

Height of Land

THUNDER BAY
FORT WILLIAM

Dog
Lake

Namakan L.
Sand Point Lake

Maligne River

Lac la Croix

Crane Lake

Loon
Lake

Crooked
Lake

Hunter Island

Kaministikwia River

Vermillion River

Cypress
Lake

Saganaga Lake

North
Lake

Arrow Lake

Arrow River

Basswood Lake

Gunflint
Lake

Rose Lake

Moose Lake
No. Fowl L.
So. Fowl L.

Pigeon R.

48°

FORT CHARLOTTE

Grand Portage

Little Fork River

ELY

Vermilion Lake

Vermilion Iron Range

TOWER

Embarrass River

Pike River

Iron   Range

LAKE

COOK

GRAND PORTAGE
POST

Trail

LAKE

SUPERIOR

ST. LOUIS

St. Louis River

TWO
HARBORS

47°

Apostle

Islands

DULUTH

SUPERIOR

CARLTON

93°   92°   91°   90°

Minnesota's Boundary with Canada

Its Evolution since 1783

By WILLIAM E. LASS

MINNESOTA HISTORICAL SOCIETY PRESS • ST. PAUL • 1980

2006 reprint of 1980 edition

ON THE COVER: *The Minnesota-Ontario boundary winds westward across Crooked Lake. Photo by Bill Tefft, courtesy United States Department of Agriculture, Forest Service.*

Library of Congress Cataloging in Publication Data:
Lass, William E
    Minnesota's boundary with Canada.

    (Publications - Minnesota Historical Society, Public Affairs Center)
    Bibliography: p.
    Includes index.
    1. Northern boundary of the United States.
2. Minnesota — Boundaries — Canada. 3. Canada — Boundaries — Minnesota.
I. Title. II. Series: Minnesota Historical Society. Public Affairs Center.
Publications.
F597.L37   341.4'2'026673071   80-21644

International Standard Book Number: 0-87351-147-6 Hard Cover
                                    0-87351-153-0 Paper Cover

Manufactured in the United States of America

TO BARBARA AND BILL
whose boundaries lie ahead

Preface

THE BOUNDARY between the United States and Canada is far more than a line on a map or a demarcation on the ground. In a broad sense, it represents the aspirations, successes, frustrations, failures, and compromises of the two largest countries on the North American continent. Behind this unfortified boundary lies an intriguing story that had its beginnings in the 18th century. By pursuing the twists and turns of the boundary's history, readers will emerge with a better understanding of American-Canadian relations as well as of the development of Minnesota and the contiguous Canadian provinces of Ontario and Manitoba.

A long-standing popular interest has existed in the portion of the boundary that lies between Minnesota and Canada. Curiosity about this region has been piqued by the presence of the Boundary Waters Canoe Area, Quetico Provincial Park, and by the chimneylike Northwest Angle, that seeming aberration of man's rationality. Over the years the United States Department of State and the Minnesota Historical Society, among other agencies, have been asked many times to explain the reason for that tag end of Minnesota isolated and alone on the Canadian side of Lake of the Woods.

My interest in the Minnesota-Canada boundary was first provoked by the necessity of explaining it to college classes in Minnesota history. I soon determined that available published sources raised as many questions as they answered. The boundary is discussed in a general way in diplomatic histories of the United States and Canada and in survey histories of Minnesota, Manitoba, and Ontario; there are also dozens of articles in periodicals dealing with various episodes in its history. But most of the available material is heavily based on secondary sources. Thus certain factual errors are repeated time and again, while other aspects of the story are never treated at all.

I therefore determined to study the topic thoroughly, using all the primary sources I could identify and to which I could gain access, with the aim of writing a comprehensive history of that portion of the United States-Canada boundary which forms the northern border of Minnesota. This book is the result. I hope it will answer many of the recurring questions concerning a fascinating and important, but often overlooked, aspect of American-Canadian relations.

During the preparation of this history I have benefited from the assistance of numerous institutions and individuals. June D. Holmquist, assistant director for publications and research at the Minnesota Historical Society, encouraged me to undertake the work and offered valuable counsel throughout. The early research was supported by grants from the Society's Public Affairs Center and the Faculty Research Council of Mankato State University. Dr. Milton O. Gustafson, chief of the Diplomatic Branch, National Archives and Records Service, Washington, D.C., was very helpful to me during periods of research in the nation's capital. Staff members in the United States and Canadian offices of the International Boundary Commission generously provided information while I was in Washington and Ottawa. I am particularly indebted to A. F. Lambert, former commissioner of the Canadian section, and to Marie A. Sheehy, former administrative officer, and Francis X. Popper, engineer, in the United States section. Several colleagues at Mankato State University also provided significant assistance. Marilyn Montgomery and Phyllis Roberts of the Memorial Library staff obtained numerous items through interlibrary loan, and Dr. Thomas L. Moir of the history department graciously answered many questions about the nature of British government and society.

Preparation of the manuscript was furthered by typists Carolyn Sandvig and June Sonju and the research assistance of Ann Regan. The front end-sheet map of Minnesota's northern border and the back end-sheet map of the entire United States-Canada boundary—both essential to following the evolution of the line—plus additional maps and the book's design are the work of Alan Ominsky. I extend special thanks to Jean A. Brookins, managing editor of the Minnesota Historical Society's Publications and Research Division, who edited and improved the manuscript. Unless otherwise credited, the maps and photographs on the following pages are from the collections of the society.

As with all of my earlier books, my wife Marilyn was a constant helpmate in her numerous roles of researcher, typist, counselor, and critic.

WILLIAM E. LASS

Contents

Maps

Introduction

THE PROCESS of defining, surveying, and marking the almost 4,000-mile border between Canada and the contiguous United States spanned nearly a century and a half. The determination of this boundary, a necessary concomitant of the western expansion of both nations, frequently strained diplomatic relations and was at times a major cause of friction between the two countries. Yet despite its significance in the diplomatic history of Great Britain and the United States, the boundary question was just one of many issues. Sometimes it was the most important point of consideration, but it was never the only one; such controversial matters as the impressment of seamen, fishing rights in the Atlantic, and Indian policy were concurrent problems at various periods over the years. Therefore, although the story of the boundary can be isolated as a historical theme, it must be told within the broad context of Anglo-American diplomatic relations.

The drawing of the entire United States-Canada boundary from the Atlantic to the Pacific was accomplished in four major agreements—the Treaty of Paris in 1783 which ended the Revolutionary War, the London Convention of 1818, the Webster-Ashburton Treaty of 1842, and the Oregon boundary settlement of 1846. All but the last of these affected the Minnesota-Canada section.

In the Paris treaty, British and American envoys agreed to separate Canada and the United States by a line running from the Atlantic Ocean to the northwest point of Lake of the Woods in what is now western Ontario. This provision, which affected the very heart of the continent, was predicated on the assumptions that the Mississippi River would be the western boundary of the United States and that a line drawn due west from the northwest point of Lake of the Woods would touch that river. Within a decade, when the geographical ignorance of the diplomats was revealed and British feelings toward the United States had hardened, Great Britain sought to modify drastically this line. Any of the several British proposals made during the 1790s would have given much of present-day Minnesota to Canada. Only after the British proved that the Mississippi River started south rather than northwest of Lake of the Woods was the United States willing to consider a change in its northern boundary. This proposed change, which was one of the subjects of a projected 1803 convention, would have closed the gap by drawing a line from Lake of the Woods south to the source of the Mississippi. Fortunately for the United States, the Louisiana Purchase agreement with France, concluded only days before the boundary treaty with Great Britain, raised a much broader question—that of the limits of Louisiana Territory.

Because the bounds of Louisiana were not fixed in the purchase agreement (and indeed were unknown), the United States chose not to limit itself in the Northwest, but rather to attempt to push its western claims at least as far as the Rocky Mountains. In 1807 Great Britain and the United States for the first time seriously considered the 49th parallel as a possible line for the vast region stretching across the plains from Lake of the Woods to the continental divide. Although this first diplomatic effort was aborted by the failure to resolve more crucial maritime issues, it opened the way for the London Convention of 1818, which extended the boundary from the northwest point of Lake of the Woods to the 49th parallel and then along the 49th to the crest of the Rocky Mountains. Projected to run from the end of the 1783 line at the northwest point of Lake of the Woods, the boundary agreed upon by the London Convention roughly divided the Minnesota-Canada portion into eastern and western sections. The eastern section from Lake Superior through the connecting waterways of the old fur trade route to Lake of the Woods was, like most of the 1783 line, a water boundary, reflecting the diplomats' preference for a natural demarcation. The western portion, however, was simply an overland course drawn across the Great Plains in keeping with the mistaken notion that the 49th parallel had earlier been selected by British and French commissioners appointed under the provisions of the 1713 Treaty of Utrecht which ended the War of Spanish Succession.

Several years before the 1818 agreement was negotiated the United States successfully resisted the last serious British effort to readjust the 1783 line. As the War of 1812 drew to a close, Great Britain, whose traders and Indian allies occupied most of the area north of the Ohio River, demanded a radical southward shift of the 1783 treaty line. During peace negotiations, however, the United States steadfastly protected the integrity of the Revolutionary War settlement and agreed only to a survey of the somewhat ambiguous demarcation of 1783 with its reference to a mysterious "Long Lake."

One of the four boundary articles in the Treaty of Ghent in 1815 applied specifically to the area that is now Minnesota as far west as the northwest point of Lake of the Woods. But the joint survey commission created under that pact did not begin its work until 1822. During four successive years of field work British and American surveyors concentrated on the section from the mouth of the

Pigeon River through the Lake of the Woods. In spite of their general belief that the Pigeon River was the unknown Long Lake specified in the 1783 treaty, both sides made extreme claims—the British seeking a boundary along the St. Louis River near present Duluth and the Americans asking for a demarcation farther north along the Kaministikwia waterway running west from Lake Superior at modern Thunder Bay, Ontario. Although these differences were finally compromised, the British and American commissioners could not settle the boundary west of Lake Superior because of a major disagreement over the disposition of navigation channels between Lakes Huron and Superior. In 1827 the last survey commission under the Treaty of Ghent adjourned *sine die*, and its final reports were shelved for over a decade.

A controversy over the eastern or New England end of the border in the 1830s and 1840s revived interest in the entire line east of Lake of the Woods. In the course of amicably settling Maine's northern boundary, Great Britain and the United States also resolved to agree on a line from Lake Superior to the northwest point of Lake of the Woods, which they thought might be a cause of future antagonisms. Believing that it was best to delineate boundaries before the land was settled, Daniel Webster, the United States secretary of state, and Lord Ashburton, Britain's special envoy, clarified once and for all the ambiguities of the 1783 document and ended the diplomatic phase of the Minnesota-Canada boundary by signing the Webster-Ashburton Treaty of 1842.

After that, the boundary story deals with surveying the line, a feat accomplished in two major projects. The first, carried out in the 1870s, surveyed the 49th parallel. The second, completed in the 20th century, resurveyed and remonumented the entire Canada-United States border. In both instances the work was necessary to calm American and Canadian settlers. That of the 1870s, from the northwest point of Lake of the Woods to the crest of the Rockies, quieted the Minnesota-inspired threat to annex much of central and western Canada. It placed monuments along the section which runs through the rich Red River Valley of the North. At that time the section east of Lake of the Woods was not an issue because frontiersmen had not yet recognized the region's potential. Before many years passed, however, miners, lumbermen, fishermen, and farmers pushed their way into the remote area to the east, which the surveyors of the 1820s had

thought so inhospitable it would not be settled for centuries. By the mid-1890s Americans and Canadians had made numerous overlapping claims to lands about the island-studded lakes of the old "voyageur's highway" of the fur trade, along which ran the border between Minnesota and Ontario. This situation prompted the systematic surveying and monumenting of the line from Lake Superior to Lake of the Woods, a project that was part of the resurvey of the entire boundary authorized by the Treaty of 1908.

Work on the Minnesota-Canada border under the 1908 treaty carried over into the 1920s, and the final reports of the survey teams were not completed until the 1930s. By 1926 the Minnesota section was at last identified on the ground by hundreds of markers. One important outgrowth was the resurveying of the elusive northwest point of Lake of the Woods, a new definition of which was included in a 1925 treaty between the United States and Canada. This agreement was the first boundary pact to be negotiated by Canada, which had by then taken over jurisdiction of its foreign affairs from Great Britain. It was also the last of the long series of boundary treaties dating back to the close of the Revolutionary War. Since 1925 Canada and the United States have co-operatively maintained their mutual border by means of a joint International Boundary Commission.

During the 142 years separating the first and the last boundary treaties, relations between the United States and its northern neighbor improved greatly. Both the British and the Americans had some difficulty allaying the residual bitterness from their two wars—the Revolution and the War of 1812. This heritage of hostilities was undoubtedly part of the reason that war was considered by the nations as a way of resolving such boundary controversies as those in New England, Oregon, and the San Juan Islands lying in the straits between Vancouver Island and the Pacific coast mainland. American Anglophobia persisted in the background as late as the 1908 treaty, and a complete reconciliation with Great Britain and Canada did not occur until the three countries experienced the unifying effects of alliance in World War I. Only since that war has there existed the tradition of good will between the United States and Canada which is reflected in a boundary that is largely unguarded. How the Minnesota portion of that line evolved over 142 years is the subject of the chapters that follow.

CHAPTER 1

The Revolutionary War Boundary Settlement

THE REVOLUTIONARY WAR is so closely associated with Lexington, Concord, Valley Forge, Yorktown, and other places on the Atlantic seaboard that its effects on the Canada-United States boundary all the way west to Lake of the Woods are sometimes difficult to comprehend. The western frontier did not figure in the causes of the war, nor were the battles generally fought there. Nevertheless the struggle enabled the United States to succeed Great Britain as the dominant power in most of the vast, unoccupied region east of the Mississippi River. The territorial gains made by the United States under the provisions of the Treaty of 1783 not only disturbed the British traders in the back country, they unsettled the new nation's French and Spanish allies as well.

Up to 1760 and Great Britain's decisive victory at Montreal during the French and Indian War, westward expansion by English colonists had been frustrated by French possession of most of the area west of the Appalachian Mountains. This ownership had not gone unchallenged, however, for Virginia and four other colonies, whose original charters had granted them great tracts of land running from the Atlantic to the Pacific, regarded the French as trespassers. Moreover New York, because of its protectorate over the Iroquois Indian confederation, had laid claim to land in the Ohio Valley. Peculiarly these western land claims were both strengthened and curtailed by the Treaty of Paris of 1763 that ended the Seven Years' War in Europe and its American phase, the French and Indian War. By this treaty France ceded to Great Britain all its land east of the Mississippi except for the settlement of New Orleans in Louisiana Territory. In the meantime France had relinquished Louisiana Territory to Spain, so the 1763 treaty really divided most of North America between Great Britain and Spain, with the Mississippi River as the western limit of British claims south of the Great Lakes. The removal of the French shadow validated colonial charters, and the English title to the lands east of the Mississippi became firmly established for the first time.[1]

The placement of a northern boundary of the English-speaking colonies developed from British efforts to provide a long-range administrative structure for Canada and the frontier. With the expulsion of France from the mainland of North America, Great Britain had finally prevailed over its perennial enemy. But the satisfaction of victory was diminished by a host of new problems. As masters of a large North American wilderness, British leaders did not wish to follow a costly war with an expensive military occupation of the frontier west of the Appalachians. On the other hand, they feared losing the area in the event of another conflict with France. Their solution was embodied in the broadly conceived Royal Proclamation of 1763, which, among other things, drew a boundary between the English- and French-speaking colonies.[2]

During their long colonial rivalry in North America, Great Britain and France had never agreed on a line separating their possessions. Once the British had a free hand, however, they moved quickly to restrict the size of Canada. Under the Royal Proclamation, Canada officially became the province of Quebec, bounded on the south by a line that followed the highlands from the Atlantic to the head of the Connecticut River in present northern New Hampshire, the 45th parallel westward from the Connecticut to the St. Lawrence, and a straight line from the St. Lawrence to the southeast corner of Lake Nipissing, a large lake about 50 miles northeast of Lake Huron. The boundary ran northeast from Lake Nipissing hundreds of miles to the head of the St. Jean River near the 53rd parallel, then southwesterly along that stream to the Gulf of St. Lawrence.

The intention of the proclamation was to sever Quebec from the interior of the continent, which had a natural geographic and economic association with the St. Lawrence Valley. Then in case Canada were ever restored to France, the boundary of the new province would help quash any French claim to the hinterland to the south and west. Allied with the motive of exterminating French claims was the fervent British desire to bring peace to the frontier by leaving the West as a great Indian reserve. By drawing the southern boundary of Quebec and forbidding settlement west of the Appalachians, the framers of the Royal Proclamation left the West outside the jurisdiction of any civil government. They reasoned that the Indians could be gradually and peacefully pushed aside in favor of an English-speaking colony in the Ohio Valley, which would provide further refutation of any latent French claim.[3]

Although Americans railed for many years against Great Britain's refusal to open the West, they ultimately benefited from the Royal Proclamation, because it established the tradition of the southern boundary of Quebec.

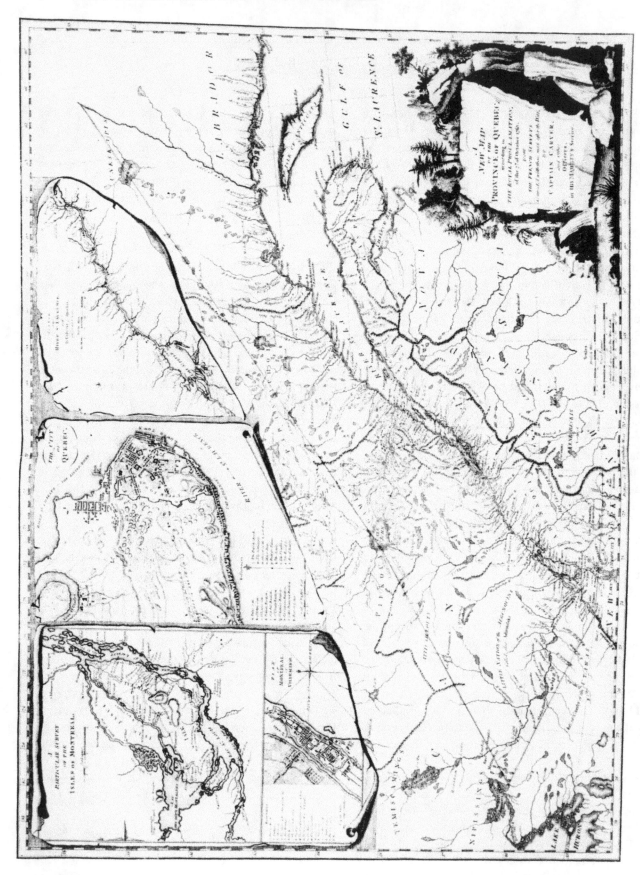

UNDER THE ROYAL PROCLAMATION of 1763 Great Britain established the boundaries of the province of Quebec, shown on this map, which separated English- and French-speaking colonies and set off the province from the interior of the continent.

It is true that this boundary was drastically, albeit temporarily, changed by the Quebec Act of 1774, which extended that province to the Ohio River on the south and the Mississippi on the west. Unfortunately for Great Britain, this act, although intended to provide a political framework for the area and to control the fur trading system to the advantage of the Indians, coincided with Parliament's notorious punitive legislation of 1774 which so incensed the colonies. It became to American patriots one of the Intolerable Acts and thus one of the causes of the Revolutionary War. Believing that the act had also violated colonial charters, members of the Continental Congress in 1779 readily swept aside any suggestions of its legitimacy.[4]

While the British restricted the westward movement of settlers, they encouraged such carefully licensed ventures as the fur trade and the search for the Northwest Passage—the supposed all-water route to the Pacific—in the area west of Lake Superior. These activities, which were a continuation of the traditional French wilderness goals, were permitted because it was believed they would not upset the Indians and could be economically rewarding. Even before the close of the French and Indian War, Alexander Henry, the elder, of New Jersey, who was to emerge as one of the principal back-country British traders, was authorized to move to Michilimackinac, the post at the Straits of Mackinac, and trade in the Lake Superior region. Henry did not cross the lake to Grand Portage in present northeastern Minnesota until 1775, but some of his men, with other Canadians, soon became regular visitors at the celebrated rendezvous there and throughout its vast hinterland stretching west beyond Lake of the Woods and Lake Winnipeg to northwestern Canada.[5]

Grand Portage served the British as it had the French—it was the break-in-bulk point where the huge Montreal canoes had to stop. At this outpost cargo was exchanged for furs, and the trade goods destined for the interior were carefully packed for the nine-mile portage overland to Fort Charlotte, a depot on the Pigeon River. The beginnings of the lively trade at Grand Portage are obscure, though some clues are provided by observant visitors. When Yankee explorer Jonathan Carver arrived in 1767, it was evident that the place had been active for some time, for he found Cree and Assiniboin Indians awaiting the arrival of the Mackinac traders with whom they had dealt in the past.

During the next decade rival traders constructed four palisaded cabins at the post. From there Montreal merchants such as Peter Pond and Joseph and Thomas Frobisher extended their activities into the present Saskatchewan country and westward to the Athabasca region of Alberta. By 1778 the business passing through Grand Portage was worth £40,000 and employed 500 people. In 1780 nearly 300 men worked the area inland from the post.[6]

In view of the flourishing British fur trade that existed before the Revolutionary War, it might be assumed that Grand Portage and its water route to the interior were well known by the time the American colonies proclaimed their independence from Great Britain. Such was not the case. The post's importance, or even its existence, was not common knowledge among either American or British political leaders. In an age when communication took months, news about the back country was neither quickly nor accurately circulated. If political leaders had any information at all, it was apt to be impressions rather than facts. Although the leading British traders later found it hard to believe that so little was known of their activities, they were virtually operating in a vacuum, cut off from the seaboard colonies and the mother country, when the American Revolution came.

During the early phases of the revolution the rebels gave little thought to the interior of the continent. But George Rogers Clark's conquest of the Illinois country, which came on the heels of the alliance with France, helped rekindle a long-standing American interest in the Ohio River Valley. Then in June, 1779, after failing to force Britain to cede Gibraltar in return for Spanish neutrality, Spain entered the war as a nominal ally of France and the American rebels.[7]

Both France and the United States believed Spain's entry would force the British to sue for peace. The French had in fact begun planning for such a contingency months before the Spanish declaration of war. On February 9, 1779, Conrad Alexandre Gérard, the French minister to the United States, notified Congress that it should prepare for negotiations at Madrid. Reacting to rumors of a possible separate peace between the United States and Great Britain, Gérard was anxious to involve the new country in a settlement that would include both France and Spain. He assumed the role of conciliator and voiced the opinion that Britain would be willing to end the war if the United States made only moderate demands.[8]

To Gérard's dismay the ensuing congressional debates over the wording of peace demands revealed fundamental differences between American expansionists and French officials. New Englanders were bent on acquiring Nova Scotia and fishing rights. Southerners, especially, wanted to extend American claims to the Mississippi and secure navigation rights on that stream. Gérard worked to minimize these territorial claims. He argued that the boundaries of the new nation should define the areas that the various states had occupied as colonies, because the Proclamation of 1763 and the Quebec Act of 1774 had stripped them of broader claims. Apparently instructed by the wily Comte de Vergennes, the French foreign minister, Gérard's aims were twofold: he wanted to be able to reassert French claims to Canadian fishing waters in later bargaining with the British, and he wanted to use the Mississippi Valley as bait to lure Spain into the war. Then as later, French diplomacy was predicated on the notion that all lands south of the Ohio River should pass to the Spanish. Obviously France did not wish to promote a large, potentially powerful United States, but preferred a division of the spoils in order to achieve a balance of power in North America.

Some New Englanders supported the French view that the United States was not fighting the war for territorial gain, because they believed that demands for western lands would lessen their chances of retaining fishing rights in the Atlantic off Canada. The advocates of westward expansion, however, pushed through Congress on March 19, 1779, a resolution calling for the northern boundary of the United States to follow the southern border of Quebec, as decreed by the Royal Proclamation of 1763, and then to continue straight west from Lake Nipissing to the Mississippi. The western boundary would follow the Mississippi southward from its source to 31 degrees north latitude—the parallel that is now the border between Louisiana and Mississippi. As a concession to critics of the northern boundary claim, Congress provided that if the line from Lake Nipissing to the Mississippi River "cannot be obtained without continuing the war for that purpose, then, that a line or lines may be drawn more southerly," but not below the 45th parallel.[9]

The March resolution was attacked by some congressmen and by Gérard, but it was only slightly modified during five more months of bickering over peace terms. The former colonies' determination to achieve the expansionist boundaries was made abundantly clear to both their reluctant allies and to Great Britain when Congress, on August 14, 1779, made the territorial demands an indispensable condition of peace. The only further congressional concession related to the northeast boundary, which was to be negotiable in the same manner as the Lake Nipissing and Mississippi River line.[10]

In framing their boundary demands, congressmen emphasized the validity of the original colonial charters of the landed states and the significance of the Royal Proclamation of 1763. Although they were well aware of Clark's conquest of the Ohio Valley, they did not base any territorial claims on it, because they did not want to suggest even obliquely the possibility of negotiating boundaries on the basis of military occupation at war's end. Instead they took the position that the West was legally part of the states before the military conquests—a philosophy that would be carried through the Paris peace negotiations of 1782–83.

The congressional peace terms of 1779, which included the demand that Great Britain formally recognize the independence of the United States, were entrusted to John Adams. He was sent to Paris as the sole minister plenipotentiary to negotiate both a peace treaty and a commercial agreement with Great Britain. After arriving in February, 1780, Adams languished for months on his abortive mission. King George III was still adamant in his war aims, and Vergennes, without openly stating his resistance to the boundary desires of the United States, persisted in his aim of limiting American territorial gains.[11]

While Adams fretted about his cool reception in Paris and John Jay, the United States minister to Spain, was having an equally frustrating experience in his efforts to enlist Spanish aid, Vergennes, through the Chevalier de la Luzerne, the new French minister to the United States, influenced Congress to adopt revised instructions on June 15, 1781. Wishing to negate the authority of the trenchant Adams, La Luzerne suggested that Congress enlarge the peace mission, dwelling on the theme that Adams acting alone had too much power. Congressmen, succumbing to La Luzerne's pressure and perhaps not trusting Adams to represent the interests of all sections, increased the mission to five by adding Benjamin Franklin, John Jay, Henry Laurens, and Thomas Jefferson. La Luzerne hoped this change might lead the American commissioners to propose peace on the basis of *uti possidetis,* or actual occupation, which Vergennes believed was a reasonable territorial request. The Frenchman's optimism was well placed. Under the new instructions, the boundary article and all other demands except independence were no longer essential. Although Congress expressed a preference for the borders it had demanded in 1779, the commissioners were simply instructed to negotiate boundaries "in such a manner as circumstances may direct, and as the state of the belligerent and the disposition of the mediating powers may require." In addition, they were to "make the most candid and confidential communications upon all subjects to the ministers of our generous ally, the King of France," and "ultimately to govern yourselves by their advice and opinion."[12]

Peace prospects appeared quite dim in June, 1781, because of the persistent British pursuit of a military victory in America, the French desire to humiliate Great Britain, and the Spanish quest for the restoration of Gibraltar. They brightened considerably, however, after General Washington's decisive victory over Lord Cornwallis at Yorktown in October. The defeat laid bare the lofty pretensions of Lord North's wartime ministry and set off in England a renewed public outcry for peace. The North administration, in the face of harshly critical public opinion and bitter attacks from its opponents in Parliament, lasted only until March 20, 1782.[13]

Presuming North's fall and anticipating the elevation of a more amiable administration, Benjamin Franklin, then the only United States commissioner present in Paris, wrote to Lord Shelburne, a previous acquaintance who he correctly thought would soon rise to a position of power. By the time he received Franklin's letter, Shelburne had become secretary of state for the southern department, which had jurisdiction over the colonies in the new ministry of Lord Rockingham. He hastened to respond positively to Franklin's expressed hope for a general peace.[14]

While Shelburne was eager to proceed with negotiations, he had no intention of facing the united allies at a grand conference and exposing his country to the risk of losing everything, including Gibraltar. Instead he hoped that a conciliatory approach might cause the United States to treat separately with Great Britain, despite American commitments under the French alliance. With this in mind, Shelburne decided that his best tactic would be to open informal meetings with Franklin. His choice of Richard Oswald for this mission is understandable only if Shelburne's desire to win the good will of the United States is kept in mind.[15]

Oswald, a 77-year-old Scottish merchant residing in London, was a man of considerable influence but woefully lacking in diplomatic experience. After a merchandising career in Glasgow he had become a supply contractor for English troops in Germany during the Seven Years' War. This business and an advantageous marriage, through which he inherited extensive properties in the American mainland colonies and the West Indies, made him extremely wealthy. He added to his fortunes after the war by engaging in the slave trade to America. Henry Laurens had worked as Oswald's agent selling slaves in Charleston, South Carolina.

Because of his American connections and his familiarity with colonial men and affairs, Oswald had often been consulted by the British government during the Revolutionary War. In 1777, while visiting Paris, he had met both Franklin and Vergennes, and he had been introduced to Shelburne by the famed Adam Smith, who profoundly influenced both Oswald and Shelburne with his advocacy of laissez-faire economics.

For Shelburne's purposes Oswald's naiveté and inexperience were more than offset by his earlier ties to Henry Laurens, his former agent and one of the United States peace commissioners, and by his previous meeting with Franklin. Shelburne followed the opening move in his peace campaign with a gesture of good will calculated to soothe American tempers: he and Oswald effected the release of Laurens from the Tower of London. Laurens had been imprisoned for over a year after being apprehended by a British warship while sailing to Europe to assume his diplomatic duties. The congenial Oswald even posted most of the prisoner's bail.

Shelburne's desire to co-operate and to restore good relations between the two countries was emphasized by Oswald in his first meetings with Franklin in April, 1782, at the latter's quarters in the Parisian suburb of Passy. The guileless Scotsman, impressed by Franklin's international fame, did not really know how to proceed. By overstressing the British wish for a reconciliation, he made it easy for Franklin to propose a simple solution to the boundary question and all related problems. The American commissioner suggested that Great Britain, as the aggressor, should be willing to make a "voluntary Offer of Canada" for the purpose of conciliation. Such a cession, he reasoned, would help rectify the great injustices of the war to the United States and would, moreover, save Great Britain the considerable expense of governing and defending Canada. Oswald readily agreed in principle with the idea and promised to impress Shelburne with Franklin's thoughts on the subject.[16]

True to his word, Oswald carried Franklin's memorandum to London and in a conversation with Prime Minister Rockingham, Shelburne, and Charles James Fox, secretary of foreign affairs, recommended Canada be relinquished. Parroting Franklin, he contended the government of Canada "was worth nothing," and England would benefit by surrendering Canada but retaining trade rights there. The ministers were noncommittal. Still Oswald was later optimistic that they would agree to his suggestions.[17]

In asking for Canada, Franklin was undoubtedly influenced by the widespread annexation sentiment in the United States and by the revised congressional instructions of August 14, 1779, which stated that the cession was "of the utmost importance to the peace and commerce of the United States." Congress, however, had not made Canada's cession an ultimatum, and, in fact, the inability to conclude peace in 1780–81 had apparently changed the government's expectations. Less than four months before Franklin first talked with Oswald, he had been sent a lengthy missive by Robert R. Livingston, United States secretary of foreign affairs, which represented a retreat from the congressional position of 1779. Although he professed to believe in the importance of the 1779 demand, Livingston said he would settle for the creation west of the mountains of an Indian state whose independence would be guaranteed by France, Spain, Great Britain, and the United States. He made it clear to Franklin that he was expressing only his personal sentiment, which did not carry the weight of congressional authority, but his statement clearly indicated that the chief foreign affairs officer of the United States was willing to make concessions.[18]

On June 10, 1782, Franklin again suggested to Oswald that Britain cede Canada, but he did not press the point. At no time did he place its cession in the form of an ultimatum.[19] If Franklin really believed Canada was attainable, would he not have demanded it? Perhaps he simply hoped the advancement of such an extreme claim would later make the Lake Nipissing line acceptable as a compromise, if the British held out for a boundary on the Ohio River. There is also the possibility that Franklin was indicating to Shelburne the United States would negotiate without its allies only in return for great favors.

Though Oswald and Franklin established a compatibility that later proved to be significant, they could do nothing conclusive. Oswald was acting only in an unofficial capacity without a commission from the British cabinet, and Franklin was awaiting the arrival of his fellow commissioners. Thus Franklin parried Oswald's invitation to negotiate separately, even though Rockingham's cabinet had on April 23 agreed to "the allowance of independence to America upon Great Britain's being restored to the situation she was placed in by the treaty of 1763." Rockingham's dissension-torn ministry, hampered by the rivalry between Shelburne and Fox, was openly concerned about French designs. Meanwhile Vergennes intrigued. He was content to let negotiations proceed between the United States and Great Britain on the one hand and France and Great Britain on the other; it was his aim to tie all of the separate agreements together in a general settlement by insisting that all powers consent to all agreements.[20]

Oswald hoped to hasten negotiations by repeatedly asking Franklin for the specific American conditions for peace. Finally on July 9, 1782, Franklin responded orally and at length. Adhering closely to the congressional instructions of 1779, he insisted on complete independence, the 1763 boundaries, and fishing rights on the Grand Banks of Newfoundland as necessary articles, and as desirable conditions he mentioned reimbursement to Americans for private property destroyed by British troops, a public acknowledgment of Britain's wrongdoing, reciprocal trade rights in British and American ports, and the cession of Canada.[21]

As Oswald and Franklin were moving toward a definition of the outstanding issues, political changes in Great Britain augured well for the United States. After Rockingham's death on July 1, 1782, Shelburne became prime minister. Shortly after Parliament convened on July 11, he sent the young political economist Benjamin Vaughan, a close friend of Franklin, to Paris with assurances that the new government fully intended to continue the drive for peace. Despite Shelburne's desires, negotiations lagged for several weeks while he consolidated his position by reorganizing the ministry and assuming full control of British diplomacy.[22]

In the meantime John Jay, who was to emerge as the most significant American negotiator, had arrived in Paris. Suspicious and legalistic, Jay had long distrusted both French and Spanish motives. In early August he opened secret talks with the Conde de Aranda, Spain's minister to France, in an effort to determine the Spanish-American boundary. It soon became apparent that the two held irreconcilable views. With a French edition of cartographer John Mitchell's map before them, Jay insisted on the Mississippi as the western border of the United States. The Spaniard, however, proposed a line from the western end of Lake Erie to Florida running about 500 miles east of the river. Jay was unwilling to settle for anything less than the Mississippi, even though Aranda was supported by Vergennes, who at last openly opposed American territorial gains in the West.[23]

The Jay-Aranda talks greatly concerned the British, who feared they might lead to a Franco-Spanish-American agreement on common war aims. These fears, compounded by the imminent Spanish assault on Gibraltar, induced Shelburne's ministers to make liberal concessions to the United States. On August 29, after strenuous urging by Shelburne, the cabinet agreed to recognize American independence before the peace treaty was negotiated and to confine Canada to the limits set down under the Royal Proclamation.[24]

The United States might very well have attained the Lake Nipissing line of 1763 if the treaty had been speedily culminated. But while Jay frittered away time with his overzealous concern about the form of Oswald's commission, the French intrigued against the United States to the advantage of Great Britain. Jay's stubbornness with Aranda convinced Vergennes that the American commissioners would not relent in their pursuit of what the French sincerely believed were unreasonable peace objectives. The French foreign minister understandably was primarily concerned about the interests of his country. With the hope of leaving the war honorably, he sent Joseph-Mathias Gérard de Rayneval, his undersecretary, to London for highly secret talks with Shelburne. Rayneval unveiled his government's strategy of working for a North American balance of power, with all parties being relatively weak, by candidly revealing the French aim to deny the United States the territory north of the Ohio and fishing rights in Canadian waters. While Shelburne concluded from these talks that French backing of the United States was faint at best, he also correctly sensed France's desire to end the war. Thus he believed there was no need to make any bargain that would support the Spanish in the Mississippi Valley and possibly restore French fishing rights off Newfoundland.[25]

Jay was still engaged with Aranda when he learned that Rayneval had slipped off to England. Sensing the import of the Frenchman's mission, Jay moved to counteract it by sending Benjamin Vaughan to talk with Shelburne. Vaughan at this time was virtually a man of two countries, a role he handled easily. His obvious sympathy for the American cause made him an extremely effective courier for Jay. On September 11 he left for London properly indoctrinated with Jay's arguments for the American case. He was to insist on the Mississippi River boundary, which would not only conciliate the United States but could possibly open up a lucrative British commerce in the interior, since the United States was prepared to give the British nagivation and trade rights on that river. Going beyond the inference that the United States stood ready to share the interior trade with Great Britain, Jay even suggested the possibility of full-scale Anglo-American reciprocity. He reasoned that the idea of free trade, which at that time found wide philosophic acceptance in diplomatic circles, was almost certain to appeal to a maritime country. The message Vaughan bore was clear. Great Britain could participate in this promising commerce only if the United States were given the Mississippi as its western boundary. Vaughan was also to insist on a commission for Oswald that specifically recognized the "United States," for Jay saw numerous hazards if Shelburne persisted in negotiating with the "colonies."[26]

Vaughan returned to Paris from London on September 27 with an ambiguously worded commission for Oswald that mentioned the "United States" but stopped short of an outright recognition of independence. Jay finally realized there was no purpose in pressing this point, since Shelburne was also willing to concede to America's boundary demands. Instead he began to work diligently with Franklin and Oswald to hammer out a preliminary treaty. The draft completed on October 5 gave to the United States land northward to the Lake Nipissing line and westward to the Mississippi, as well as fishing rights and independence. Significantly the document also provided "That the navigation of the river Mississippi, from its source to the ocean, shall forever remain free and open, and that both there and in all rivers, harbors, lakes, ports, and places belonging to his Britannic majesty or to the United States, or in any part of the world, the merchants and merchant ships of the one and the other shall be received, treated, and protected like the merchants and merchant ships of the sovereign of the country." The agreement of October 5 embodied everything Jay desired. Not only did it include his boundary demands but it appeared that the United States—even though an independent country—would not lose the commercial advantages of being within the British empire, for Oswald had agreed to free trade.[27]

Oswald had obviously negotiated in the spirit of the cabinet's decision of August 29, 1782, but by the time the draft reached London on October 11, England's situation had changed for the better and the cabinet's mood had stiffened. News that Gibraltar had successfully withstood Spanish attack was circulated in London on September 30. This triumph alone would have been sufficient to strengthen Great Britain's bargaining position, but when French disenchantment with the United States became obvious, Shelburne's ministers were moved to reconsider their earlier stance. In a crucial session on October 17, the cabinet reversed its August decision by rejecting Oswald's agreement and laying down new and stricter peace terms. Oswald was again sent to Paris, even though he had been greatly maligned by some cabinet members. His orders were to demand the Ohio River rather than the Lake Nipissing line as the northern boundary, unless the United States was willing to permit the settlement of Loyalists in the Northwest. Oswald, who in the cabinet's opinion could no longer be trusted to act alone, was to be assisted by Henry Strachey, the experienced and highly regarded undersecretary of state in the colonial office.[28]

Even Shelburne was caught up in the cabinet's assertiveness and supported its resolves on boundaries, debts, and Loyalists. He had by no means abandoned his intention of dealing generously with the United States, but political expediency if nothing else dictated that he reflect the cabinet's goals. Moreover Shelburne, like most of the ministers, was now responsive to various pressures from fur traders, American Tories, and English creditors who wanted a treaty that looked after their interests. He felt obligated to bargain with the American commissioners, but he well realized the hazards of adamancy which might cause a break in negotiations. His hold on power was very weak, and he had staked his political future on his ability to end the war; he knew it would be to his advantage to reach an agreement before November 26, when Parliament was to convene. The prime minister's uncertain political tenure and the American commissioners' belief that they could achieve the best terms while he was still in office imparted both a sense of urgency and a need for cooperation to the treaty talks.[29]

The British and American negotiators moved rapidly toward an amicable solution of the northern boundary and other issues, but they did so only after some blunt talking. On October 29 Strachey proposed to Jay that the United States be limited on the west by a longitudinal line east of the Mississippi. To this restatement of the Aranda-Rayneval idea Jay replied that if the line "was insisted upon it was needless to talk of Peace," because the United States "never w[oul]d Yield that point." The following day Jay and Franklin were joined in a meeting with Oswald and Strachey by John Adams, who had recently returned to Paris to assist his fellow commissioners. There "some torrid conversation" took place in a discussion of the outstanding issues.[30]

Jay, Adams, and Franklin worked with Oswald and Strachey at a feverish pace for nearly a week. Although Jay had flatly rejected Strachey's longitudinal line, he and his colleagues realized the need to retreat from the Lake Nipissing border, because the cabinet was now adamantly against a boundary that would sever the routes of Canadian fur traders. The Americans found it easy to compromise, for Congress in 1779 had expressed only a preference for such a boundary, while specifying that the war should not be continued for the purpose of acquiring territory north of the 45th parallel. Also influencing the compromise was Strachey's determination to acquire a portion of the Northwest for the resettlement of Loyalists. Although Franklin later wrote that "We did not choose such neighbors," it is apparent the Americans did not simply reject the proposition out-of-hand, but linked their refusal with a boundary concession.[31]

Diligently following the 1779 instructions, the American treaty makers proposed that the international boundary follow the 45th parallel from the Connecticut River to the Mississippi. In effect they were offering to extend the parallel-line portion of the 1763 Quebec boundary westward from the St. Lawrence River.[32] Such a line from St. Regis, New York, to the present Twin Cities would have cut across the St. Lawrence and Lakes Huron and Michigan, leaving what is now southern Ontario to the United States and portions of present-day Michigan, Wisconsin, and Minnesota to Canada. By cutting off the natural river and lakes route, the boundary would have been an immediate nuisance to fur traders and conceivably would have caused incalculable harm to future commerce.

No doubt prompted by British concern over the inconvenience to fur traders of a boundary based on a parallel, the Americans then offered an alternative. The northern boundary, they suggested, could proceed from the point where the 45th parallel struck the St. Lawrence westward via the middle of the lakes and streams to the northwest corner of Lake of the Woods. Once the commissioners had agreed upon the Mississippi as America's western boundary, they had only to close the gap between it and Lake of the Woods to complete the border. Consulting Mitchell's map, they concurred that this could be accomplished simply by drawing a line due west from the northwest corner of Lake of the Woods to the Mississippi, which appeared to rise in Canada.[33]

Since such a northern boundary apparently would give Great Britain access to the Mississippi in Canada, the commissioners discussed joint navigation on that river—the lone remnant of Jay's earlier proposal of complete reciprocity. Shelburne and his ministers felt a certain philosophical sympathy for free trade, but they sacrificed it to the economic realities of the British navigation laws during their debates in October. Thus stripped of the broader question before their November talks, the treaty makers agreed simply "That the navigation of the river Mississippi, from its source to the ocean, shall forever remain free and open."[34]

On November 5 Strachey left for London satisfied that he and Oswald had improved the boundary stipulations. The American commissioners had agreed to the St. Croix rather than the St. John River as the northeastern boundary of the United States, and they had offered two alternatives to the Lake Nipissing proposal, which to Strachey were "both better than the original line." Shelburne and his cabinet agreed. In a meeting on November 11, they accepted the water boundary to the northwest corner of Lake of the Woods and the due-west line to the Mississippi, mainly because it was less likely to disturb the Canadian fur traders' activities on Lakes Ontario and Erie. Shelburne accommodated the fur traders because he had to win parliamentary support for any final treaty. He needed the approval of Scottish members of Parliament who traditionally voted as a bloc and would be influenced by the fate of their countrymen in the Montreal fur trade.[35]

The American commissioners saw the British acceptance of the lake-and-river line as advantageous to the United States. Two weeks after the preliminary treaty was signed in Paris, they reported to Robert Livingston that the boundaries "appear to leave us little to complain of and not much to desire." The particular advantage of the line through the Great Lakes, explained the negotiators, was that it "divides the Lake Superior, and gives us access to its western and southern waters, from which a line [on the parallel] in that latitude would have excluded us." Did these men foresee the commercial importance of Lake Superior, or were they merely concerned with giving Americans an opportunity to compete in the fur trade? Twelve years after the Paris negotiations, Jay offered an explanation of the mutual acceptability of the national border: "as the waters would form a line which could never be mistaken, and afforded great conveniences to both parties, the line of the waters was preferred by both."[36]

For a time in November the boundary question and, for that matter, the entire negotiations were imperiled by the British cabinet's concern for the Loyalists. On November 15 the ministers issued instructions to Oswald (whom some had denounced as "an additional American negotiator") and Strachey, calling for the restitution of Loyalist property confiscated by the various states. The Americans pointed out that the federal government of the United States could not restore the property because it did not have the power to order the states to do so. Realizing the gravity of the situation, Oswald proposed an acceptable compromise under which the treaty makers agreed Congress would recommend to the states that Loyalist property be restored. Once this and the question of private

American debts to British creditors had been resolved to the cabinet's satisfaction, the preliminary treaty was returned to Paris. There on November 30, 1782, it was signed by Oswald for Great Britain and Jay, Franklin, Adams, and Laurens for the United States.[37]

The final treaty was ratified by the United States on April 15, 1783, and by Great Britain on August 6, 1783. While the ratifications were pending, Shelburne fell from power; nevertheless the preliminaries signed at Paris remained essentially unchanged. In fact Charles James Fox and David Hartley, the successors of Shelburne and Oswald, respectively, were openly cordial toward the United States. They made no effort to change the northwestern boundary provision, even though there was some reason to believe that it was inaccurately conceived. As early as February 21, 1783, Benjamin Vaughan, somehow alert to the possibility that a line drawn due west from the northwest corner of Lake of the Woods would not strike the Mississippi, had suggested to Shelburne that the provision be amended. He proposed it be changed to read: "and from thence [*Lake of the Woods*], by a line which shall describe the shortest course for reaching the Mississippi" or "and from thence on a due south course to the Mississippi."[38]

The complete northern boundary provision of the final treaty, reflecting both Great Britain's generosity and a marked Anglo-American ignorance of geography, read: "From the north west Angle of Nova Scotia, Vizt. that Angle which is form'd by a Line drawn due north, from the Source of St. Croix River to the Highlands, along the said Highlands which divide those Rivers that empty themselves into the River St. Laurence, from those which fall into the Atlantic Ocean, to the northwesternmost Head of Connecticut River; thence down along the middle of that River to the 45th. Degree of North Latitude; from thence by a Line due West on said Latitude, untill it strikes the River Iroquois, or Cataraquy [*St. Lawrence*]; thence along the middle of said River into Lake Ontario; through the middle of said Lake, untill it strikes the Communication by Water between that Lake and Lake Erie; thence along the middle of said Communication into Lake Erie, through the middle of said Lake, untill it arrives at the Water Communication between that Lake and Lake Huron; thence along the middle of said water communication into the Lake Huron; thence through the middle of said Lake to the Water Communication between that Lake and Lake Superior; thence through Lake Superior northward of the Isles Royal & Phelipeaux, to the Long Lake; thence through the middle of said Long Lake, and the water Communication between it and the Lake of the Woods, to the said Lake of the Woods, thence through the said Lake to the most Northwestern point thereof, and from thence on a due west Course to the River Mississippi. . . . " The two countries agreed that the Mississippi was to be the western boundary from the point of intersection west of Lake of the Woods south to the 31st parallel.[39]

The peace terms gained by the United States rather surprised Vergennes, who was also understandably resentful that France had not been informed about the details of the preliminary treaty until after it had been signed. Writing to Rayneval, he commented, "You will notice that the English buy the peace more than they make it. Their concessions, in fact, as much as to the boundaries as to the fisheries and the loyalists, exceed all that I should have thought possible. What can be the motive, that could have brought terms so easy, that they could have been interpreted as some kind of surrender?" Historians of the negotiations have generally concurred with Vergennes' view that British officials yielded far more than required and Americans gained far more than they could have reasonably expected. Canadian Edgar W. McInnis aptly concluded that it was on the British "readiness to yield rather than on the vigor of American insistence that the final decision rested."[40] Why then was Great Britain willing to give up so much?

Lord Shelburne and his associates were influenced by past actions of their government, by war fatigue, by a genuine desire to placate the United States, and by their belief that British title to the entire interior was not important. They could not escape the significance of the Royal Proclamation of 1763, which provided the United States with a tangible boundary demand from which the American commissioners only grudgingly retreated. Furthermore nearly two decades of experience as the ruler of the wilderness had taught Great Britain that such a role was costly. As far as the government was concerned, protecting the interior had served only to strain the national budget and to benefit one special interest group—the Canadian fur traders. It is no small wonder that many British statesmen regarded the interior as a burden rather than an asset.[41]

In his desire to end the war Shelburne reflected the public mood in Great Britain, but at the same time he carefully made it seem that this goal could be attained only through negotiating separately with the United States. Many of Shelburne's contemporary critics seemingly ignored the fact that, by concluding a separate peace with the United States, he saved his country from the almost certain disaster of a collective treaty with the Americans' allies.[42]

Shelburne predicated his entire diplomatic course on the premise that he was dealing with the United States as a future friend rather than a past enemy. But unfortunately for the prime minister, the blunt, unsophisticated Oswald was incapable of bargaining with the American emissaries as conditions improved for Britain; consequently Shelburne was not able to take full advantage of either the defense of Gibraltar or the Rayneval mission. In relating the seeming necessity for conciliation to the boundary question, Shelburne showed a preference for the United States over Spain as a neighbor. He saw a hazard in a British boundary on the Ohio River that might bring his country face to face with a hostile Spain and push an angry United States firmly back into the French alliance. Fifteen years after the negotiations, Shelburne explained his thinking to an American acquaintance: "I may tell you in confidence what may astonish you, as it did me, that up to the very last debate in the House of Lords, the Ministry did not appear to comprehend the policy upon which the boundary line was drawn, and persist in still considering it as a measure of necessity not of choice. However it is indifferent who understands it. The deed is done; and a strong foundation laid for eternal amity between England and America."[43]

Strongly steeped in a materialistic frontier heritage, Americans have always attached great importance to land acquisition, which accounts for a certain difficulty in their understanding of British reasoning in 1782. Partially because of their country's experience in the interior, but also because of a lack of knowledge and appreciation of the land north of the Ohio, British politicians deduced that boundaries and title to the land were secondary to the essential question of use of the interior. John Jay was clearly attuned to British thinking when he interwove his boundary demands with his proposition for reciprocity.[44]

By offering mutual navigation of the Mississippi and reciprocity, Jay was saying in effect that Great Britain as a trading nation could enjoy the fruits of the interior commerce without heavy outlays for military protection and Indian annuities. Even though Jay's reciprocity proposal was shelved, Shelburne's ministry was impressed by the commercial prospects held out in the article on navigation of the Mississippi. With persistent talk of a future commercial union, it was natural for the British negotiators to emphasize access to the interior rather than title to the land. The cabinet in all likelihood decided to accept the line through the lakes precisely because it offered that access. At the time the boundary article was concluded, commissioners for both sides anticipated moving rapidly to consider a commercial treaty, which they believed might revive reciprocity. Such a treaty also would have underscored the boundary agreement which made British trade in the interior geographically possible. Since the commercial treaty was not realized, the boundary soon became much more meaningful than the treaty makers had intended, because there was a tendency for both sides in a strained postwar mood to regard it as a hard dividing line separating opposing interests.

Even though Shelburne had good cause to deal magnanimously, the treaty probably exceeded his intentions. Once the negotiations were under way, he was caught up in a maze of crosscurrents that obfuscated issues and catapulted Great Britain into accepting a hastily drafted document which the prime minister, delicately poised amid conflicting political interests and public pressures, could only choose to endorse. Despite the later, rather common British view, especially among Canadian fur traders, that a feckless Oswald was responsible for Canada's boundary problems, there is sufficient reason to believe, in light of all the other circumstances and motives, that Great Britain would have concluded essentially the same treaty regardless of the negotiator.

It appeared to Oswald and the American commissioners that, in a spirit of good will, they had solved the major issues between Great Britain and the United States. They could hardly have foreseen the later litigious relationship between the two countries. But there were flaws in the treaty, particularly in the northern boundary provision, that made later troubles unavoidable. The very forces that dictated the hurried negotiations would have made it impossible for the commissioners to study the geography of the boundary country had they been so inclined, which is doubtful. Working without expert geographical advice or up-to-date information, the negotiators confidently placed their trust in the highly reputed Mitchell map, first issued 27 years earlier.

John Mitchell's map was destined to become "the most important and the most famous map in American history"—largely because of its relatively few shortcomings rather than its many virtues. It was the handiwork of an Anglo-American physician and botanist, whose international fame was embellished by prolific writings on diverse subjects. Born in Virginia in 1711, Mitchell attended school in Scotland and returned to live at Urbanna on the Rappahannock River, where he practiced medicine and wrote on botany and zoology. In 1746 he moved to England in search of a more salubrious climate to ease his ill health.[45]

The talented Mitchell was attracted to cartography by his desire to illustrate the French threat to British lands in North America. By 1750 he had produced a North American map that so impressed the lords of the Board of Trade that they asked him to continue his work with the aim of preparing another one more complete and detailed. Drawing upon a wide variety of primary and secondary sources, including information from ship captains, colonial scientists, travelers, geographers, and historians, Mitchell had his map ready within five years.

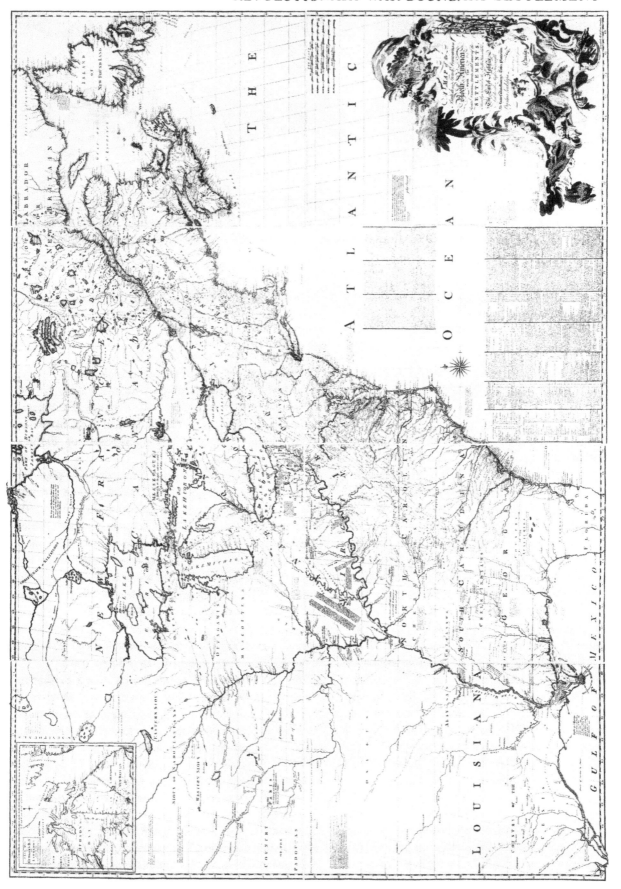

JOHN MITCHELL'S famous map of North America, first published in 1755, was used by negotiators of the Treaty of 1783 in defining the northern boundary of the United States. Courtesy James Ford Bell Library, University of Minnesota.

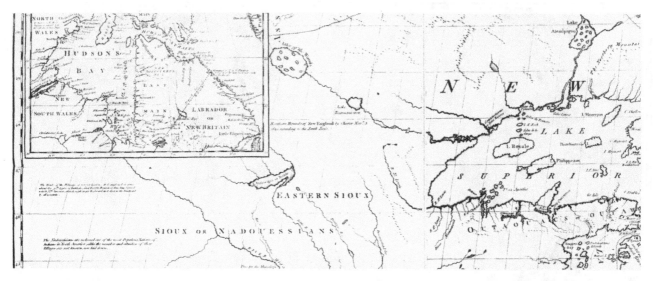

THIS ENLARGED SECTION of Mitchell's map of the region between Lake Superior and Lake of the Woods reveals the location of the mysterious Isle Philippeaux and includes his statement that "The Head of the Missisipi is not yet known." Courtesy James Ford Bell Library, University of Minnesota.

In February, 1755, the first edition entitled *Map of the British and French Dominions in North America with the Roads, Distances, Limits and Extent of the Settlement* was published in London. Mitchell's intention, as evidenced by the map, was to show the division of British and French claims and those of the various British mainland colonies rather than topography. The western edge of the map was carried beyond the Mississippi, apparently to portray the colonial sea-to-sea charter claims, but the supposed headwaters of the Mississippi River were obscured by an inset of Hudson Bay and Labrador placed in the upper left corner. To account for the Mississippi, which so mysteriously flowed from under the inset, Mitchell inscribed on the map: "The Head of the Missisipi [*sic*] is not yet known: It is supposed to arise about the 50th degree of Latitude, and Western Bounds of this Map."[46]

The diplomats' references to "Mitchell's Map" left the impression there was but a single edition of it. In fact the popular map had been issued in many and varied editions between 1755 and the time of the Paris negotiations. Before 1782 at least seven French and two Dutch editions had appeared, and a plagiarized version had been printed in Venice, Italy. Four English editions were published, the last appearing in 1775, seven years after Mitchell's death. There were three impressions of the first edition and two of the third, thus the English map was actually issued seven times. Interestingly all bore the same date—February 13, 1755—but no two of them were exactly the same. Although Mitchell did not change the map greatly from the first to the second edition, he corrected a point of latitude and another of longitude. More significantly for

its later bearing on the United States-Canada boundary, he changed the location of the St. Croix River in the Maine-New Brunswick area. Most of the differences, however, including some orthographical inconsistencies and a slightly varied title for the fourth edition, did not alter the basic features.[47]

Mitchell's map was no more and no less than a pictorial representation of geographical facts as he knew them. Like all cartographers of his time, he labored with North American data that were often incomplete and unreliable, because much of the area portrayed was known only in a general way. This was especially true of the interior regions of the continent that had never been professionally explored. In his original research, Mitchell worked among the records in the archives of the Board of Trade. All too often he had to rely on maps that at best offered evidence several times removed from the original source, which may well have been inaccurate in the first place.[48]

Mitchell's faulty information is particularly evident in his portrayal of the Northwest. He not only erred with regard to the source of the Mississippi, but he also misrepresented the watershed of the Great Lakes. His basic error in the latter lay in the relationship of Lake Superior to Lake of the Woods, which was shown as outflowing southeastward to Lake Superior by a large, unidentified river whose estuary was designated "Long Lake." Consequently anyone relying on Mitchell's map could only conclude that Lake of the Woods, rather than lying within the Hudson Bay watershed, was the head of the Great Lakes-St. Lawrence drainage system and that it could be easily reached by a direct all-water route. On the map, that route across Lake Superior was particularly imaginative. It stayed north of "I[sle] Philippeaux," now known to be nonexistent, and neighboring Isle Royale before entering "Long Lake," which, because of its relationship to Isle Royale and the Kaministikwia and St. Louis rivers, could only have been a misrepresentation of the Pigeon River.

Some of the errors were unavoidable because none of the French voyageurs on Lake Superior was a trained cartographer, and even eyewitnesses could not always accurately describe what they had seen. James White, the eminent Canadian geographer, later concluded that Isle Philippeaux simply resulted from varying reports about the location of Isle Royale. He believed that someone skirting the south shore of Isle Royale had probably mispositioned it southeast of its actual location and duly reported the discovery of another large island, which soon found its way onto maps.[49]

Other inaccurate features of Mitchell's map seem to have been largely the creation of various cartographers. Long Lake was first designated on a sketch drawn in 1730 by an Assiniboin chief, known as Ochagach or Auchagah, for French explorer Pierre Gaultier de Varennes, Sieur de la Vérendrye. The elliptically shaped Lake of the Woods, with only nine islands, appeared on a map published in 1744 in Arthur Dobbs's *Remarks Upon Captain Middleton's Defence*. The misplacement of the upper Mississippi was illustrated by Guillaume Delisle in his 1722 map and by Henry Popple in his English map published 11 years later.[50]

Mitchell's map became very popular in Europe and America, as evidenced by its many editions. Certainly it was known to anyone who had an interest in North American geography. Its reputation was such that European statesmen considered it unquestionably authoritative. In 1779, when the French first had to grapple with Congress' proposed boundaries of the United States, Conrad Alexandre Gérard urged Vergennes to study the suggested lines on an edition of the map executed by French cartographer Georges Louis Le Rouge. Subsequently various other editions were regularly used by French, Spanish, English, and American negotiators. Aranda and Jay consulted a Mitchell map during their discussions, and the Spaniard sent to Floridablanca, his country's principal minister, a marked Mitchell edition showing Aranda's proposed demarcation between Spanish territory and the United States.[51]

Although Oswald and the American commissioners did not mention Mitchell's map in the treaty, they definitely followed it in drawing the boundary. On December 14, 1782, two weeks after they signed the preliminary treaty, Adams, Franklin, Jay, and Laurens reported to Livingston that "The map used in the course of our negotiations was Mitchell's." Less than two years after the Paris negotiations Adams, in response to an inquiry about the already controversial northeastern boundary, wrote: "We had before us, through the whole negotiation, a variety of maps; but it was Mitchell's map, upon which was marked out the whole of the boundary lines of the United States." In two letters written in 1786 Adams reasserted the reliance on Mitchell's map, and on August 2, 1796, he reported to James Sullivan, American agent for the commission to determine the true St. Croix River of the northeastern boundary, that "Mitchell's map was the only one which the ministers plenipotentiary of the United States, and the minister plenipotentiary of Great Britain, made use of in their conferences and discussions relative to the boundaries of the United States, in their negotiation of the peace of 1783, and of the provisional articles of the 30th of November, 1782. Upon that map, and that only, were those boundaries delineated." Adams' testimony was supported by his fellow negotiators. Jay recalled Mitchell's map "was frequently consulted for geographical information," and Franklin, only nine days before his death, reported to Secretary of State Thomas Jefferson, "I now can assure you, that I am perfectly clear in the remembrance that the map we used in tracing the boundary, was brought to the treaty by the commissioners from England, and that it was the same that was published by Mitchell above twenty years before."[52]

It has been impossible to identify the copy of the Mitchell map used and marked by Oswald and the American commissioners, because they neither signed it nor attached it to the treaty. During the long boundary history there has been both diplomatic and academic interest in any marked map that could be directly associated with the treaty, because it would show the intent of the negotiators. It is reasonable to assume more than one map was marked during negotiations or shortly thereafter. In 1842, American historian Jared Sparks discovered that on December 6, 1782, Franklin had sent Vergennes a map on which he had "marked with a strong red Line, according to your Desire, the Limits of the Thirteen United States, as settled in the Preliminaries between the British and American Plenipotentiaries." This particular map, which would have great evidential value, has never been located, but a presumed copy of it provoked considerable debate after the Webster-Ashburton Treaty of 1842.[53]

Lawrence Martin, the foremost authority on Mitchell's map, concluded that it is impossible to prove any of the existing copies were actually used by the negotiators in 1782. He believed, however, that two extant copies—the Jay copy and the King George copy—were in use in 1782, but there is no evidence they were the ones consulted during the final Paris negotiations.[54]

The failure to locate a Mitchell map marked by the negotiators caused great inconvenience in determining the northeast boundary, but the intent of the commissioners

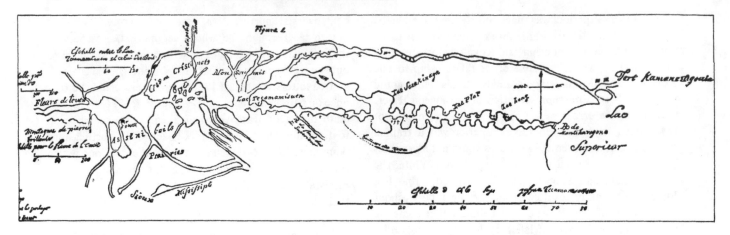

THE EARLIEST KNOWN MAP showing "Long Lake" was a sketch made in 1730 for Sieur de la Vérendrye by an Assiniboin chief known as Ochagach. In this and other versions, the Pigeon River and the border lakes between Lake Superior and Saganaga Lake have the appearance of a dinosaur's vertebrae, much as they looked on Mitchell's 1755 map. From N. H. Winchell and Warren Upham, *The Geology of Minnesota* (1884).

IN 1722 French cartographer Guillaume Delisle placed the headwaters of the Mississippi River in an area far to the northwest of Lake Superior on his map of North America. Courtesy Map Division, University of Minnesota Libraries.

regarding the northwest boundary was abundantly clear from the wording of the treaty. They intended to follow the St. Lawrence waterway to its source—supposedly Lake of the Woods. By placing their trust in Mitchell, the treaty makers worked to the later advantage of the United States. Had their knowledge of geography been accurate, they would almost certainly have brought the boundary through Lake Superior to the St. Louis River and then west, probably from the head of that river, to the northern sources of the Mississippi. In effect, the use of Mitchell's map saved the Mesabi and Vermilion iron ranges for Minnesota and created the aggravating problem resulting from the impossibility of drawing a line due west from the northwest corner of Lake of the Woods to the Mississippi.[55]

The error in closing the northwest boundary gap was understandable, for the negotiators were unaware of the inadequacies of the Mitchell map. While there were other charts showing different versions of the Northwest, there was no truly accurate map; had there been one, there would not have been any way to determine which it was.[56] The hurried pace of the negotiations, the lack of staff, and perhaps a mutual feeling that the northwest boundary was not really important prevented the American and British negotiators from carefully investigating the geography of the wilderness. If they had undertaken a critical examination of the area, they would no doubt have seen what Vaughan soon saw—that the locations of Lake of the Woods and the Mississippi as shown by Mitchell were doubtful. Part of the explanation for the mistake in the treaty has to be that no one involved cared to raise thorny questions. There was time after Vaughan's alert and before the treaty was ratified to attempt to change the wording of the northern boundary provision. None of the parties involved chose to press the point, however, probably out of fear of aborting the agreement. There seems to have been a mutual interest in giving the boundary provision an immediate finality, perhaps in the mistaken notion that a categorical statement in the treaty would preclude future difficulties. No doubt the negotiators also saw the advantages of a precise boundary stipulation, rather than one that could be determined only after further topographical data had been obtained. A precise boundary could have the effect before long of creating a British presence on the Mississippi that would not only discomfit Spain, the possessor of the lower Mississippi, but would also stimulate commerce to the advantage of both the United States and Great Britain.

The inadequacies of Mitchell's map would almost certainly have been exposed if Shelburne and his ministers had been more concerned about the Canadian fur traders who were intimately acquainted with parts of the country west of Lake Superior. London merchants, who in all probability could have obtained information about the back country from Canadian sources, were not included in the negotiations. A story circulated years later in Canadian fur trade circles that Oswald had admitted he was unaware of the existence of British trading posts in the interior in 1782.[57] Ignorance to this degree defies belief. The only likely reason Shelburne and his associates did not seek the merchants' advice is they did not wish to open the way for direct involvement of a special interest group in the territorial settlement.

When the terms of the preliminary treaty became public, London merchants interested in the Canadian fur trade were not so easily shunted aside. In a vigorous protest sent to Shelburne on January 31, 1783, they complained that the boundary had deprived them of a number of significant posts, including Grand Portage, and had jeopardized the trade based in Quebec. As a result of this letter, Oswald met with a committee of merchants six days later. By his account he assured them the boundary was not a barrier to their activities because the treaty did not prohibit British trade in American territory. After adjourning to a London coffeehouse, the merchants composed a letter to Shelburne. In it they asked that the government make arrangements to permit the traders to hold their posts south of the border for three years and to obtain for them perpetual use of the portages and waterways in the border country.

The Montreal traders were similarly shocked and dismayed by the northwestern boundary provision. They instantly recognized that "Long Lake" was the Pigeon River, and they seemed to have feared an immediate American takeover of British posts south of the border— including Grand Portage, their principal access to interior Canada. To the traders there was only one explanation for this catastrophic turn of events: they had been betrayed by conniving British diplomats. They neither understood nor cared about American claims based on colonial charters, preferring a settlement based on actual possession of the land. They were afforded some solace when Great Britain had retaken the Illinois country after Clark's much publicized expedition, but they recognized an accomplished fact and had no choice other than to live with the new boundary.

In a desperate effort to retain Grand Portage, which was vital to the continuation of their business, the traders questioned "Long Lake," even though they knew perfectly well where it was located. Benjamin Frobisher, one of Montreal's key traders and a leading figure in the newly organized North West Company, commented to an associate on the "ambiguous sence [*sic*] of the late Treaty of Peace." He observed that "there is no such thing as a Long Lake as expressed in the Treaty, the only communication from Lake Superior is by that tract of land known by the name of the Grand Portage." He reported that instead of a Long Lake west of the small river reached by the portage there "is rather a Chain of Lakes, few of which have any visible inlet or communication with each other." As an immediate solution to the problem, Frobisher suggested "a survey of the Carrying Place and the Country adjacent will be highly necessary to assertain [*sic*] and fix unalterably the Line in that Quarter, while on the other hand it will give us time to discover another passage if such a thing exists."[58]

Fully realizing such a survey could not be done promptly, Frobisher and his North West Company partners decided to search on their own for an alternative to the Grand Portage route. Knowledge of the Kaministikwia passage had somehow been lost during the half century since it was drawn on La Vérendrye's map by the Indian chief, so the traders sought a route far to the north. In June, 1784, they sent Edward Umfreville to explore westward from Lake Nipigon. Umfreville was quite satisfied with the canoe route he followed from Lake Nipigon to Rat Portage, the outlet of Lake of the Woods, although it was more difficult than the Grand Portage route and was really too far north of the existing posts.[59]

The North West Company partners did not have to use the Nipigon route, however, for they soon concluded that their immediate salvation lay not in new discoveries, but in the rapid emergence of a formal British policy of retaining the posts south of the border. Canadian distress over the boundary settlement was so acute that, in order to soothe tempers, William Pitt's ministry decided not to order the evacuation of the posts. The decision to retain them was made in April, 1784, before the official reason for it—America's inability to honor the treaty stipulation regarding collection of private American debts by British creditors—was given.[60] Thus the British traders stayed south of the border and the United States was powerless to evict them. This left the question of the northwest boundary dormant until the discovery several years later of the impossibility of the specified line between Lake of the Woods and the Mississippi.

CHAPTER 2

The Northwest Boundary Gap

ALTHOUGH the Canadian fur traders had quickly discerned the Long Lake error in the peace treaty, they were apparently ignorant for some time of the impossibility of drawing a line due west from the northwest corner of Lake of the Woods to the Mississippi. Then, almost a decade after the boundary had been set, George Hammond, the young British minister to the United States, received a map from Montreal which showed the source of the Mississippi well to the south of Lake of the Woods. Choosing to believe the map valid, Hammond in February, 1792, called this probable shortcoming to the attention of Lord Grenville, secretary of state for foreign affairs. In so doing he opened the question of the boundary gap, which subsequently plagued British and American statesmen intermittently for the next 26 years.[1]

After the British refused to evacuate the posts south of the border in 1784, the only way the United States could hope to assert its ownership was to push aggressively westward into the area north of the Ohio River. This, however, was not easily accomplished. The land surveying and governance systems established by the Ordinances of 1785 and 1787 encouraged only a modest influx of Americans into the Northwest Territory—too few to weaken British occupancy of such places as Niagara, Detroit, and Michilimackinac. Britain's fur trade continued to flourish, especially through Detroit and Michilimackinac, which were clearly south of the border, and Grand Portage, which the Canadian traders privately believed was on American soil.[2]

Futile American efforts in the early 1790s to vanquish the Indians in the region north of the Ohio coincided with an increasing British awareness of the importance of the fur trade in lands claimed by the United States. Canadian traders, smarting from the treatment meted out under Shelburne's peace, began to believe that a boundary adjustment might be possible after the king tacitly supported their views by refusing to abandon the posts south of the Great Lakes. Spokesmen for the traders, aware of Oswald's professed ignorance of their activities in 1782, hoped to prevent the reiteration of a similar excuse by informing British leaders of the importance of their commerce. On May 31, 1790, merchant John Inglis wrote to Lord Grenville that Canadian fur exports for the preceding ten years had averaged £200,000 annually, with half of this value coming from furs brought in from the area south of the Great Lakes. About £40,000 worth of furs was gathered each year in the interior beyond Lake of the Woods, prompting him to observe that to concede the American claim to the lake would give the United States control of the canoe routes to the interior and would result in the loss to Canada of the trade in the far northwest.[3]

By the time George Hammond was apprised of the boundary gap, he was aware of the significant Canadian fur trade and the American military failures; he also knew the United States was dangerously close to war with Spain over land disputes in the lower Mississippi River area. His map find, coming at a time when the United States appeared to be vulnerable, emboldened him to propose a virtual undoing of the 1783 treaty's northwest boundary provisions. He had far more in mind than merely rectifying the line from Lake of the Woods to the Mississippi, however. He hoped to use his new-found information to reopen for discussion a whole range of outstanding issues between the United States and Great Britain.

When Hammond informed Grenville of the boundary error on February 2, 1792, he argued that the intention of the peace treaty's Article 2 on boundaries and Article 8 on mutual navigation had been to create a boundary which guaranteed the British access to the Mississippi. The newly discovered map proved the treaty line as specified would not accomplish that intent and mandated the reopening of the boundary question. He then suggested the line be redrawn so that British claims would extend to the Mississippi at some point below the Falls of St. Anthony, located within present-day Minneapolis. The navigation of the Mississippi was important to Hammond, who, attuned to British commercial interests, had a sense of the potential richness of the river valley and relished the possibility of adding the area to Canada.[4]

Hammond found a receptive audience in Lord Grenville, who had conceived of yet another plan to deprive the United States of the Northwest. By March, 1792, after months of deliberation, Grenville had fully elaborated the idea of converting the region into an Indian buffer state. On March 17 he instructed Hammond to offer "the good offices" of Great Britain in mediating between the United States and the Indians north of the Ohio River with the object of securing for the natives "their Lands and hunting Grounds, as an independent Country." To that area both the United States and Great Britain would renounce any claims. If the United States accepted his proposal, Hammond was to promise British abandonment of the posts south of the Great Lakes.[5]

Within a matter of weeks Grenville had pooled his and Hammond's ideas, and on April 25 he wrote new instructions. Hammond was to press the United States on all three issues which had been recently raised—boundary rectification, access to the Mississippi in the north, and creation of the Indian state. Grenville anticipated that the United States, despite its known unwillingness to negotiate the Indian question, would probably be forced to do so because of its difficulties with the tribes. He also thought the United States might agree to a southward shift of the northwestern boundary and even to British access to the Mississippi by way of the Fox and Wisconsin rivers.[6]

Hammond was frustrated at every turn by United States Secretary of State Thomas Jefferson, who suspected that the Indian state idea was nothing more than the opening wedge in a British move to reclaim the area south of the Great Lakes. With regard to the other two issues, Jefferson contended the boundary could be corrected by intersecting a line drawn due north of the northern source of the Mississippi with one extending west from Lake of the Woods. There was, he insisted, no connection between the boundary and navigation articles, which were separated in the treaty text by five others. He claimed that the provision for mutual free navigation of the Mississippi really related to the southern boundary.[7]

Hammond's hopes were kept alive by Treasury Secretary Alexander Hamilton, who was eager for a commercial agreement and an alliance between the United States and Great Britain. Fearing war with Spain because of differences in the Southwest, he believed the United States should make concessions to Great Britain in order to win a strong ally, and he was openly alarmed at Jefferson's rigidity. Consequently he indicated his sentiments to Hammond, buoying the British minister's aspirations. Like Jefferson, however, President George Washington believed the very essence of American sovereignty was at stake; therefore he would not consider an undoing of the peace treaty. Thus by the end of 1792 none of the three issues had been resolved.

Relations between the United States and Great Britain soon worsened. The British, at war with revolutionary France, flagrantly violated the neutrality of American ships, and affairs on the northwestern frontier simmered menacingly as Great Britain stubbornly clung to its posts in the face of renewed American efforts to bring the Indians under control. As General "Mad Anthony" Wayne's troops lay poised on the edge of the Indian country during the winter of 1793-94, the natives were incited to new heights of anti-American feeling because of an unexpected action by Lord Dorchester, the governor of Quebec. In an address to an Indian council he not only predicted war with the United States, but encouraged the tribesmen to block American expansion in the Ohio region. The bellicose Dorchester, who had acted without his government's sanction, was rebuked. His indiscretion had a sobering effect. Both countries realized that war could erupt at any time, and they agreed to meet in London to negotiate their differences.[8]

For this mission the Washington administration chose the experienced and prestigious John Jay, then chief justice of the Supreme Court. He was instructed by Edmund Randolph, who had replaced Jefferson as secretary of state, to negotiate a commercial agreement and "to draw to a conclusion all points of difference . . . concerning the treaty of peace." The importance of Jay's assignment was underscored by Randolph's statements that failure of the negotiations would almost certainly lead to war.[9]

When Jay arrived in London during the summer of 1794, he held a diplomatic advantage. Great Britain was faced with the alarming prospect that Sweden and Denmark would lead the way in forming a new League of Armed Neutrality in retaliation for British interference with neutral shipping. But Jay was unable to press his advantage, as Foreign Secretary Grenville dallied, awaiting developments that might improve his country's position. After leisurely preliminaries Grenville finally sent Jay specific proposals on August 30. With reference to the northwest border, Grenville reiterated Hammond's contentions that the peace treaty articles on the boundary and on the Mississippi River were related and that freedom of navigation implied freedom of access without passing through foreign land. Therefore, suggested Grenville, the United States should agree to extend British territory to a navigable portion of the Mississippi by relinquishing either the land north of a line drawn due west from the mouth of the St. Louis River at present Duluth, or the area lying west of a north-south line from the mouth of the St. Croix River at present Prescott, Wisconsin, to the waterway connecting Lake Superior and Lake of the Woods as defined in the 1783 treaty.[10]

Jay rejected Grenville's overture politely but firmly. If it were true that the Mississippi could not be intersected by a line west from Lake of the Woods, he stated, this merely showed "that the northern and western lines of the United States do not meet and close, and, therefore, that it is necessary to fix on a line for closing them." But, he contended, there should be no cession of territory "further than what such closing line may possibly render unavoidable."[11]

Noting that William Faden's 1793 map, which Grenville had sent with his proposal, did not identify the source of the Mississippi, Jay questioned the existence of "good evidence" proving no point on that river would be struck by a line west from Lake of the Woods. His proposed solution to the northwest boundary problem was that the two countries jointly survey the area and, if it was determined that the Mississippi did not lie west of Lake of the Woods, an adjustment would be made a matter for further negotiation. While it was obvious the primary purpose of his proposal was to fend off Grenville's initiative, Jay nonetheless made a telling point, for Grenville could not prove the existence of the boundary gap.

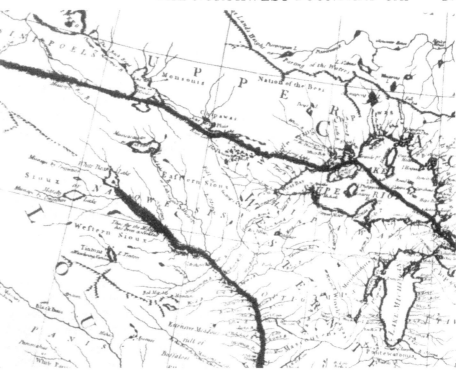

BECAUSE the Mississippi's source was not yet known in 1793, mapmaker William Faden identified two streams as the Mississippi "by Conjecture" and labeled a third "Red lake river, or Lahontan's Missisipi." Faden's map supported John Jay's argument in 1794 against British claims to navigation rights to the river.

Like Jefferson two years earlier, Jay denied any connection between the boundary and the British right to navigate the Mississippi. He stated that the Paris negotiators had not intended to give Great Britain land contiguous to a navigable portion of the Mississippi, for if they had, the navigation article would have been worded more explicitly, and the boundary article would have included a stipulation that the line would be adjusted according to the actual lay and navigability of the river. Jay further contended that if Great Britain had been concerned about navigation in 1782, Shelburne's ministry would have opted for the 45th parallel as the boundary, rather than the river-and-lake line which provided less chance of British claims extending to a navigable portion of the river.

Although both Grenville and Jay had intended their opening proposals to be a starting point for further discussions, their exchanges on the northwest boundary issue were poles apart. Grenville held out for a territorial cession if it should prove impossible to reach the Mississippi by a line west from Lake of the Woods. Jay's response was a formal call for a survey of the upper Mississippi and Lake of the Woods incorporated in his draft of September 30, when he still believed he could negotiate a good treaty.

Jay was toppled from his advantageous negotiating position when Grenville received news from Hammond on September 20 that the American threat to join a League of Armed Neutrality was only a bluff. Hammond's information came from an unimpeachable source—Alexander Hamilton, whose fears of further alienating Great Britain caused him to betray his country's interests. Hamilton dashed Jay's chances of winning a good commercial agreement, and only Anthony Wayne's decisive victory over the pro-British tribes at the Battle of Fallen Timbers on August 20, 1794, assured limited success on the frontier issues.[12]

In the treaty signed on November 19, Great Britain agreed to evacuate the posts in the United States on or before June 1, 1796. British and American citizens, however, were permitted to travel and trade freely in the boundary areas of the United States and Canada, except in lands of the Hudson's Bay Company. Although it was reciprocal, this provision enabled the British traders who were already among the tribes to maintain their stranglehold over the fur trade in the American Northwest.[13]

The boundary question was dealt with when Jay's survey proposal was accepted in modified form. Article 4 of the treaty provided for a joint survey of the Mississippi from one degree of latitude below the Falls of St. Anthony to its principal source. If the survey proved that the river could not be intersected by a line drawn due west from the northwest point of Lake of the Woods, the diplomats agreed their countries would "proceed by amicable negotiation" to determine the boundary in that area.

Jay's Treaty, while not highly successful, relieved a great deal of tension and at least postponed the outbreak of war between the United States and Great Britain. It also stimulated the resolution of some issues, but the boundary gap was not among them. The survey of the Mississippi was never conducted. Instead Great Britain and the United States gave priority to the treaty provisions calling for the organization of joint commissions to deal with the problems of the war debts and the northeastern boundary.[14] By the time the way was clear to establish the upper Mississippi survey commission, the availability of new information about that area removed any need for it.

Because Jay and Grenville had done nothing to clarify the boundary puzzle at "Long Lake," the Grand Portage post remained in a state of diplomatic limbo. When the British surrendered Detroit and Michilimackinac in 1796, the Canadian traders apprehensively retained Grand Portage. But because they believed a boundary determination, which they considered imminent, would result in a Pigeon River line, they again attempted to find a usable route north of that stream.[15]

Their rediscovery of the Kaministikwia route was accidental. In 1798 Roderick McKenzie, a cousin of Alexander Mackenzie, the famed transcontinental explorer, learned of it from some Indians at Height of Land Portage. With the aid of a single guide, McKenzie followed the passage from Lac la Croix to Lake Superior. He found it "most astonishing" that the North West Company had not known of the route earlier, because, although it was "apparently new," it lay "at the door of Grand Portage" and had been "formerly used by the French." The Nor'westers began to refer to their new route as the "Old Road." The same label was used on a map illustrating Alexander Mackenzie's journals, published only three years after the route's rediscovery.[16]

Although the partners of the North West Company were generally pleased with Roderick McKenzie's find, they regarded it as inferior to the Grand Portage route. The Kaministikwia waterway was much swampier and nearly 60 miles longer than that via Grand Portage, and some of its numerous portages needed bridges and corduroy roads before they could be used efficiently. Thus it was natural that the North West Company partners preferred to remain at Grand Portage as long as possible. There, however, they soon had to reckon with an American threat.[17]

In 1800 a Yankee customs collector working out of Michilimackinac landed at Grand Portage. His purpose, according to the later recollection of David Thompson, the prominent British explorer and surveyor in the Canadian Northwest, was to tell "the British fur traders, [that] the bay, and carrying place were within the United States territory, and he would levy duties on all the merchandize and furrs that should be landed in the bay, or pass on the carrying place." North West Company partners William McGillivray, William Mackay, and Hugh McGillis also later swore that they were forced out of Grand Portage because American army officers and customs officials at Michilimackinac threatened to occupy it, insisting it was in the United States.[18]

Americans at Michilimackinac probably did speak to North West Company traders in those terms, because the official United States position was that the Grand Portage post and trail were within American jurisdiction and British goods passing through there were liable to American duties. This position was based on Article 3 of Jay's Treaty, which, while giving certain assurances about the "free" passage of commodities, applied only to portages and waterways on the common boundary.[19]

Facing ruin with the likely American takeover of Grand Portage, the Nor'westers scurried about for an alternate route—one better than the Kaministikwia. Alexander Mackenzie himself reconnoitered the north side of the Pigeon River, but found only rugged, forested hills, which made a portage from Lake Superior to Fort Charlotte, above the rapids, impossible. In 1801 two more exploration parties were sent out by the company partners gathered at Grand Portage for a critical meeting. The first, led by William Mackay, traveled with great difficulty from Rainy Lake to Lake Superior over the Kaministikwia passage. The second, headed by William McGillivray and Mackay, examined the route from the Kaministikwia's mouth to Lac la Croix. Both found the travel "so dangerous and laborious" that the partners looked without success for another alternative before deciding the Kaministikwia would have to suffice. The following year they sent workmen to improve some of its most challenging swamps.[20]

As this work got under way, the company speeded up the removal of its depot from Grand Portage to a large post constructed at the mouth of the Kaministikwia. New Fort, as the place was originally called, was virtually completed by late 1803, and four years later it was officially named Fort William.[21]

While the search for a more northern route to replace the Grand Portage Trail was going on, the mystery of the relative locations of Lake of the Woods and the Mississippi River was being unraveled for the North West Company. During 1797-98 surveyor David Thompson traveled from Grand Portage through Lake of the Woods to Lake Winnipeg and across the plains to the Missouri River before returning to Lake Superior by way of the upper Mississippi. Considering the number of men and posts the company had in the interior, it is likely that partners McGillivray and Mackenzie already knew the Mississippi did not extend north of Lake of the Woods. Thus their instructions to Thompson were probably not to discover that fact, but to prove it.[22]

While passing through Lake of the Woods, Thompson measured certain points but did not really map the lake. Canoeing rapidly and directly across it, he failed to chart its irregular shoreline and to determine accurately its size. As a result his map drawn on the basis of his measurements showed the lake's exit at Rat Portage (now Kenora) as its northwesternmost point, its shape as an inverted pear, and its placement too far east. Despite these errors, Thompson accomplished his main purpose of determining the lake's latitude.[23]

On his return trip Thompson was guided to Turtle Lake, about ten miles north of present Bemidji. On April 27, 1798, he declared it to be "the Source of the famous Mississippi, in the most direct Line, all the other little sources are reckoned to be subordinate to this, as they are longer in forming so considerable a Stream."[24] He passed out the east side of Turtle Lake through present Fox Lake and calculated that the Mississippi began where Turtle Brook left Fox Lake at 47° 37′ 19″ N. and 95° 8′ 35″ W. Thompson's latitudinal measurement of Turtle Lake was within approximately a mile of modern surveys, but his longitudinal measurements placed it about 15 miles too far west. This error, when combined with the mispositioning of Lake of the Woods, caused him to conclude that the source of the Mississippi lay south but slightly west of the northwest point of Lake of the Woods.

Thompson's superiors must have been pleased with his report proving that no part of the Mississippi lay due west of Lake of the Woods. His observations and his map were well publicized in 1801 with the issuance of Alexander Mackenzie's account of his transcontinental expeditions to the Pacific and Arctic oceans. In a prefatory history of the fur trade, Mackenzie triumphantly reported that "Mr. Thompson, astronomer to the North-West Company," had proved that a boundary line from the northwest point of Lake of the Woods due west to the Mississippi "can never happen, as the North-West part of the Lake du Bois [*Lake of the Woods*] is in latitude 49. 37. North, and longitude 94.31 West, and the Northernmost branch of the source of the Mississippi is in latitude 47. 38. North, and longitude 95.6. West." Furthermore, Mackenzie noted, Thompson had "determined the Northern bend of the Missisoury [*Missouri*] to be in latitude 47. 32. North, and longitude 101. 25. West; and, according to the Indian accounts, it runs to the south of West, so that if the Missisoury were even to be considered as the Mississippi, no Western line could strike it."[25]

Mackenzie's interest in the border was far from academic. He realized Thompson's determinations necessitated a boundary rectification. As one possibility, he suggested that if the line were "to follow the principal waters to their source, it ought to keep through Lake Superior to the River St. Louis, and follow that river to its source; close to which is the source of the waters falling into the river of Lake la Pluie [*Rainy River*], which is a common route of the Indians to the Lake du Bois." On the other hand, Mackenzie advised, "if the navigation of the Mississippi is considered as of any consequence" by Great Britain, the "nearest way to get at it" would be provided by a boundary from the St. Louis River through the Savanna Portage to the Mississippi. But this man, who had twice crossed the continent, was too farsighted to limit his view to the upper Mississippi; his eyes were also on the future fur trade of the Columbia River basin. So, concluded Mackenzie, if Great Britain had a right to enter the Mississippi "along the line of division," it would have to do so below the latitude of the river's source, and then "the line must be continued West, till it terminates in the Pacific Ocean, to the South of the Columbia."[26] American statesmen, however, who without question accepted the results of Thompson's survey, thought in terms of a far less radical closure.

The northwest boundary issue was soon caught up in plans for quieting contention over the northeast boundary, where a survey conducted under Jay's Treaty had solved one problem only to uncover two others. Jay and Grenville had agreed to the creation of a joint commission to identify and locate the St. Croix River, which on Mitchell's map emptied into the Bay of Fundy. Samuel de Champlain, the founder of New France, had also designated a St. Croix River in the area in 1604, but no river of that name existed during Mitchell's time in what is now the Maine-Nova Scotia borderland. Soon after the 1783 peace treaty, rival American and Canadian land seekers were in open disagreement. Matters were further complicated because three streams, each regarded as a possible St. Croix, flowed into the Bay of Fundy; the Cobscook and the Schoodic were quite close together, and about 50 miles east of them was the Magaguadavic. Americans, particularly those in Massachusetts, which claimed the area under its colonial charter, insisted the easternmost river was the St. Croix; the British determinedly held that the honor belonged to the Schoodic.[27]

The joint British-American commission agreed in 1798 that the Schoodic should be regarded as the St. Croix. The traditional name was restored, and the stream was surveyed and marked to its source. The land north of the river's headwaters did not conform to the "highlands" referred to in the peace treaty, however, and the boundary out from its mouth—which affected the ownership of islands and navigation rights in Passamaquoddy Bay, an arm of the Bay of Fundy—had never been clarified.[28]

These problems became critical to the administration of President Thomas Jefferson after the Massachusetts legislature called on the federal government to settle the disputed ownership of certain islands in Passamaquoddy Bay. Secretary of State James Madison therefore instructed Rufus King, American minister to Great Britain, to resolve all outstanding boundary differences.[29]

For guidance on the northwest boundary gap Madison had turned to Mackenzie's recently published *Voyages*. He concluded that, contrary to the provisions of the peace treaty, a line drawn due west from the northwestern point of Lake of the Woods would not strike the Mississippi, whose highest source "It is now well understood . . . is South of the Lake of the Woods. . . . To remedy this error," Madison instructed, "it may be agreed that the Boundary of the United States in that quarter shall be a line running from that source of the Mississippi which is nearest to the Lake of the Woods and striking it Westwardly as a tangent and from the point touched along the Watermark of the Lake to its most Northwestern point at which it will meet the line running thro' the Lake."[30] His apparent anxiety to close the northwest gap was probably influenced strongly by Mackenzie's assertions that Great Britain should seek a southward revision of the boundary west of Lake Superior. He evidently thought his solution was logical and reasonable, since the United States had no territorial claims west of the proposed closure line, but instead he nearly blundered into a major diplomatic disaster.

In the absence of the vacationing King, preliminary negotiations on the boundary convention were conducted by Christopher Gore, United States chargé d'affaires in London. On August 24, 1802, Gore first mentioned the proposed boundary settlements to Lord Hawkesbury, British secretary of state for foreign affairs, and in a conference on September 28 he gave him Madison's proposals in detail.[31]

Although outwardly courteous and avowedly desirous of "removing all causes of future dispute," Hawkesbury responded dilatorily to American advances throughout the negotiations. He may have been inclined to mistrust American motives, or he may merely have been preoccupied with more important continental affairs. In any event, he delayed opening the conferences with Gore in order to confer with George Hammond, undersecretary of state for foreign affairs and former minister to the United States. Then, following the September 28 meeting, Hawkesbury indicated "it may perhaps be necessary" for him "to obtain information from persons in this country on some of the subjects which are likely to be brought into discussion." Not only was the British foreign secretary unhurried, he was also inclined to quibble over the northwest boundary. Gore interpreted his remarks to mean that Great Britain expected an American land cession in order to give British subjects access to the Mississippi.[32]

Madison concluded that "the proposition for adjusting the boundary in the North West corner of the United States is not relished by the British Government." On December 16, 1802, he wrote to King, who had by then assumed responsibility for the negotiations in London, that President Jefferson considered the proposition "as a liberal one, inasmuch as the more obvious remedy for the error of the Treaty, would have been by a line running due North from the most Northern source of the Mississippi, and intersecting the line running due West from the Lake

of the Woods." It appeared to Madison that Great Britain was about to spurn a gracious concession which might give it access to a navigable portion of the Mississippi. He instructed King that, since the British did not share Jefferson's views on the northwest boundary proposal, "it should not for the present be pursued; and that the other questions of boundary should be adjusted with as little delay as possible." Nevertheless, Madison desired that King continue to try to interest Hawkesbury in a joint survey of the Mississippi headwaters area.[33]

The ambassador was ultimately successful in reaching an agreement with Hawkesbury, but along the way he became exasperated with the British minister's apparent unconcern for the boundary negotiations. On February 28, 1803, King reported some progress, but only on the Passamaquoddy Bay portion and this by virtue of conferring with Thomas Barclay, who had been the British commissioner on the St. Croix River survey. Barclay, according to King, agreed in principle to the American proposal with respect to the Passamaquoddy line, so King foresaw "nothing to impede a settlement of this boundary, except the difficulty of engaging the minister [*Hawkesbury*] to bestow upon the subject sufficient time to understand it." In due course an agreement was reached on all three boundary areas, and early in April King sent Hawkesbury a draft. The Convention of 1803 was signed on May 12 "without the alteration of a word of the original draught." King had every reason to be pleased with the agreement, because it conformed closely to Madison's original directive. Article 1 gave the United States everything it desired, including a navigable channel, with the single exception of rights to one island in Passamaquoddy Bay; Articles 2 and 3 called for the naming of commissioners who were to determine the boundary from the source of the St. Croix to the "North westermost Head of Connecticut River."[34]

Article 5 provided that the northwest boundary gap was to be closed through the simple expedient of drawing a direct line from the northwest point of Lake of the Woods to the nearest source of the Mississippi, both of which were to be determined by three commissioners who were also to run and mark the connecting line. King regarded the direct line as "equally advantageous" as that proposed by Madison. Using Thompson's and Mackenzie's incorrect information, King concluded that the direct line would lie west of any part of Lake of the Woods until it struck the most northwest point.[35]

Had they ever been appointed, the commissioners would probably have accurately mapped the area. But such was not to be, for only two days after signing the convention, King hastily and somewhat embarrassedly notified Hawkesbury that on April 30 the United States and France had completed the Louisiana Purchase treaty in

Paris. During the convention negotiations King had apparently used Madison's reasoning that perhaps there was a navigable portion of the Mississippi west of the northwest boundary line. He now assured Hawkesbury that in drafting the Louisiana Territory treaty "care has been taken so to frame the same, as not to infringe any Right of Great Britain in the navigation of the River Mississippi."[36] King was correct enough in his observation that the Louisiana treaty did not "infringe" British navigation rights to the Mississippi, but his statement that this was deliberately achieved by the United States was a gross distortion. In simple truth, the British had not been excluded from the Mississippi by the limits of Louisiana because the United States had purchased a territory with undefined boundaries.

The difficulty in delineating Louisiana lay partially in the obfuscated wording of the treaties whereby it was ceded from France to Spain in 1762 and retroceded to France in 1800. According to the Treaty of San Ildefonso, the retrocession document, Spain was to transfer "Louisiana with the Same extent that it now has in the hands of Spain, & that it had when France possessed it." Interestingly enough the territory had never been clearly defined when France possessed it before 1762.[37]

This vagueness was perpetuated by Napoleon's ministers, even though they had some sense of Louisiana's extent. Before selling Louisiana, French foreign minister Charles Maurice de Talleyrand stated in a secret memorandum that the Mississippi had been set as its eastern boundary by the Anglo-French treaty of 1763. He contended, however, that its southern and southwestern boundaries were formed by the Rio Grande River to 30 degrees north latitude (about 200 miles southeast of modern El Paso, Texas). From that point northward, he observed, the boundary was uncertain because it had never been fixed by an international agreement. Likewise there had never been a demarcation of Canada and Louisiana. Such a line would have been pointless, he noted, because both areas had belonged to France before 1763, and no boundary had since been drawn between them.[38]

None of this information was shared with Robert Livingston, United States minister to France, or special envoy James Monroe, who assisted him late in the negotiations, even after Napoleon had decided to sell all of Louisiana. Not wishing to ruin an admittedly wise purchase because of undue concern with the legal niceties of boundaries, Livingston and Monroe agreed to buy Louisiana "with all its rights and appurtenances as fully and in the Same manner as they have been acquired by the French Republic" under the Treaty of San Ildefonso.[39]

The nature of the problem and the depth of French diplomatic guile are indicated in Livingston's résumé of a conversation he had with Talleyrand several weeks after the treaty had been signed. "I asked the minister what

were the east bounds of the territory ceded to us?" wrote Livingston. "He said he did not know; we must take it as they had received it. I asked him how Spain meant to give them possession? He said, according to the words of the treaty. But what did you mean to take? I do not know. Then you mean that we shall construe it our own way? I can give you no direction; you have made a noble bargain for yourselves, and I suppose you will make the most of it."[40]

Jefferson's administration suspected Talleyrand of laying the groundwork for future boundary squabbles between the United States and the neighboring claims of powerful Great Britain and Spain. Nevertheless, it proceeded to "make the most of it" by claiming a grand Louisiana stretching from the Perdido River (the present western boundary of the Florida panhandle) across the lands drained by the Mississippi and Missouri rivers. But Article 5 of the King-Hawkesbury Convention inadvertently threatened to undercut American ambitions for a liberal northern boundary of Louisiana. Jefferson came to this realization during the summer of 1803. His initial solution, described in a paper entitled "An Examination into the Boundaries of Louisiana," dated September 7, 1803, was to call for a northern boundary which would run "round the heads of the Missouri & Mišipi & their waters."[41] Still seeking a closure of the northwest boundary gap, however, he continued to study the question.

When Congress reconvened in October, Jefferson wanted the Senate to act immediately on the Louisiana Purchase treaty. Despite political opposition and some constitutional misgivings on the part of the president, the treaty was rushed through the Senate in three days. Ratifications were promptly exchanged with France on the following day, October 21.[42]

On October 24, after the Louisiana treaty was incontestable, Jefferson submitted the King-Hawkesbury Convention to the Senate. The agreement's delimiting fifth article was quickly detected as a threat to Louisiana's northern extent. Amid some sentiment to delete the article, and even some feeling that the entire convention should be rejected, the senators on November 15 referred the agreement to a committee of three headed by John Quincy Adams. The committeemen were particularly troubled by the timing of the French and British treaties. Knowing that King had signed his agreement nearly two weeks after the Louisiana Purchase treaty, they feared he might have surrendered certain territorial rights that the United States had just gained in Paris. Therefore, in order to determine the circumstances of King's negotiations, they inquired of Secretary of State Madison if the convention with Great Britain "was concluded with any reference whatsoever to that with the French republic, or with any right or claim which the United States have acquired by it." Madison no doubt informed Adams of a letter he had received from King, who by then was back in New York. King assured him that at the time he signed the agreement he "had no knowledge of the treaty with France; and have reason to be satisfied that Lord Hawkesbury was equally uninformed of it. It results, that the convention with Great Britain was concluded without any reference whatsoever to the treaty of cession with France."[43]

King's statement should have satisfied the Senate that it was unnecessary to delete the fifth article. Still the senators proceeded at an unhurried pace while awaiting more information. On January 15, 1804, Jefferson concluded a supplement to his earlier "Examination" entitled "P.S. The Northern boundary of *Louisiana*, Coterminous with the Possessions of *England*." In this postscript Jefferson unknowingly reiterated a historical fiction by contending that commissioners appointed under the 1713 Treaty of Utrecht had agreed on the 49th parallel as the boundary between Louisiana and Canada. The authorities for Jefferson's findings were American geographer Thomas Hutchins' *Topographical Description of Louisiana* and John Mitchell's by-then-famous map of North America. On the Mitchell map a wavering, broken line ranging from below the 49th parallel to nearly as high as the 51st parallel and passing north of Lake of the Woods was labeled "Bounds of Hudsons Bay by the Treaty of Utrecht." Jefferson inferred that it had been the intention of the peace commissioners in 1782 to close the northwest boundary gap by following the 49th parallel from Lake of the Woods to the Mississippi, which was then supposed to rise north of that line.[44]

Further, explained Jefferson, the intention of the King-Hawkesbury negotiation had been to complete the provisions of the peace treaty by closing the gap between Lake of the Woods and the Mississippi, which, as it developed, lay south not west of the lake. But once Louisiana had been acquired with the 49th parallel as its northern limit, the president insisted, Article 5 of the convention with Great Britain was unnecessary, because it applied to territory that lay solely within the United States.

Jefferson's brief paper soon became the basis for the government's position on the question of Louisiana's northern boundary. On January 31, 1804, Secretary of State Madison wrote to Livingston in France that "The northern boundary, we have reason to believe, was settled between France and Great Britain by commissioners appointed under the treaty of Utrecht, who separated the British and French territories west of the Lake of the Woods by the 49th degree of latitude." Livingston was instructed "that no time should be lost in collecting the best proofs which can be obtained" to support these "just claims" of the United States. In particular, Madison wanted the minister to obtain an authenticated copy of

Crozat's charter, "the proceedings of the commissioners under the treaty of Utrecht," and other documents, including maps.[45]

Not surprisingly, by the time the Senate returned to the King-Hawkesbury Convention most of its members were troubled by the possibility that Great Britain could use Article 5 in the future to limit the Louisiana Purchase. Consequently, on February 9, 1804, the Senate approved the convention with the deletion of Article 5.[46]

Five days later Madison sent the altered convention to James Monroe, King's successor in London. Madison instructed him to press vigorously for British ratification, pointing out that the United States should not be expected to compromise Louisiana's northern boundary by agreeing to Article 5. Monroe was to present the deletion of the fifth article as an insignificant matter, because Louisiana would only "remain the same in the hands of the United States as it was in the hands of France; and may be adjusted and established according to the principles and authorities which would in that case have been applicable." The "principles and authorities" Madison had in mind were clearly based on Jefferson's belief that the boundary west from Lake of the Woods had been fixed at the 49th parallel by commissioners appointed under the Treaty of Utrecht. As in his earlier letter to Livingston, Madison showed some misgivings about the administration's basis for the claim, so Monroe was to be mindful of "the necessity of recurring to the proceedings of the Commissioners as the source of authentic information. These are not within our reach here, and it must consequently be left to your own researches and judgment to determine the proper use to be made of them."[47]

By the time Monroe received the boundary convention, its fate was virtually foredoomed by the state of Anglo-American relations, which had deteriorated rapidly after Napoleon's resumption of war in May, 1803. The British government had understandably reacted angrily against American shippers who supplied France and her allies. Consequently the Royal Navy forcibly searched American merchant ships and impressed certain sailors who were alleged to be British subjects.[48]

Monroe was delayed for several months in broaching the boundary question to Hawkesbury, not only because of the contentious issues of maritime rights and commerce, but also because of a political crisis within the cabinet of Prime Minister Henry Addington. Monroe, who found both Addington and Hawkesbury adamant on the question of neutral rights, bided his time until they were replaced by William Pitt and Lord Harrowby.[49]

Feeling that he could now deal with a stable government, Monroe initiated discussions with Harrowby on the whole range of outstanding issues. At their first meeting Harrowby learned the United States had ratified the

King-Hawkesbury Convention with the exception of the fifth article and, Monroe reported, he "censured" the action "in strong terms." The American could only conclude from the manner in which Harrowby suggested postponing a settlement of issues that the foreign minister's "will had settled the point." Subsequent events bore out this judgment.

On September 5, having become pessimistic about his chances of resolving the impressment issue, Monroe presented Harrowby with a memorandum of the American case for acceptance of the boundary convention. His statement essentially reiterated the main points of Jefferson's study and Madison's instructions, differing only in emphasis. Whereas Jefferson had merely implied that the peace commissioners in 1782 had intended the 49th parallel be the boundary west from Lake of the Woods, Monroe boldly stated that this had been their "obvious intention." His presentation was to no avail and, as he observed later, "The conduct of Lord Harrowby in this business was essentially the same with that of his predecessor." Harrowby then procrastinated in referring the matter to the cabinet, and it and all other questions were left in abeyance when Monroe left England in October, 1804, for a special mission to Spain. The question of the boundary settlement was not reopened upon his return the following summer, and the Convention of 1803 quietly died.[50]

In the form it was presented to Great Britain, the convention could have had no effect on the northwestern boundary of the United States. As Alfred L. Burt aptly pointed out, the "real tragedy" of the convention's failure was that the Maine-New Brunswick line along the highlands remained undefined to cause serious difficulties later.[51] Why did the British refuse to act on the convention? Lord Harrowby's position was that the British government would not sanction an agreement unilaterally altered by the United States. This sounds like the official rather than the real reason, which was no doubt related to the inability of the two governments to reach accords on the other, more significant problems leading to the War of 1812. Perhaps Harrowby regarded approval of the convention as a form of accommodation to the United States, and considering his stance on the maritime questions, he would not have been willing to countenance any such diplomatic good will.

CHAPTER 3

The Northern Boundary of Louisiana Territory

WITH THE PURCHASE OF LOUISIANA in 1803 American interest shifted from closing the boundary gap between Lake of the Woods and the Mississippi River to the broader question of defining Louisiana Territory's northern extent. That problem was not resolved until 15 years after Jefferson first contemplated it. Then, following another abortive boundary convention and the War of 1812, the line was settled along the 49th parallel in keeping with his original suggestion.

After Jefferson advanced his claim to the 49th parallel boundary, his administration sought more substantial proof than Mitchell's map and Hutchins' reference. Jefferson and Madison hoped to find good primary evidence, such as the actual records of the boundary commissioners appointed under the 1713 Treaty of Utrecht. Accordingly Ambassadors James Monroe in England and Robert Livingston in France were enlisted in the search. On September 17, 1804, Monroe informed Madison that he had not yet obtained the commissioners' report, "tho' all the bookshops have been ransacked for it, by an agent whom I employed for that purpose." The ambassador was able to secure more secondary evidence, however, including a 1755 map by English cartographer Ellis Huske, which showed the boundary line running west "indefinitely" on the 49th parallel from a point several degrees east of Lake of the Woods. Monroe reported that he "did not hesitate" to rely on the Huske map and "other documents which supported it" as authorities for the American claim to the 49th parallel. In actuality he was uneasy about the nature of his proof and therefore advanced what was to become the official American position on the northern boundary question: "The report of the Commissaries must be in possession of this [*the British*] government, so that if there is any error in my statement it is in its power to correct it."[1]

As Monroe suspected, there was error in his statement. He was passing on as fact an intriguing myth that had somehow gained wide acceptance over more than a century. Although he and his British counterparts never knew the accurate history of the boundary question in relation to the Treaty of Utrecht, the myth of the 49th parallel dividing line had a certain foundation in truth.

The original proposal to use the 49th parallel to divide British and French claims had grown out of the desires of the Hudson's Bay Company to limit French access to the interior streams of the far north. The idea of formally setting a border between the two countries' lands dated back to 1686 and had been expressed several times by company officials. Negotiators of the Treaty of Utrecht in 1713, unable to agree on a specific settlement, stipulated in Article 10 that French and British commissioners would convene within a year to fix the line in the Hudson Bay region and other areas. Amid indications of imminent boundary negotiations in 1714, the Hudson's Bay Company suggested a boundary starting on the Atlantic at Grimmington Island, just below the 58th parallel, and running southwesterly through Lake Mistassini to the 49th parallel, which would be followed west indefinitely.[2]

The presumption that a boundary commission would be convened in 1714 proved to be false. Because of a variety of domestic and international crises, five years elapsed before the British and French returned to the matter of implementing Article 10 of the Treaty of Utrecht. Even then the commissioners' conferences during the fall of 1719 and early 1720 came to naught, because the French steadfastly refused to consider any cession southward to the 49th parallel and, in fact, counterproposed that the British and French boundary be drawn along a line running between Hudson Bay and Lake Mistassini. The Hudson's Bay Company was not easily dissuaded. Thirty-two years after the joint Anglo-French commission had abandoned its work, the company in a renewed effort asked the Board of Trade for assistance in establishing the requested borders. Again in 1755 the firm reminded the board that its request had languished for three years and offered to provide further information in support of the desired boundaries.[3]

Ironically the company's futile solicitations came at the very time that the myth makers—including Dr. John Mitchell, who was then working for the Board of Trade—were reporting that the 49th parallel had been established as the international boundary by commissioners appointed under the Treaty of Utrecht. Somehow these various efforts to define the line, which were always associated with the Treaty of Utrecht, caused some English historians to report that an international boundary had actually been set in North America.[4]

These circumstances were not known to Monroe in 1804; consequently it was logical for him to expect the British to prove that his case was ill founded. As he returned to his post in London during the summer of 1805, the grave maritime questions of the day threatened to plunge the United States and Great Britain into another war. When Monroe could not reconcile differences with the Pitt ministry, possibly because of his well-known Anglophobia as well as some social difficulties, President Jefferson, with some urging by Congress, sent William

THE MYTH that the northwestern boundary had been set along the 49th parallel by the Treaty of Utrecht in 1713 was perpetuated by such cartographers as Ellis Huske, who produced this map of North America in 1755.

Pinkney of Baltimore to assist him. Special envoy Pinkney did not land at Liverpool until June 19, 1806, and then talks with British officials were delayed many weeks while Foreign Minister Charles James Fox struggled against a fatal illness.[5]

Monroe and Pinkney had been explicitly instructed by Secretary of State Madison to settle outstanding naval and commercial differences with Great Britain in an agreement that was to include British revocation of the principle and practice of impressment. At about the same time, Madison advised Monroe that he should continue to work on a resolution of the boundary questions covered in the 1803 convention. As negotiations progressed during the fall of 1806, it became increasingly evident to the Americans that they could not persuade the British to renounce impressment. On November 11 Monroe and Pinkney informed Madison that they had failed to reach an agreement on this matter. Then, in direct violation of their instructions, they continued to work on a commercial agreement, which was finally signed on the last day of the year.[6]

Undoubtedly the Americans would have preferred knowing their government's reaction to the trade agreement signed on December 31, 1806, before they resumed talks with the British. That, however, was precluded by slow mail service. While they waited, they opened negotiations on a supplemental convention dealing with United States-Canada trade and boundaries.[7]

Monroe and Pinkney and their British counterparts, Lord Holland and Lord Auckland, agreed on certain boundary principles with little difficulty. Rather than rework the 1803 convention per se, they would write a new treaty. They would, however, include the earlier articles pertaining to Passamaquoddy Bay and the highlands above the St. Croix River essentially unchanged. But with respect to the controversial northwest boundary closure, they would forsake the Lake of the Woods-Mississippi River line in favor of recognizing American claims to the area west of Lake of the Woods.[8]

The wording of Article 5, providing for the boundary west of Lake of the Woods, caused some differences. Holland and Auckland preferred that the line be drawn due west from the lake along the 49th parallel as far as the territories of the United States extended. Monroe and Pinkney, however, insisted that the starting point for a boundary extension had to be the "most northwestern point of Lake of the Woods," from which a due north-south line would be followed to the 49th parallel. They also objected to any reference to the extent of American claims west of Lake of the Woods, which they feared could be interpreted in a way that would limit the United States. As they well knew, such powerful men as Thomas Douglas, Earl of Selkirk, then a member of the House of Lords and a colonizer of eastern Canada, were contending that occupancy was the only valid means of determining ownership of disputed territory.[9]

The British commissioners agreed to the stipulation concerning the most northwestern point of the lake but balked at the omission of the reference to American territorial extent. While they were determined to have such a reference, they at least agreed to make it reciprocal. The version acceptable to Holland and Auckland provided that the 49th parallel was to be the boundary "westward of the said lake, as far as their said respective territories extend in that quarter." Even though this version carried the implication that Great Britain as well as the United States might be limited, Monroe and Pinkney still preferred their own wording. The seeming British generosity in agreeing to the 49th parallel boundary was probably part of a bargain whereby the United States conceded in Article 6 that British subjects and goods would be granted free access through American territories to the Mississippi.

In his reaction of July 30 Madison made little effort to disguise his displeasure with the supplemental convention. He was particularly disturbed by the inference that American and British claims extended west of the Rocky Mountains. The language of Article 5, he warned, would be "an offensive intimation" to Spain and must be stricken from the final agreement. Furthermore, he was adamant that British access to the Mississippi was not to be allowed.[10]

Madison's views made little difference, for he realized by late July that no agreement could be reached. His hopes of a year before had been completely dashed by a series of disastrous events which enlarged the specter of war. While Monroe, Pinkney, and the British negotiators were meeting in London, Napoleon mandated a blockade of Great Britain in his Berlin Decree. The responding British Order in Council served to pinch neutral traders further and make President Jefferson more insistent on a formal British renunciation of impressment. Consequently, when Jefferson learned on February 1, 1807, that Monroe and Pinkney had failed to reach an agreement on impressment, he reacted quickly. He hastily convened his cabinet members, who unanimously agreed they would neither accept nor consult the Senate on any treaty that did not ban impressment.[11]

By the time Madison relayed this decision on February 3, the agreement of December 31, 1806, which included no reference to impressment, had been en route to Washington for a month. When Jefferson received the official copy on March 15, he simply refused to consider it, and Madison ordered Monroe and Pinkney to resume negotiations with the aim of reaching an agreement on impressment. Suddenly tensions were further heightened by the so-called "Chesapeake" affair—the unwarranted and unprovoked attack on June 21, 1807, by the British warship "Leopard" on the United States frigate "Chesapeake" only about ten miles from Norfolk, Virginia. When news of this incident reached London late in July, the American negotiators immediately recognized that their Convention of 1806 and the supplemental Convention of 1807 were doomed.[12]

The supplemental Convention of 1807 was never approved, but the fact that both nations' envoys had agreed on the principle of a boundary line at the 49th parallel was significant, for it reinforced a premise that would reappear in later negotiations. The intriguing question is why the British negotiators agreed to it. Monroe had made clear his position on the evidential value of the sources supporting a boundary at the 49th parallel set by commissioners under the Treaty of Utrecht. This left Holland and Auckland with the challenge of producing better sources, if the British had them.

Although the Englishmen could not be troubled with research in British government records, they were curious enough about the 49th parallel tradition to confer with officials of the Hudson's Bay Company. The company's response indicated that, at least officially, it believed its southern limits had been set at the 49th parallel by commissioners appointed under the Treaty of Utrecht. But, the firm reported, "after a diligent search" it could find "no traces" of the commissioners' report. This reply, though far from being positive evidence, was enough to satisfy the British negotiators, who obviously were not greatly concerned about proof. They apparently assumed nothing better than the 49th parallel boundary, for which there was some precedent, could be gained from prolonged bargaining.[13]

Throughout the years devoted to negotiating the abortive Conventions of 1806 and 1807, the British maintained their control over the fur trade of the upper Mississippi region. In 1805–06, when the youthful Lieutenant Zebulon M. Pike wintered there—the first American on record to visit the Minnesota country—he found the area occupied by employees of British trader Robert Dickson and his associates. Although Pike negotiated with the Dakota Indians and acquired land at the confluence of the Mississippi and Minnesota (then called the St. Peter's) for the site of a future military post, his brief sojourn did not ruffle Dickson's men. They continued trading in the United States, despite the lieutenant's warning that they were trespassing on American lands.[14]

It was not long, however, before British traders became bitterly anti-American as they felt the impact of the United States' newly invoked trade restrictions in the years just before the outbreak of the War of 1812. The Embargo and Nonintercourse acts, intended to exclude British goods from the United States, hampered but did not stop the traders, who simply resorted to smuggling. Another irritant was the American contention that Article 3 of Jay's Treaty, which permitted Canadian traders to operate in the United States, did not apply to Louisiana Territory. This prohibition, first invoked by military proclamation in 1805, was intended to keep them out of the Missouri River area. The traders therefore welcomed the War of 1812 as an opportunity to solidify their position in the Northwest and to rectify their losses under the Treaty of 1783.

When the United States declared war on June 18, 1812, the British and their Indian allies were far better prepared for hostilities on the frontier than were the Americans. The island fortress of Michilimackinac, which was the key to control of the western Great Lakes, fell to the British less than a month after the start of the war. With forceful Indian assistance, the British effected the evacuation of Fort Dearborn (in present Chicago) and occupied vital posts at Green Bay and Prairie du Chien, Wisconsin, located at either end of the Fox-Wisconsin waterway connecting Lake Michigan and the Mississippi. As they made more and more wartime inroads into the area northwest of the Mississippi watershed, the British also began to pose a threat to American fur traders on the upper Missouri. In August, 1812, the first of Lord Selkirk's settlers arrived at the heart of his colony—the junction of the Red and Assiniboine rivers in what is now modern Winnipeg. This straggling settlement was but a speck in the earl's vast land grant that included present southern Manitoba, southeastern Saskatchewan, and the Hudson Bay watershed of North Dakota and Minnesota. But Americans, naturally suspicious of any British activity on the frontier, soon saw Selkirk and his colonization scheme as a threat to their northern flank.[15]

In light of the British traders' achievements, their belief that they and their Indian allies had won the conflict, at least in their region, is understandable. In 1814, when peace talks appeared imminent, they envisioned a diplomatic triumph in keeping with their victory in the field. On May 7, 1814, the London firm of Inglis, Ellice and Company, acting as the agent of Canadian traders, represented their view of boundary rectification in a lengthy memorial to Lord Bathurst, the colonial secretary. Contending that a radical adjustment was necessary to preserve the fur trade and to protect Britain's Indian allies,

the company suggested four possible lines, all of which would have pushed the United States back from the Great Lakes. The most extreme asked for a boundary on the Ohio, Mississippi, and Missouri rivers. Although Bathurst was initially cool to these proposals, Prime Minister Liverpool's cabinet, stimulated by its *continental successes* and increasingly in a mood to punish the United States, soon became more aggressive and accepted the Canadian traders' philosophy that Great Britain should gain territorially from the war in America.[16]

By the time the British and American peace commissioners convened at Ghent on August 8, 1814, prospects for a British victory in North America had been brightened by the transfer of thousands of the Duke of Wellington's veterans of the Napoleonic wars. Consequently the British negotiators were able to make demands in keeping with anticipated military successes. Conversely the American negotiators were hampered by their instructions from the war-weary Madison administration, which had been forced to temper its aims in the weeks before the Ghent conference opened.[17]

In his original instructions to the peace commissioners on April 15, 1813, Secretary of State James Monroe had specified that a ban on impressment was an indispensable condition of peace. Two months later he directed that any territorial agreement should be based on the principle of *status quo ante bellum*. The administration adhered to this aim, but as the dispirited, factionalized country limped through the following year without notable military accomplishments, Monroe abandoned the effort to negotiate an end to impressment.

The peace negotiations held intermittently in the summer and fall of 1814 included numerous boundary considerations. The British initially demanded that a permanent Indian territory be established in the Northwest with an eastern boundary following the line set by the Treaty of Greenville in 1795. This meant the Indians would gain approximately a third of the state of Ohio and retain all United States land to the west and north of it. Great Britain then asked for a portion of Maine to enable the construction of a direct road from Halifax, Nova Scotia, to Quebec; it also insisted that the boundary west of Lake Superior be changed.[18]

After refusing to negotiate on such terms, the Americans assumed the conference would end, but the British kept the proceedings alive by sending further written explanations of their government's position. It was obvious the Foreign Office did not want to conclude an agreement until Britain's military standing in North America improved. Hoping for a conquest of the Lake Champlain area, the British were stunned by the smashing American naval victory on the lake and by the failure of British forces to seize Fort Erie and Baltimore. These three major reverses jeopardized any chance Great Britain had of gaining territorial concessions from the United States. The British diplomats in Ghent received newspapers carrying the stories of these setbacks on October 20, along with revised boundary instructions. They were ordered to insist that each nation retain the territory under its control at war's end, except for the area west of Lake Superior, where the Foreign Office wanted the Mississippi-Lake of the Woods line of the 1803 convention.[19]

In their carefully drafted counterproposal, delivered to the British on November 10, the Americans promoted the mutual restoration of territories as the guiding principle. Regarding the boundary delineated in 1783, they asked that the entire line—with the exception of the established eastern segment following the St. Croix River—be clarified later by joint commissions. They also considered the extension of the boundary beyond Lake of the Woods. Acquisition of Louisiana and the Convention of 1807 virtually precluded their acceptance of a Lake of the Woods-Mississippi River line. To safeguard the interests of the United States, the American commissioners proposed a return to the Convention of 1807. Article 8 of their draft was exactly the same as that of 1807. Thus it included the controversial wording that the 49th parallel was to be the dividing line as far as the "respective territories" of the two nations extended west of Lake of the Woods.[20]

The British response was delivered at Ghent on November 26 in the form of marginal notes on a copy of the American proposal. On most of the articles there was little disagreement, with suggested changes usually consisting of the alteration of single words. Article 8, however, was completely rewritten. The British were willing to accept the 49th parallel boundary, but only with their wording of 1807, which left the way open to limit the extent of American claims west of Lake of the Woods. They also added the stipulation that British subjects were to be given free access to and free navigation of the Mississippi River. During the negotiators' ensuing discussions the Americans realized they could achieve the 49th parallel boundary only if they compromised on the provisions respecting Mississippi navigation and the United States right to fish in the Atlantic off Canada. Fearing such concessions would undermine the validity of the Treaty of 1783, they chose to omit any references to all three sensitive issues.[21]

Inability to agree on the 49th parallel brought both nations' negotiators to accept the future clarification of the line, as delineated in 1783, by joint survey commissions. Most of the brief treaty signed on Christmas Eve, 1814, dealt with their establishment. Article 4 provided for the Passamaquoddy Bay survey and Article 5 for that from the head of the St. Croix River to the St. Lawrence. Article 6 called for two commissioners, one from each country, to supervise the survey of the water boundary from the point where the 45th parallel struck the St. Lawrence to Lake Superior. The same two commissioners

were designated by Article 7 to chart the line from "the water communication between Lake Huron and Lake Superior to the most North Western point of the Lake of the Woods" after they had completed the work of Article 6. The seventh article also required the commissioners to "particularize the Latitude and Longitude of the most North Western point of the Lake of the Woods, and of such other parts of the said boundary as they may deem proper." All four articles provided for arbitration by a "friendly Sovereign or State" in the event the commissioners failed to agree on their final recommendations.[22]

The Treaty of Ghent was a bitter disappointment to the Canadian traders and the Indians, who again had been deserted at the conference table. Firmly in control of the upper Northwest, they neither understood nor accepted the broad circumstances which had caused the British to forsake them. From the standpoint of Anglo-American relations, the peace was a sensible conclusion to an unproductive war, but to many it looked more like a truce. The Ghent negotiators had ignored rather than solved the fundamental differences which caused the war. Strained relations continued, although the two nations signed a short-term commercial convention in 1815 and, two years later, the Rush-Bagot Agreement providing for the demilitarization of the Great Lakes.[23] These two accomplishments were overshadowed by the issues left unresolved—impressment, the fisheries, and the northern boundary of Louisiana—issues which loomed as threats to any lasting peace.

The unsettled boundary west of Lake of the Woods was troublesome to the United States in its strenuous postwar effort to curtail illicit British trade on the upper Mississippi and subject the area's Indians to American policy. A congressional measure of April 29, 1816, prohibited the issuance of Indian-trade licenses to foreigners unless the president authorized specific exceptions. The act, however, was virtually unenforceable in the Red River Valley and upper Missouri regions, where Canadians openly plied their trade. Robert Dickson, after years of economic failure, fell in league with Lord Selkirk, and the two concocted various schemes to establish trading posts and even colonies in the upper Red River Valley. Although the plans were never acted upon, Selkirk secured a lease from the Indians of lands reaching from the mouth of the Red upstream to the Grand Forks at the mouth of the Red Lake River, a move that greatly concerned American officials.[24]

To bolster its frontier, the United States sent Major Stephen H. Long to the upper Mississippi in 1817 to select a site for a military post. The spot chosen by Long at the junction of the Mississippi and Minnesota rivers was on one of two tracts of land secured by Pike when he treated with the Dakota in 1805. Shortly after Long's reconnaissance the government began plans to establish this post, as well as a sister installation at the mouth of the Yellowstone River, for the purpose of safeguarding northern Louisiana from incursions by British traders and Selkirkers. There was also considerable interest in projecting the northern boundary of Louisiana beyond the Rockies, because of friction over the question of American jurisdiction in the Pacific Northwest.

While all of these matters were important, the most pressing concern of President Monroe's administration was renewal of the 1815 commercial treaty with Great Britain, which was due to expire in July, 1819. When Richard Rush, the newly appointed United States minister, left for London in November, 1817, he carried instructions from Secretary of State John Quincy Adams to work for an extension of the agreement. Lord Castlereagh, the British foreign minister, was willing to consider the commercial treaty, but he also suggested to Rush that it was "a favourable time" for settling claims to territory. Referring to the northwest boundary gap, Castlereagh spoke in terms of a line from Lake of the Woods to the Mississippi and offered to submit the question to a joint survey commission like those provided by the Treaty of Ghent.[25]

Unprepared for this proposition concerning the boundary, Rush waited until the next day to remind the foreign secretary that the closure line agreed upon by King and Hawkesbury in 1803 had been expunged by the United States because of its possible interference with the Louisiana Purchase. Rush concluded he would have to defer to his government for further instructions, and the British would be free to renew the proposal at any time in the future.

Adams was distrustful of Castlereagh's amicableness because of his own frustrations as Rush's predecessor in London, and because he did not yet recognize that Britain's sincere desire to reach an accord with the United States was due to an impending diplomatic crisis in Europe. Nonetheless he urged Rush to propose "an immediate general negotiation." To support his efforts the Monroe administration named Albert Gallatin, then minister to France, as Rush's conegotiator.[26]

Anticipating British acceptance of the proposed convention, Adams sent detailed instructions to Gallatin and Rush on July 28. "The President," he wrote, wanted the commercial convention of 1815 "continued without alteration for a further term of eight or ten years." Adams also reviewed the northwest boundary question at length, touching not only on the origin of the gap in the Treaty of 1783 but on all subsequent developments. Believing that Great Britain "can have no valid claim" south of the 49th parallel, Adams authorized Rush and Gallatin to agree to the boundary defined by the 1807 convention. Because he

suspected the real British motive was to gain access to the Mississippi River, he bluntly ordered them to reject any line that abutted that stream.[27]

Meanwhile Castlereagh had assented on July 23 to a general convention, informing Rush on the same day that Henry Goulburn, one of the Ghent commissioners, and Frederick John Robinson, president of the Board of Trade and a member of the cabinet, would be Great Britain's negotiators. Castlereagh took time to assure the success of the Anglo-American convention by agreeing to a broad agenda, including such problems as the fisheries, the northern boundary, title to the Columbia River area, and even the impressment issue. The British foreign secretary was far ahead of public opinion, however, and considerably more liberal than his cabinet peers in his willingness to consider relinquishing impressment.[28]

The negotiations, which opened on August 27, dragged on for weeks, primarily because of disagreements over the terms of an impressment article. Finally in mid-October the impatient Gallatin threatened to leave for Paris. His move—recognized by the British as an ultimatum—spurred a hasty, but relatively satisfactory, conclusion to the convention on October 20, although there was no provision for ending impressment.[29]

In closing the northwest boundary gap, the Anglo-American negotiators relied on the Utrecht settlements of the 49th parallel and turned to the Convention of 1807 for guidance. The tone of the boundary article was set by the opening American pronouncement that the United States would not accept any provision which would bring British territory to the Mississippi River. Goulburn and Robinson then retreated from Castlereagh's earlier suggestion of a restatement of the Lake of the Woods-Mississippi line and accepted the principle of the 49th parallel, but they attempted to couple it with a stipulation that Great Britain would have access across American land to the Mississippi. They further asked that British subjects be permitted free navigation of the entire course of the river in conducting their trade. Since Gallatin and Rush had been expressly forbidden to concede any sort of British access to the river, they could not accept these stipulations, and the convention was signed with no reference to the avowed British navigation right which had plagued the United States since 1783.[30]

Article 2, which extended the boundary from Lake of the Woods, read: "It is agreed that a Line drawn from the most North Western Point of the Lake of the Woods, along the forty Ninth Parallel of North Latitude, or, if the said Point shall not be in the Forty Ninth Parallel of North Latitude, then that a Line drawn from the said Point due North or South as the Case may be, until the said Line shall intersect the said Parallel of North Latitude, and from the Point of such Intersection due West along and with the said Parallel shall be the Line of Demarcation . . . to the Stony Mountains."[31]

By agreeing to the boundary westward to the continental divide, the diplomats eliminated the objectionable, ambiguous wording of the 1807 convention that had left the western terminus unspecified, thus providing mutual assurances against encroachments on the western plains. Article 2 also pointed directly to the Pacific Northwest, the disposition of which the United States and Great Britain, recognizing that Spain was no longer a significant factor, were now free to consider. After discussing various proposals, including the American suggestion to extend the 49th parallel boundary to the Pacific Ocean, the diplomats agreed to postpone determination of title to the Oregon country for ten years.[32]

Rush was disappointed that the Convention of 1818 did not contain articles on impressment and American trade with the West Indies; nonetheless the treaty was a signal achievement for the United States. It extended the commercial agreement of 1815 for ten more years; it contained generous provisions for the continuance of American fishing rights in Canadian waters; it closed the boundary gap, and it relaxed tensions in the Columbia River area. In terms of its long-range import, the convention brought to an end the period of poor relations between the United States and Great Britain that had existed since the Revolutionary War and, by solving some of the particularly troublesome issues, reduced the danger of future wars.[33]

With the Convention of 1818 the United States-Canada boundary was settled in principle from the Atlantic to the continental divide. Since the survey parties designated by the Treaty of Ghent were already in the field, it appeared that the line would soon be specifically determined and marked from Passamaquoddy Bay on the east to the northwest point of Lake of the Woods.

CHAPTER 4

Organizing the Wilderness Survey in 1822

ACCORDING to the provisions within two documents— the Paris Treaty of 1783 and the Convention of 1818— the United States and Great Britain had agreed to a boundary that nearly spanned the continent. By the time the second agreement was signed, however, the inadequacies of the first had not yet been resolved. The Treaty of Ghent in 1814 had seemed to promise a ready solution by designating three survey commissions to determine the boundary from the Atlantic to the northwest corner of Lake of the Woods, excepting only the already settled St. Croix River line in New England. Within two years after the negotiations at Ghent, the three survey commissions had been organized, and they seem to have been expected to move with dispatch. In the immediate wake of the War of 1812, however, there was no way of foreseeing the many problems created by geography, transportation difficulties, the personalities of the commissioners, and, for that matter, the changing diplomatic moods of the countries— all of which would delay until 1842 the final settlement of the boundary first described in the 1783 treaty.

The commission established under Article 4 of the Treaty of Ghent was to complete a survey of, and define the boundary line through, Passamaquoddy Bay. That under Article 5 had the unenviable task of determining the line from the head of the St. Croix River westward through the "highlands" (referred to in the Treaty of 1783) to the 45th parallel, and along it to the St. Lawrence.[1]

As its commissioner for both Articles 4 and 5, Great Britain named Thomas Barclay, a former Loyalist who had fled from his native New York City to Nova Scotia during the Revolutionary War. After serving as Britain's boundary commissioner on the St. Croix River survey, he returned to New York in 1799 as the British consul general, a post he held for the next 13 years. His close ties with London were further tightened during the War of 1812, when he served as the agent for British prisoners of war held in the United States. It is unlikely that Great Britain could have found a boundary commissioner more dedicated to its interests.

The work of the commissions under Articles 4 and 5 began with a meeting at St. Andrews, New Brunswick, on September 23, 1816. Within 14 months the survey of Passamaquoddy Bay was completed, and the boundary line it established was accepted by both nations early in 1818. On the other hand, the work under Article 5, from the St. Croix westward, progressed neither efficiently nor satisfactorily. At the commission's final meeting on April 1, 1822, the complete disagreement of the American and British commissioners was made clear in their separate reports. During the next five years arrangements were made to submit the complex boundary case to the king of the Netherlands for arbitration.[2]

From the point where the 45th parallel struck the St. Lawrence River at St. Regis, New York, to the northwest point of Lake of the Woods, the surveying was to be done by a commission authorized by Articles 6 and 7 of the Treaty of Ghent. Once the area prescribed in Article 6, extending from St. Regis to the western end of Lake Huron, had been determined, the same commission was to proceed with the work of Article 7, which was to carry the boundary up the St. Marys River into Lake Superior and on through the wilderness to the northwest point of Lake of the Woods. Great Britain named John Ogilvy of Montreal as its commissioner for Articles 6 and 7, and the United States selected Peter B. Porter of Black Rock (now part of Buffalo), New York. These choices were in keeping with the general sentiment in both countries not to make significant boundary concessions.[3]

Ogilvy, a Scotsman who moved to Canada about 1790 to begin a career as merchant in the fur trade, had been a partner, successively, in the firms of Parker, Gerrard, and Ogilvy, the XY Company, and the North West Company. Thus he represented that tightly knit fraternity of traders who had been angered ever since 1783 over the extraordinary American acquisitions gained at Paris and who had long hoped for a drastic readjustment of the boundary.[4]

In contrast, Peter Porter came from the borderlands and had been caught up in the rampant expansionist mood characteristic of the War of 1812. Soon after his election to Congress in 1809, he earned a reputation as one of the leaders of the "War Hawks," a group of comparatively inexperienced congressmen mainly from the West who advocated war with Great Britain in order to acquire Canada. During more than 11 years as commissioner for Articles 6 and 7, Porter was never fully engaged with his boundary duties, even though he was paid for continuous service. He devoted much of his time to politics and to business in the Black Rock area.

The British and American commissioners meeting jointly as a board were to evaluate the accuracy and validity of the data and evidence gathered by the surveys and reach conclusions on the specific course of the boundary. Although the commissioners were to act as judges rather than as advocates of their country's case, they obviously could not be completely impartial. In practice, the judgeship role meant the commissioners did not participate in the arguments at board meetings, but listened to presentations by each of the agents, whose principal responsibility was to collect and report the evidence best representing his country's aims.[5]

Agents therefore were expected to spend a great deal of time with the survey parties, and as a general rule the surveyors received specific directions from the agent rather than the commissioner. At other times the surveyors were almost entirely on their own, except for written instructions received from the agent, the commissioner, or both. Given this situation, it was important that the commissioner and agent act in concert, because any fundamental disagreements or countermanding of orders would have undermined the work.

The British agent under Articles 6 and 7 was John Hale, a well-known figure in Quebec and the province of Lower Canada. In 1808 he gained his first political office as a member of the Legislative Council of Lower Canada. This position, which he retained for the rest of his life, by itself probably would not have detracted greatly from his ability to fulfill assignments as commission agent. But additional political involvement as a member of the Executive Council of Lower Canada and later as the provincial receiver-general undoubtedly interfered with his duties. Hale therefore spent most of his time in Quebec, consistently deferring boundary matters to the British commissioner.[6]

The influence of the American agent, on the other hand, ultimately surpassed that of the commissioner, largely because of Porter's preoccupation with private affairs in New York. Joseph Delafield, destined to become the dominant figure in the Article 7 survey, was the second agent named to the United States commission. The first was Samuel Hawkins, a former army colonel and, like Porter, a friend of Delafield's. Hawkins simply did not get along with Porter, and he was gradually eased out in favor of his dedicated, ambitious, and hardworking former assistant.[7]

Throughout their efforts to determine the boundary, both Porter and Delafield corresponded directly with the secretary of state, often about related matters, although they were careful to keep each other informed of their activities. Since all of the United States boundary commissions operated within the Department of State, the secretary was the ultimate authority to whom they reported. Both the State Department and the Foreign Office, which controlled the British surveys, permitted the commissions surprising autonomy. The governments' attitude essentially was that since the commissioners and agents were competent, it was best not to interfere except in unusual circumstances.

The staffs of the American and British survey commissions were roughly prescribed by Article 8 of the Treaty of Ghent. Each was authorized "to appoint a Secretary, and to employ such Surveyors or other persons as they shall judge necessary." In establishing the Article 7 commissions the United States and Britain turned to the precedent set by the St. Croix survey. Consequently, in addition to a commissioner and an agent, each employed a secretary, a surveyor trained as an astronomer, and an assistant surveyor who was also a draftsman.[8]

One commission's secretary served as the board secretary and the other as his assistant who kept accounts of joint activities, such as the records and official journal of board meetings. The assignment of these two positions was made by lot. Initially the British secretary served the board, and Donald Fraser, the American, was the assistant. In 1817, when the British position was vacant, Fraser assumed the role of board secretary. After Dr. John J. Bigsby was added to the British party three years later as its secretary and surgeon, he became assistant secretary for the joint commission.[9]

Of the British and American surveyors and their assistants only David Thompson, the famous explorer and mapmaker of the North West Company, served throughout the work of both the Article 6 and 7 commissions. After his first year with the Nor'Westers, when he traveled and explored full time to complete his Lake of the Woods-Mississippi River survey, Thompson surveyed part time while engaging in the fur trade in the Canadian Rockies and along the Columbia River. At the time he joined the British commission, he was 46 years old and his major explorations lay behind him.[10]

Thompson was the key figure on Ogilvy's commission during the British survey of the St. Lawrence water line upstream from St. Regis, New York, and through Lakes Ontario and Erie during 1817–19. But the alliance of the old fur traders was abruptly terminated by Ogilvy's sudden death on September 28, 1819, from a fever he contracted while working in the swamps near Detroit.[11]

Ogilvy's death was first reported to the Foreign Office by the opportunistic Thomas Barclay, who promptly recommended his youngest son, Anthony, as the commissioner's successor. Whatever aspirations British agent John Hale had for the position were thwarted by Barclay's peremptory suggestion, which was readily accepted in London. Anthony, 27 years old when he was named in January, 1820, to head the British commission for Articles 6 and 7, had worked as secretary of his father's commission under Article 4 of the Treaty of Ghent.

Barclay and Porter proceeded amicably with the Article 6 work, although their methodical trigonometrical surveys necessarily slowed the effort. During 1820 and 1821 the surveyors covered Lake Huron and refined their determinations on the St. Clair River. By the end of the latter season the commissioners were in fundamental accord, and all that remained was to complete the maps and formalize the agreement.[12]

In the meantime a budget-minded Congress, eager to have the boundary settled, had reacted negatively to the survey commissions. The inability of the Article 5 commission to settle the Maine boundary and the lingering work under Article 6 persuaded Congress that the commissioners and agents would move faster if their positions were less remunerative. Near the end of the session in March, 1821, the annual salaries of these officials were reduced from $4,444.44 to $2,500. Porter especially was embittered by this action because the British government continued to pay Barclay at the old rate. Although he became increasingly irate over the commission's finances, the New Yorker stayed in his position. Under the pressures of congressional criticism and periodical urging from the secretary of state, he even promised a hasty completion of the Article 7 survey, which he and Barclay discussed at length when they met in Philadelphia from January 29 to February 5, 1822, to work out the details of the Article 6 agreement.[13]

After the Philadelphia meeting Porter visited Washington, D.C., to inform Adams about the next season's work. The survey through "remote and comparatively unimportant country" would be done by British and American parties of 10 to 12 members each, working independently but close enough together to co-ordinate their activities. He expected it would be impossible to complete the work in one season, but he "confidently believed that it can be done in two." Possibly this prediction was sincerely made in the expectation that, by abandoning the trigonometrical survey method used in the Article 6 work and adopting the "most summary methods," the project could go ahead rapidly. But it is also possible that Porter, who was openly concerned about congressional scrutiny, thought it politically unwise to suggest a long tenure for the Article 7 commission.[14]

Porter knew the act Congress had passed on March 3, 1821, limited appropriations for boundary surveys to January 1, 1823, so any request for funding beyond that date would have to be based on complexities unforeseen before the work was under way. Thus he rather optimistically told Adams that only the measuring of the northwest corner of Lake of the Woods would have to be done with "great care and accuracy," because it would influence the location of the northern boundary of the United States westward. Then, perhaps to remind Adams of the enormity of his mission—in case he needed to retreat from his prediction that it could be completed in two years—he described the territory to be surveyed. It "embraces an extent of one thousand miles," he wrote with some exaggeration, running "through a totally wild and uninhabited country affording no means for the comfort or even subsistence of the persons employed in this service." In addition, he made much of the cold, inhospitable climate, which would limit work to a "small portion of the year."

Barclay agreed that the latitude would have to be determined only at the northwest corner of Lake of the Woods, but he refrained from offering the Foreign Office a speedy conclusion of the survey. In fact, even before discussing the Article 7 work with Porter at Philadelphia, he reported that he did not anticipate the need to determine the lake's northwestern point before the autumn of 1823, which would almost certainly carry the work over into the next year.[15] Barclay, who never attempted to hurry the commission's business, could afford to be less concerned about finishing than Porter. His salary was adequate and assured, he was far removed from his immediate supervisors in London (who therefore had to rely on him as their principal source of information), and unlike Porter he had no political past, which relieved him, to a degree, of parliamentary criticism.

Both men were awed by the prospect of venturing into the unmapped wilderness west of Lake Superior. They knew the Paris Treaty of 1783 had specifically mentioned only four places west of Lake Huron—Isles Royale and Phelipeaux, Long Lake, and the northwest point of Lake of the Woods. Isle Royale was known only by its general location, and Lake of the Woods, though it had appeared on many maps, had never been scientifically surveyed. The commissioners were also quite certain there was no Isle Phelipeaux in the western part of Lake Superior near Isle Royale, but they could not declare it nonexistent before they looked. Moreover there was always the possibility that they might later agree to proclaim some island in that vicinity as Phelipeaux. Likewise they had been reliably informed by fur traders that there was no Long Lake near the Pigeon River as shown on Mitchell's map. But they knew there were three principal routes leading to the interior from the western end of Lake Superior—the Kaministikwia on the north, the old Grand Portage Trail (via the Pigeon River) in the middle, and the St. Louis River on the south. Was any one of the three a more likely Long Lake than the others? In 1822 Barclay and Porter seemed to think so. Since Mitchell's map showed all three routes with Long Lake at the mouth of the middle one, the commissioners assumed, without formally agreeing, that the mouth of the Pigeon River was Long Lake.[16]

These geographical questions prompted Porter and Barclay to plan the survey with the idea that the country they would find differed from what the treaty makers had thought it was in 1783. They agreed to survey adjacent areas "in order to determine—not where the line must go to conform with the description of the treaty, for that is deemed impracticable—but where it ought to be established to comport best with the views of the parties at the time of making the treaty." Porter interpreted this to mean that the treaty makers intended the boundary to be a water line running from Lake Superior through the Pigeon River and its connecting waters to the northwest point of Lake of the Woods. Whatever misgivings Barclay had in 1822 about the Pigeon River being Long Lake, he apparently did not commit them to paper. Thus as the British and American parties readied for the season's field work, they intended to survey only the Pigeon River below the site of Fort Charlotte and the old fur trade route from that point to the northwest corner of Lake of the Woods.[17]

Before launching the 1822 work, Porter and Delafield had to reorganize their crew. William A. Bird, the astronomical surveyor during the last years of the Article 6 project, chose not to continue. His assistant, 24-year-old James Ferguson, who had served the commission since 1819, was then elevated to chief surveyor. One of Delafield's principal last-minute tasks was to find an assistant surveyor who was also a competent draftsman to take the main responsibility for preparing maps. After soliciting applications in New York City, he hired George Washington Whistler, a 21-year-old army lieutenant.[18]

Compared to David Thompson, Ferguson and Whistler were young and completely inexperienced in the rigors of prolonged wilderness travel. In search of helpful advice, Delafield turned to various fur traders, notably Ramsay Crooks, the general manager of the American Fur Company. Crooks advised that west of Mackinac the surveyors would have to live as the traders did, because there was no place beyond that station to depend on for supplies.[19]

Porter assisted in making some of the arrangements, but it was Delafield who led the surveyors to the Article 7 area. He traveled with them to Mackinac, where he met with Robert Stuart, agent of the American Fur Company, who agreed to act as their supplier and agent. As part of his business deal with Stuart, Delafield instructed Ferguson to give preference to American Fur Company posts if it became necessary to obtain additional supplies and to use Hudson's Bay Company posts only in emergencies. After a few days at Mackinac the surveyors moved westward to Sault Ste. Marie, where they were to begin the St. Marys River survey and await the arrival of David Thompson. Delafield left Ferguson and Whistler at the river and returned east, apparently satisfied that the surveyors were equipped for two years.[20]

During his stay at Mackinac and Sault Ste. Marie, Delafield had learned enough about the country west of Lake Superior to doubt whether any of the three principal routes to Rainy Lake afforded a direct water communication. He noted the British traders had long since abandoned Grand Portage in favor of the northern route; he also commented, "The Southern or Fond du Lac route, does

not seem to be in question, altho it has by some persons been improvidently suggested." Delafield was apparently upset because that suggestion, he claimed, had been made by American "gentlemen"—specifically Henry R. Schoolcraft—of the 1820 exploring expedition headed by Lewis Cass, governor of Michigan Territory, which passed up the lower St. Louis River on its way to Cass Lake, then the supposed source of the Mississippi. From the start Delafield regarded the St. Louis River as "no route at all" and certainly not worthy of consideration as a possible boundary. The northern route by way of the Kaministikwia was of more interest to him.[21]

Despite Delafield's efforts and the good intentions of the commissioners, the opening of the Article 7 survey was poorly co-ordinated. Porter and Fraser stayed at Black Rock preparing for the last meeting of the Article 6 commission at Utica, New York. Barclay, who did not return from his winter home in Savannah, Georgia, until late May, was more concerned with arranging the Utica meeting than with Article 7 matters. John Hale, the British agent, was quite content to leave his field preparations to David Thompson, who made no particular effort to plan his work in co-operation with the American party. Ferguson and Whistler had been told to work on the St. Marys River only until they received the commissioner's specific instructions from Utica. But when the anticipated co-ordination with Thompson did not materialize, and the instructions from Utica were delayed, they were virtually left to their own devices.[22]

During their month of surveying on the St. Marys, Ferguson and Whistler gathered information on the area west of Lake Superior, particularly about the prospects of wintering there. Ferguson had hoped to winter at Rainy Lake, but he learned from William Morrison, head of the Fond du Lac district of the American Fur Company, that this would be impossible. Morrison told of the great distance to Rainy Lake and the slowness in forwarding supplies through his department along the St. Louis River. He was hardly more encouraging about the routes via the Kaministikwia, which he said had some 36 portages, or the old Grand Portage Trail, which "has not been travelled for so long a period . . . it is said to be hardly passable at present." It was also obvious that the trader did not care to be bothered with assisting the surveyors. Ferguson had crews for only two canoes but enough provisions and baggage for four, thus he had to alter his plans to forward the cargo through Morrison's post at Fond du Lac. Under the circumstances, he thought it best to winter at Fort William.[23]

Meanwhile Porter and Barclay had closed the Article 6 commission at Utica on June 21, and had set down instructions to the Article 7 surveyors. Secretary Fraser was told to send them to Ferguson at the Sault, but, like the steamboat supplies, they were delayed in transit and arrived after the surveyor's departure on July 15. Consequently Ferguson had far more leeway in determining the nature of the initial work than anyone intended.[24]

Thompson likewise set out without his instructions. Arriving at Sault Ste. Marie on June 23, he left five days later after advising Ferguson that he was going to proceed along the south shore of Lake Superior. He also told the American he intended to return to Montreal for the winter, which no doubt prompted some of Ferguson's later misgivings about his plan to remain west of Lake Superior.[25]

The two men soon met again at Fort William when Thompson arrived on July 31, two days after Ferguson's group. There they discussed the survey and agreed that both parties would work on different portions of the old Grand Portage route during the brief remainder of the 1822 season. Earlier Ferguson had thought of exploring the Kaministikwia, but he changed his mind after Alexander Stewart, the factor at Fort William, informed him it offered no uninterrupted water passage to the Height of Land, whereas the old Grand Portage route was the shortest and the most expeditious. Ferguson was willing to examine the Grand Portage route first, because, he said, it "has always been considered the boundary."[26]

Thompson, however, commented that the waters of the St. Louis River "approximate most nearly to those emptying into the Lake of the Woods," and that after his inspection, Barclay would determine if this route should be examined. Ferguson, perhaps with a premonition of disagreements to come, alertly interpreted Thompson's remarks as a sign of British interest in the St. Louis River route; consequently he looked about for a counterbalancing passage to the north.

Although disturbed by Thompson's remarks about the St. Louis River and by his own failure to find quickly its counterpart to the north, Ferguson did not really think there was a serious threat to a Pigeon River boundary. Like Porter and Delafield, he believed the stream's mouth was obviously Mitchell's Long Lake. As he plunged into the wilderness west of Lake Superior, Ferguson thought a routine identification of a water route from the Pigeon to the northwest point of Lake of the Woods would fix the boundary.

CHAPTER 5

The Uncertain Boundary, 1822–25

As FERGUSON AND THOMPSON stood ready to launch their separate expeditions before freeze-up in 1822, neither man could possibly have foreseen that the field work would span four successive seasons. Nor could they imagine that, after five years of surveying and arguing, the commission would end without settling the boundary from Lake Huron to the northwest point of Lake of the Woods.

In early August, 1822, after acquiring provisions and a new North canoe at Fort William, Thompson moved inland from Grand Portage. He explored for less than three weeks west of Arrow Lake, where on August 20 he met Ferguson. Thompson was on his way back to Montreal, but he had made plans for the reconnaissance work to continue in his absence. On August 17 he had hired a Fort William trader, John Charles Sayer, to work until June, 1823. Sayer was to obtain information from the Indians about all the rivers emptying into Lake Superior between Fort William and the St. Louis River and about all the streams leading to Rainy Lake. He was also to find out whether the Indians knew of a Long Lake and, if so, to determine its location and extent. Thompson instructed Sayer to have the Indians draw maps with ashes on birch bark, giving the native names of the lakes and streams. The following May, Sayer was to bring the maps to Fort William, where he would meet the British surveying party and serve as its guide and interpreter.[1]

Ferguson, meanwhile, had experienced a frustrating introduction to the wilderness due primarily to labor problems. By the time he arrived at Fort William, the surveyor was completely disenchanted with his guide and interpreter, claiming he was guilty of either "misconduct or ignorance," for he had twice misrepresented the nature of the coastline, thereby delaying the voyage. In addition Ferguson discovered that accomplished steersmen were essential to the safe navigation of birch-bark North canoes. Regrettably he had not learned this at Mackinac, so he hired only one. Thus he was forced to change plans and operate with only one canoe rather than two. With considerable help from factor Alexander Stewart, whom Ferguson found to be "very civil," the American party finally got under way early in August.[2]

Before going to the site of the Grand Portage post and moving up the trail, Ferguson and Whistler attempted to paddle up the Pigeon River from its mouth, hoping the stream would prove to be the navigable water communication required by the 1783 treaty. The two men soon found that there was a good reason for the Grand Portage Trail. The lower Pigeon was decidedly not navigable. They were "obliged to return after encountering some difficult rapids and cutting large trees with which the bed of the river was obstructed." It is unlikely that they moved any farther upstream than Pigeon Falls, about two miles from Lake Superior, for that barrier alone certainly would have proved the unnavigability of the lower river.[3]

On August 7 the two surveyors determined the latitude and longitude at the site of Grand Portage and, after struggling up the abandoned trail, took similar measurements at its western end on August 12 and 13. Moving west during the next several weeks, they recorded the latitude and longitude of the lower ends of Fowl Portage and the portage from Moose Lake to the Arrow River, the upper end of Height of Land Portage, the first island in North Lake (which they called Height of Land Lake), and the entrance to Saganaga Lake, where they arrived on September 5.[4]

In addition to locating significant points astronomically, Ferguson and Whistler determined the size and shape of the waters through which they passed and made sketches showing the locations of the islands near what was thought to be the middle line through the lakes and streams. Because they had been forewarned about the significance of a water communication, they also traced the courses of rivulets that joined the Pigeon. While engaged in such exploring, they discovered that the old route of the voyageurs deviated from the most continuous water line, which left the Pigeon at its junction with the Arrow River, followed that stream northwesterly to Arrow Lake, and rejoined the old voyageur route east of Height of Land Portage at what is now Rose Lake. In reporting this discovery to Porter, Ferguson wrote, "I have reason to believe that Mr. Thompson is unacquainted with it."[5] This find would later influence the United States commission in its decision to contend that the old voyageur route was really a part-water and part-land course, which did not conform to the 1783 treaty's specification of a water communication.

Ferguson turned back toward Fort William after he had surveyed to about the center of Saganaga Lake. His aim was to reach Lake of the Woods during the 1823 season and to examine Isle Royale over the winter. He seems to have been satisfied with his brief 1822 efforts, which he claimed had covered half the distance from Lake Superior to Rainy Lake. Even after discovering the Arrow River problem, he believed the work could be completed in 1823, unless the commissioners ordered surveys of the St. Louis River and the mysterious Long Lake.[6]

After exhausting its provisions, the survey party reached Fort William on September 19. There Ferguson immediately made plans to chart Isle Royale, a task that occupied him for 20 days in late September and early October. The survey was important because Isle Royale was explicitly named in the peace treaty, which dictated that any boundary through Lake Superior was to stay north of the island; thus it was thought such a line might point directly to the elusive Long Lake. Although intimidated by the cold winter weather, Ferguson also ventured out in January to measure the small offshore islands between Fort William and Grand Portage.[7]

When they were not working, Ferguson and his men joined in the social life of Fort William, which the chief surveyor found "tremendously dull." Nonetheless he and his party were well accepted by the post's 60-odd residents, about half men (including the survey crew) and half women and children. Ferguson, in fact, furnished liquor for the New Years' Day celebration attended by the inhabitants plus a like number of visiting Indians. This gesture proved to be his greatest wintertime expense, but he justified it by explaining, "we were obliged to be civil." More regular entertainments were the fortnightly dances with music provided by the post's lone instruments, two fiddles and a triangle. It was Ferguson's belief that the company leaders encouraged the dances "to keep their men in spirits, and prevent them from growing morose and savage."[8]

Although bored at times, Ferguson found pleasure in the company of Stewart, who furnished the American party with milk, vegetables, and occasional fresh beef. He also became acquainted with many of the post's other inhabitants and struck up a fortuitous friendship with Thompson's guide, Sayer, who returned to Fort William on January 14, 1823. Sayer was "very communicative"; he not only told Ferguson the nature of his mission for Thompson, but the results of it as well. Thus the American learned—even before Thompson—that the headwaters of the St. Louis River started south of Vermilion Lake and did not mingle with the watershed of Lake of the Woods. Ferguson had earlier suspected Thompson's belief that the waters of the St. Louis River approximated those of Lake of the Woods was based solely on "Mr. Schoolcraft's Journal," and he was relieved by Sayer's intelligence. But the very fact that the guide had been sent on such a mission only confirmed American suspicions that the British were interested in the St. Louis River as the boundary.[9] Sayer's information would also influence Delafield's plans concerning the Kaministikwia route when he went into the field himself later in the year.

After leaving Ferguson at Mackinac in the spring of 1822, Delafield journeyed to Washington, D.C., where he delivered the journal and maps of the completed Article 6 commission to Secretary of State Adams. During their discussions about the survey of the Lake Superior area, Adams showed Delafield what the agent believed to be "the [Mitchell] map upon which the Boundary Line was traced as described in the Treaty of 1783." Noting that Long Lake was shown near old Grand Portage, Delafield concluded that it was "probably" the same as the Pigeon River. Porter agreed, indicating that "with proper certificates of its authority," the map would immediately and conclusively resolve the Long Lake question. Delafield soon became convinced that the map proved "there is no longer any serious question open as to the general course that the Line is intended to be run." As a result he expected the commissioners to agree on the Pigeon River boundary after the return of the surveyors in 1823.[10]

Barclay, however, had been interested in the St. Louis River from the start of the Article 7 work, and he was not persuaded by Delafield's contention that the State Department's copy of Mitchell's map proved Long Lake was near old Grand Portage. He asked George Canning, Britain's secretary of state for foreign affairs, to send him a copy of the map marked by the treaty makers in 1783. Such a map, he believed, "would throw a light upon the intentions of the framers of the Treaty, which might prove beneficial to His Majesty's interest." In requesting the marked map, Barclay was probably relying on information obtained from his father that an original map used in Paris was extant. The Foreign Office failed to find such a document, so it merely sent Barclay a copy of Mitchell's map. Neither the British nor the American party, of course, had the original map upon which the diplomats in Paris had marked the boundary with a bold red line.[11]

Despite indications there might be contention over the boundary course west of Lake Superior, Porter at the end of 1822 claimed "we have every reason to believe that we shall complete the survey in the course of the [next] season." Barclay, however, accepted David Thompson's judgment that it could not be completed before the fall of 1824.[12] After the end of the 1822 work, the commissioners did not meet to set a concerted plan for the following year. Instead they independently sent their surveyors into the Pigeon River-Lake of the Woods area in the spring, apparently content to rely on chance meetings of the crews to avoid duplicate efforts.

Barclay was still in Savannah when Thompson left Montreal in May to lead the British party to the northwest point of Lake of the Woods. He was accompanied throughout 1823 by John Bigsby, who, despite his dual position of commission doctor and assistant board secretary, spent most of his time collecting rock and mineral specimens and studying the geology of the Lake Superior area.[13]

After stopping at Fort William, Thompson and Bigsby moved to the Grand Portage Trail, where they were "greatly annoyed by mosquitoes and the closeness of the air, the path, such as it was, being overgrown by briers and coppice." From the site of Fort Charlotte they followed the old voyageur route to Lake of the Woods. Thompson commenced surveying on South Fowl Lake and took some measurements on almost every lake and stream. For nearly three weeks the tedium of surveying was broken only by a stop for supplies at the Hudson's Bay Company post on the north bank of the Rainy River just below Koochiching Falls near the outlet of Rainy Lake. This post, the only one of significance between Fort William and Lake of the Woods, was an outfitting point for both the British and United States surveyors. There Thompson and his party were received by Dr. John McLoughlin, chief factor, and William McGillivray, a member of the board of advisers of the Hudson's Bay Company who happened to be visiting. Aside from the small station of the American Fur Company opposite the Rainy River post and a farmhouse built by former North West Company employee Vincent Roy at the mouth of the Little Fork River, Thompson and Bigsby saw no other habitations on their trip.[14]

Using the "most summary methods" instead of a trigonometrical survey, as directed by the boundary commissioners, Thompson fixed the latitude and longitude of certain principal points, then measured from point to point by compass. Thus the shape and dimensions of any given lake were determined by paddling at a particular compass azimuth, carefully timing that movement, and making an estimate of the distance traveled. Bigsby noted that the canoe rate was "found to be 120 yards per minute, or rather less than four miles per hour," but this was not an unvarying standard. For example, on July 9 in Crooked Lake Thompson moved 2,300 yards on an azimuth from 9:37 to 9:55 P.M., and on July 17 in Lake of the Woods he traveled 6,000 yards from 5:57 to 8:03 A.M. Throughout the long days—which sometimes started at 4:30 A.M. and ended after 9:00 at night—Thompson logged all azimuths, times, and estimates. These records became the basis for the field maps he sketched en route.[15]

Within two days after leaving the Hudson's Bay Company post, the party traveled the length of the Rainy River, reaching Lake of the Woods on July 16. Thompson's principal goal was to determine the lake's northwesternmost point, which a quarter century before he had assumed to be at Rat Portage, its outlet. Since he also had to survey the lake, he undoubtedly hoped its most northwest point would be identified in the course of his routine measuring. Therefore he proceeded along the south shore past the mouth of the Warroad River before turning north and investigating the indented western shoreline all the way to Rat Portage, which he identified as the "supposed North West corner of the Lake of the Woods." By July 28 the crew was back at the mouth of the Rainy River, having circumnavigated the entire lake in less than two weeks.[16]

Three and a half weeks after leaving Lake of the Woods,

Thompson and his group arrived at Fort William. On the way they spent 12 days surveying Rainy Lake, which presented special problems because of its size and numerous islands. From Fort William en route to his home in Montreal, which he did not reach until November 9, Thompson surveyed for two weeks on the St. Marys River.[17]

The United States surveyors, like Thompson's crew, worked their way from Fort William to Lake of the Woods in the spring of 1823. Before the season started, Porter had written to Adams that either he or Delafield or both would join Ferguson in the field. Only Delafield, however, made the long trip from New York, while Porter stayed in Black Rock, continuing in his role of armchair commissioner.[18]

From May 3 to June 13, 1823, Delafield traveled from New York City to Mackinac. He outfitted there with the assistance of Robert Stuart, completed his crew at Sault Ste. Marie, and set off for Fort William in a "large bark canoe." The agent was cordially received at the post by both Alexander Stewart and Roderick McKenzie, who was about to succeed Stewart as factor. After purchasing a North canoe, Delafield embarked on July 9 for the Grand Portage Trail, hoping to overtake Ferguson and Whistler, who had left for Lake of the Woods far in advance of his arrival at the fort.[19]

From Fort William to Saganaga Lake Delafield was guided by copies of Ferguson's maps, which he had received at Mackinac. Hence he was well aware of the Arrow River deviation, which, he noted, "we consider to be the Boundary Line." Delafield did not travel up the Arrow, however, but stayed on the old voyageur route, although he also knew about another deviation Ferguson had followed to the north—that around what came to be known as Hunter Island. In his search for the most continuous water passage, Ferguson had discovered that Saganaga Lake drained to the northwest via a water passage connecting to Sturgeon Lake on the Kaministikwia route, which then followed the Maligne River to Lac la Croix and there merged with the traditional voyageur track from Grand Portage. Delafield was tempted to try the more northern route despite its reported "many bad rapids," but he did not do so because of the inexperience of his hired guide. Nevertheless the agent concluded that the boundary should follow the most continuous water line north of Hunter Island (see front end sheet map).

At Lac la Croix Delafield learned that the most direct connection from it west to Namakan Lake was by the Namakan River, which ran in a fairly straight course, whereas the commercial route looped southward through Loon, Little Vermilion, and Sand Point lakes. After passing through Namakan and Rainy lakes, Delafield reached the Hudson's Bay Company's Rainy River post, where he stayed overnight before pushing on in search of Ferguson and Whistler. While descending the Rainy he met

Thompson and Bigsby, who were returning upstream after completing their work on Lake of the Woods. Thompson, who had not seen Ferguson there, offered the opinion that the northwest point of the lake had to be in the vicinity of Rat Portage. Delafield was somewhat distressed to learn there would be no joint survey of Lake of the Woods during the season and Ferguson was apparently "following the circuit after Mr. Thompson." He traveled nearly the length of the lake before he finally found the Americans encamped near Rat Portage. They had indeed canoed around the south and west shores in Thompson's wake, duplicating many of the Britisher's observations.

On August 2 Ferguson and Delafield went together to Rat Portage, where the surveyor took observations for latitude. There they remained for two days, because "The N.W. point of the Lake of the Woods we find is not an easy point to ascertain." Although they could not fix the northwest point for want of a guiding principle, Delafield felt sure it had to be near the portage. He predicted that it would "be North more than half a degree probably of Par[allel] N[orth] 49°, so that the line to be drawn South again to Par. 49°, will have a curious effect here."

For the return trip to Fort William, the combined parties divided at Lac la Croix, with Delafield and Whistler taking the Kaministikwia passage and Ferguson the old Grand Portage route. Delafield's men traveled from Lac la Croix to Fort William in only nine days. Even though Whistler accompanied him, the agent did not attempt to survey any part of the area, but made general observations along the way. He apparently wanted only to see the northern route in order to lend legitimacy to any future claim he might make concerning it.[20]

After 17 months in the field, Ferguson and Whistler returned with Delafield to Black Rock in October, 1823. Reporting to Secretary of State Adams, the agent admitted that his "former conjectures as to the completion of the work were founded in error," and that the survey of the area between Lake Superior and Lake of the Woods would "occupy at least another year of diligent application." He told the secretary of the numerous islands in some lakes—a reported 450 in Lac la Croix, 289 in Saganaga, and "several thousand" in Rainy Lake—which made it difficult to determine a middle course for a boundary. He also informed Adams that, in his opinion, the United States should not expect to acquire valuable land as a result of the Article 7 work. The country from Lake Superior to Rainy Lake was extremely rocky as well as mountainous, he pointed out, but at Rainy Lake there was some soil that could be cultivated; he had seen Indian corn there and on islands in Lake of the Woods. His overall impression, however, was that "In an agricultural sense the country is of no possible value. . . . I do not foresee

any inducement, but the fur trade, that can ever draw the people of the United States, to this part of the Indian N.W. Territory. The climate would forbid, if its rocky wastes did not. . . . Notwithstanding this gloomy reality," Delafield concluded, "the Indian trade carries a great number of people, annually over the routes I have described. The American trader has a strong desire that the Line should be determined."[21]

By the close of their second season Thompson and Ferguson had surveyed much of the pertinent country between Lake Huron and the northwest point of Lake of the Woods, and it seemed likely that the remaining work could be completed in 1824. They had measured parts of the Neebish Channels in the St. Marys River and had circumnavigated Lake Superior and recorded all compass courses and distances in addition to Ferguson's astronomical observations in the western part of the lake. Isle Royale had been surveyed, but Isle Phelipeaux had not been identified. In the area between Lake Superior and the northwest point of Lake of the Woods, the land along the old voyageur route had been surveyed from the Pigeon River end of the Grand Portage Trail to the west shore of Saganaga Lake, including the Arrow River deviation, and from Lac la Croix through Lake of the Woods, including the Namakan River cutoff.[22] The remaining work consisted principally of establishing the most northwest point of Lake of the Woods, identifying the lake's islands adjacent to the boundary line, surveying both the old voyageur route and the most continuous water route from Saganaga to Lac la Croix, as well as the Pigeon River below the western end of the Grand Portage Trail, and refining many of the observations taken in 1822 and 1823.

The need to review the Article 7 work was apparent to both commissioners after the 1823 season. Before leaving for Savannah, Barclay suggested to Porter that a board meeting with all the British and American agents and surveyors present be arranged for January or February. The first official gathering of the Article 7 commission was subsequently held at Albany, New York, February 16–24, 1824.[23]

Because nearly two years had passed since their conference at the Article 6 Utica meeting, it was necessary for Barclay and Porter to take care of such routine business as balancing accounts and filing oaths before they could consider the Article 7 survey results. The Treaty of Ghent specified that all expenses were to be equally defrayed by the two governments. In practice each paid its own employees and purchased its own supplies and provisions independently. Under the treaty's moiety arrangement, the boundary commissioners periodically adjusted their accounts and determined any balances due. The moiety principle was followed throughout the work under Articles 6 and 7, with the sole exception of the commissioners' *salaries*, which were determined and paid by the commissioner's own country.[24]

At the Albany meeting Delafield and Hale approved the Article 6 expense accounts and examined and approved Article 7 expenditures up to January, 1824. Balancing the accounts was a laborious and somewhat strained effort, because the frugal Porter regarded Barclay as a spendthrift who billed the United States for half his excesses. Disturbed by Barclay's expenses during the Article 6 survey, Porter told Adams early in the Article 7 work that the moeity agreement ought to be abandoned — a suggestion the administration considered improper.[25]

Reconciling the accounts proved to be the easiest part of the work at the Albany meeting, for the anticipated differences over the boundary route from Lake Superior to Lake of the Woods soon dominated the proceedings. When David Thompson filed his report, he stated that the estuary of the St. Louis River was the most likely Long Lake. But he also pointed out that 13 other streams flowing into Lake Superior between the St. Louis and Pigeon rivers needed to be investigated.[26]

Delafield's response was emphatically negative. The agent argued that the boundary line west from Lake Superior should start on the Pigeon River, which was the Long Lake shown on Mitchell's map. He was so convinced of the "indisputable position of Long Lake" that he considered himself "precluded from the right . . . of following the direct water communications by the River Kamanistiquia from Lake Superior." It seems strange Delafield would speak so strongly at the outset for the Pigeon River when he knew the British would probably claim the St. Louis, for so firm a stand left him without a more extreme position from which to compromise.[27]

Delafield urged Barclay and Porter to refrain from ordering surveys of either the St. Louis or Kaministikwia routes or of "any other place north or south of Long Lake near the old Grand Portage." The boundary survey, he contended, could be expeditiously ended by completing measurements of the continuous water route from the mouth of the Pigeon River to the northwest point of Lake of the Woods. John Hale countered by asking for additional investigation of all water routes leading west from Lake Superior. It would be inappropriate, he stressed, to abandon any of them, as Delafield suggested, as long as the boundary's starting point on Lake Superior had not been decided.

Ascertaining the location of Long Lake was only one of the three puzzles emanating from the Treaty of 1783 which faced Barclay and Porter at their Albany meeting. The other two concerned Isle Phelipeaux and the northwesternmost point of Lake of the Woods. The commissioners were not pleased that no Isle Phelipeaux had been found by either Ferguson or Thompson, who both reported that the local traders were also unaware of such an island. They were equally distressed that the 1823 operations had not conclusively ascertained the elusive northwest point of the Lake of the Woods. Porter hoped Rat Portage would prove to be correct. Barclay preferred "a more western point," no doubt because the British traders had already persuaded him that American control of Rat Portage, one of the key places on their pathway to the Canadian interior, would be disastrous.[28]

Although they hoped for different outcomes, both commissioners recognized that the northwesternmost point would have to be determined by mathematical principles and astronomical measurements. Therefore they asked Thompson to explain the necessary procedures. The veteran surveyor's opinion was formally presented in writing to the board on February 23. The northwest point, he wrote, would be that place which combined the highest latitude and the greatest longitude — measurements which could be ascertained only through astronomical observations. A reference point on the lake, he stated, could be determined by drawing a line due south from the north end and another due east from the west end. From the spot where the two lines intersected, it would be possible to judge which point on the lake had the greatest longitude and the highest latitude. Barclay and Porter were apparently satisfied that Thompson would be able to fix the northwestern point on the ground. Although the records of the meeting do not show Thompson was formally named for this duty, it is evident the commissioners intended him to work on Lake of the Woods during the 1824 season without assistance from Ferguson and Whistler.[29]

The instructions to the surveyors co-issued by Barclay and Porter carefully avoided any steps which would have aggravated their differences. They left open the question of the boundary's starting point on Lake Superior by ordering a continuation of the survey of the middle route and, in what was clearly a concession to the British, by allowing that the surveyors could "(if you have time and it appears necessary) make further examinations thro[ugh] the Fond du Lac and, while in that part of the Lake Superior, endeavor to discover the island intended by the isle Phillipeaux." Porter knew the United States had nothing to gain by any operation in the Fond du Lac area. But he feared that a "rigid adherence to our own views would probably break up the Commission, and we have therefore thought it better to yield" to the wishes of the Canadian people and the British government. Although Barclay agreed that the first order of business in 1824 should be the completion of the middle-route survey, it was obvious by the close of the Albany meeting that he would not agree to a boundary without first seriously considering the St. Louis River.[30]

The meeting in Albany was a turning point in the relationship between Porter and Barclay, which saw a noticeable hardening of attitudes. Little remained of the amicability that had characterized the Article 6 work, as both commissioners lost patience with cultivating each other's good will.[31]

After the Albany meeting it was agreed to convene another board session in Montreal on October 25, 1824. Both countries then turned to preparations for the 1824 season. Porter and Fraser returned to Black Rock; Delafield went home to New York City to ready a summary report of the meeting for Adams and to continue his search for proof of the veracity and reliability of Mitchell's map. Ferguson and Whistler prepared for their third season beyond Lake Superior, and Thompson made ready to act on Barclay's instructions to establish "the precise parallel" of 49 degrees on the west shore of Lake of the Woods.[32]

Barclay, like Delafield, was well aware of the peculiar boundary configuration that would result from a line literally drawn according to the 1783 and 1818 treaties. He believed the simplest solution to the problem would be a boundary in Lake of the Woods following the water line called for in the 1783 treaty to the 49th parallel and then running due west. This would save the time and expense of determining the northwest point, he reasoned, and "might also prevent future controversies" over ownership of the lake's islands.[33]

The British commissioner did not reveal his contemplated modification to the Americans, but he shared it with George Canning, the foreign secretary. The latter was receptive to Barclay's notion that such a change "may be of some advantage" to the Hudson's Bay Company, which would then be "free" from foreign interference. Canning in turn asked his undersecretary, Joseph Planta, to solicit a reaction from Lord Bathurst, secretary for colonial affairs. As might be expected, Bathurst turned to the Hudson's Bay Company for advice. Nicholas Garry, the company's deputy governor, expressed alarm at the possible American occupation of Rat Portage. Its retention, he said, was "essential . . . to the trade of the Hudson's Bay Company, and to British interests."[34]

Choosing to accept Garry's views as those of the Hudson's Bay Company, the Foreign Office requested a legal opinion from the advocate general. In light of the differences between the treaties of 1783 and 1818, Planta wondered "how far His Majesty's Government are warranted in pressing the line—pointed out by the Hudson's Bay Company." Advocate General Christopher Robinson responded promptly. Since the northwest point was specifically named in the Treaty of 1783, he said, it was precise and could not be superseded by the Treaty of 1818. Any

thought of making the 49th parallel the boundary through Lake of the Woods, he ruled, would have to be the subject of a "further Arrangement" with the United States.[35]

Canning contemplated having the British chargé d'affaires in Washington suggest to the United States that the treaties of 1783 and 1818 be adjusted as a "matter of right." Instead he decided to order a private survey, entirely separate from the boundary commission's work, "*with the express view* of determining on scientific principles, the most N.W. point of the Lake of the Woods." Completing independent observations for this sole purpose, he believed, was the only way to avoid error. Barclay was instructed to prepare for the private survey and to postpone any decisions until it was completed.[36]

During the summer of 1824, while Canning evolved the independent survey project, Thompson focused his efforts in the Lake of the Woods area. Leaving Montreal on May 5, the surveyor traveled to his destination by way of the Ottawa River, Lakes Huron and Superior, and the Grand Portage route. From the Pigeon River to Lake of the Woods he surveyed some places that had not been fully explored. Once on the lake he marked the 49th parallel on the shore of Muskeg Bay with "a heap of large stones with several pickets well driven into the ground." Proceeding northward to what is now Northwest Angle Inlet, which he identified as the "first angle" of the lake, Thompson moved to its northwesternmost point. "There being no stones within several miles," he erected "a square monument of logs, twelve feet high by seven feet square, the lower part of oak, the upper part of aspin [*sic*], and nailed to it a Tin Plate marked the North West corner of the Lake of the Woods No. 1." North of Angle Inlet he raised two more stone pyramids to mark other possible "most northwest" points. That at the western end of Monument Bay was seven feet high with a four-foot base and a pierced-tin plate identifying it as "The North West corner of the Lake of the Woods No. 2." At the western end of Portage Bay, the other pyramid was similarly labeled as northwest corner "No. 3." The British party explored several miles beyond Portage Bay, but because the shoreline turned eastward and did not have any inlets Thompson headed homeward. He was satisfied that it was not necessary to resurvey Rat Portage, the fourth possible northwesternmost point, since it had been positively located the previous year.[37]

Thompson had identified four possible northwest points, but he made no effort to single out one of them as the most northwest. The question of why he failed to apply his own method of doing so, which he had convincingly described to the commissioners, remains unanswered. Perhaps he was not completely satisfied with his data, or he may have refrained from making a choice because he had seen nothing in 1824 to change his long-standing opinion that Rat Portage was the most northwest point.

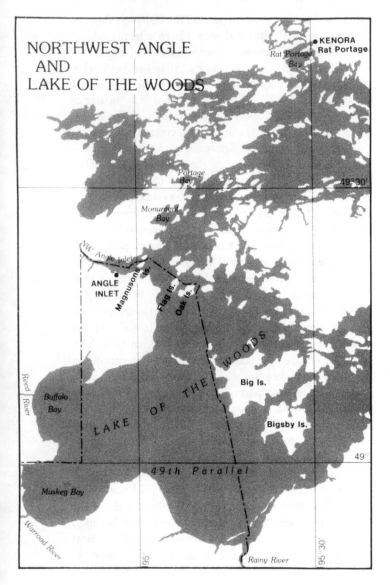

NORTHWEST ANGLE
AND
LAKE OF THE WOODS

if taken with the location of Long Lake shown on the map, would be sufficient to convince the British at the Montreal board meeting that the treaty makers intended to run the boundary via the Pigeon River and the most continuous water route to Lake of the Woods.

On October 25, 1824, at the opening of the four-day Montreal meeting, Delafield proposed that the starting point for the boundary west of Lake Superior be set. He reiterated his belief that Long Lake was the Pigeon River, offering as proof Mitchell's map and the statements by Adams and Jay. In rebuttal John Hale concurred that Mitchell's map had been used in Paris, but, he argued, it contained inaccuracies and was not irrefutable proof of the intent of the 1783 treaty. The British agent reasoned that if Mitchell's map was to be strictly followed there would have been no need for the joint boundary commission. In conclusion Hale called for more investigation of the possible starting points on the west shore of Lake Superior. He was, of course, interested in only one point—the estuary of the St. Louis River. Nearly two months before the Montreal meeting, Hale had been informed by the old North West Company director, William McGillivray, that the St. Louis River was the main stream leading into western Lake Superior, and as such it should have been designated as the boundary in 1783.[40]

Neither Delafield nor Hale changed anyone's mind. Porter insisted that no more surveys were necessary west of Lake Superior. Barclay urged an investigation of the St. Louis River, which he pronounced "the most practicable way, and expeditious route to the interior," because it was a necessary prerequisite to any final agreement. When Porter refused to join Barclay in ordering it, the enterprising Britisher wrangled a concession that either commissioner acting alone could order surveys. On the last day of the Montreal meeting he announced that his surveyors would explore and map the St. Louis River route in 1825.[41]

Although Barclay's action ended the meeting on a sour note, the commissioners had made some progress. They had agreed that the needed surveys—some trigonometrical observations on the St. Marys River and locating and measuring Caribou Island in eastern Lake Superior—were to be completed during the 1825 season, and they had ordered the surveyors and draftsmen to spend the winter of 1824–25 finishing a series of maps. Specifically they asked for a map of the St. Marys River, one of Lake Superior, and a "succession of maps" of the surveyed region from Lake Superior to Lake of the Woods. The latter were to show the old voyageur route commencing at Grand Portage as well as the most continuous water route starting at the mouth of the Pigeon River and deviating from the voyageur route at the Arrow River, Hunter Island, and the Namakan River. Lastly, the commissioners requested a map of Lake of the Woods showing the several

On the return trip to Fort William via Grand Portage, Thompson surveyed portions of Crane Lake, Lac la Croix, and Basswood, Saganaga, and Gunflint lakes. At the fur post, he learned the American party had arrived on August 23 and left four days later. During the season Ferguson and Whistler had spent nearly two months surveying the water route from Saganaga Lake to Lac la Croix on the north side of Hunter Island and examining the Pigeon and Arrow rivers.[38]

While the surveyors pursued their 1824 work, Delafield stayed in the East to continue his research on the intention of the treaty makers in 1783 regarding the boundary west of Lake Superior. He obtained copies of the old 1784 and 1796 statements by Adams and Jay concerning their dependence on Mitchell's map, but the original marked copy could not be found.[39] The agent thought these statements, possible northwest points plus the location of the 49th parallel and such measurements of longitude as had been determined. Barclay evidently remained silent about his 49th parallel boundary scheme, which was then under consideration by the British Foreign Office.[42]

After the Montreal meeting, Porter and Delafield were pessimistic about the chances of finishing the boundary survey within a year. The commissioner informed Adams that, unless otherwise directed, he intended to refuse any British request for surveys beyond 1825. Delafield, meanwhile, braced himself for the expected British claim to the St. Louis River. Although he was entirely convinced the line should start on the Pigeon River, the agent now advised Adams he was prepared to counter by proposing that the boundary run through the Kaministikwia River.[43]

Despite his growing certainty that Barclay would propose a St. Louis River boundary, Delafield continued to think the Pigeon River line would prevail if only he could produce better proof of the intent of the 1783 negotiators. Since both Jay and Adams were still living, the agent set out to get firsthand evidence from these makers of history. He was obviously disappointed with Jay's response that he could not speak "with sufficient certainty" and Adams' reiteration that only the Mitchell map had been used in Paris.[44]

With the approach of the 1825 season of the Article 7 survey, the outlook of the American and British commissions diverged markedly. Delafield and Porter were satisfied that the necessary surveying was virtually done. Once the maps were finished, they believed, the commissioners would have all the data they needed to make a decision, which should be a boundary by the most continuous water line from Lake Superior to the northwest point of Lake of the Woods. Despite the strong possibility they would have to claim the Kaministikwia route, the Americans chose not to survey it. Barclay, on the other hand, actively prepared for the 1825 work both because of his desire to advance the St. Louis River as an alternative and because he had become directly involved in the Foreign Office's plans for an independent survey of the northwest point of Lake of the Woods.

Foreign Secretary Canning's December, 1824, order for a private survey marked the first time he had actively asserted himself in the affairs of the boundary commission. Not only did he direct that the survey be made, but he named the astronomer as well. His choice, who was not popular with either Barclay or Thompson, was the German emigré, Johann Ludwig Tiarks.[45]

Tiarks had impressive academic and professional credentials. With a doctor of philosophy degree in mathematics he moved to London, where he taught briefly before becoming the assistant librarian of Sir Joseph Banks, a famed naturalist. While in that position Tiarks compiled longitude data for major European commercial centers. Then from 1817 to 1821 the talented German served as Thomas Barclay's astronomer on the Article 5 commission, surveying between the Connecticut and St. Lawrence rivers.[46]

After the completion of the Article 5 survey, the elder Barclay recommended that the government retain Tiarks because he was the man best qualified to mark latitude. The Foreign Office contemplated assigning him to Anthony Barclay's commission in 1822, but the young man did not share his father's enthusiasm for the German astronomer. Tiarks was subsequently employed by the British government's Board of Longitude. Late in 1824 Canning remembered him as "the very able astronomer" he needed for the private survey.[47]

Canning personally talked with Tiarks several times after he received Barclay's information and charts on Thompson's 1823 survey of Lake of the Woods showing Rat Portage as the likely most northwest point. Intrigued by the irregular shape of the lake, Canning asked how, theoretically, should its northwest point be determined? The astronomer responded that "The most N.W. Point of this lake (or of any other object) is that spot which a due North East line first touches, when approached to the lake from a N.W. direction." He was then asked to apply this principle to Thompson's drawing of Lake of the Woods. First, Tiarks answered, one should not assume that the chart was perfect. The difference between Rat Portage and the spot marked southwest of it at Angle Inlet was so "trifling" that "a survey made for the express purpose, might produce a different result."[48]

When asked to be specific in explaining the procedure for such a survey, Tiarks briefly outlined his proposed method and illustrated it with a rough drawing. First, he said, it would be necessary to determine compass variation, and then start a survey of the southernmost inlet on the western shore of the lake. At the western extremity of this bay, designated "A" on his drawing, a true northeast line would be run. If examination of the shore north of this point showed that the line would touch water to the northeast, then point A was not the most northwest. This process was to be repeated at points B through E, and, as he illustrated, the northeast line from E did not touch water, hence it would be the most northwest. In practice it would be necessary to examine closely the starting point at each inlet and to investigate the shoreline carefully, because the entire area of the lake had not been authoritatively surveyed, and even a slight difference in selecting the western extremity of a bay could affect the outcome.

Anthony Barclay, with no choice but to accept Canning's appointee, admitted he could "not at present vouch, that the survey already made will suffice." Begrudgingly he informed the Foreign Office that the German might as

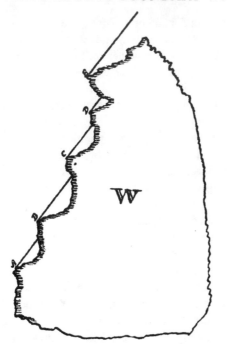

THIS DRAWING illustrated Dr. Johann L. Tiarks' plan for determining the most northwestern point of Lake of the Woods. Courtesy Public Archives of Canada.

well do the work because Thompson had enough to do in 1825, and it would be difficult to obtain other "competent persons, on this side of the Atlantic." Probably because he chose not to explain the private survey to Porter and Delafield until it was an accomplished fact, Barclay advised the Foreign Office it would be best if the Americans did not know the British government had sent Tiarks to ascertain the northwest point of Lake of the Woods. Let it appear, he wrote, that when Tiarks arrived in New York "his accidental meeting with the opportunity, which my journey thither presents, induced him to accept of it, as convenient to his views."[49]

Tiarks arrived in New York on May 12, 1825; four days later he left with Barclay for Lake of the Woods. The party also included Ferdinand R. Hassler, a Swiss scientist-mathematician who was the Americans' astronomer on the Article 5 survey and the first superintendent of the United States Coast Survey. At Sault Ste. Marie the group was joined by David Thompson and his son Samuel, who were to survey the St. Louis River watershed. After stopping at Fort William, the party moved on to Grand Portage, where illness forced David Thompson to return to the fur trade post, leaving his son in charge of the St. Louis River survey while Barclay and Tiarks proceeded along the old voyageur route to Lake of the Woods.[50]

Barclay and Tiarks reached the northwestern side of Lake of the Woods in late July. After studying Thompson's maps, which incorporated his 1824 observations, Tiarks concluded there were only two possible most north-

west points—Rat Portage and monument No. 1 in Angle Inlet. He made his observations of both on eight successive days. To determine latitude he used a Troughton sextant with a nine-inch radius; for his longitudinal measurements he used pocket chronometers, resulting in readings of unprecedented accuracy in that region.[51]

After taking dozens of readings at both places, Tiarks concluded that Thompson's monument No. 1 was farther northwest than that at the portage, but he was bothered by the slightness of the difference. A line drawn due northeast from the marker in Angle Inlet ran less than a mile west of Rat Portage. Therefore he was reluctant to claim Angle Inlet as the most northwest point, because he thought the Americans would challenge his results, charging that the difference of less than a mile was probably due to an error in his mathematics. Anxious to avoid any questioning and possible reversal of his measurements, Tiarks thought of a simple solution to his dilemma: he would not base his observations on Thompson's monument. After investigating Angle Inlet, he concluded that monument No. 1 was not placed at the most northwestern point of the inlet because the bay really ended in a small pond about a mile beyond the marker. He paddled to the northwest end of the pond and declared it to be the most northwestern point of Lake of the Woods. A due-northeast line drawn from that point cleared Rat Portage by a margin sufficient to remove any question of mathematical accuracy. When Tiarks left Lake of the Woods, he was satisfied that the northwest point "unquestionably corresponds with that which His Majesty's Government is desirous of procuring in these points."[52]

By August 22 Tiarks and Barclay were at Fort William where they probably met the Thompsons. Samuel had completed his survey of a possible boundary line through the St. Louis, Embarrass, and Pike rivers, Vermilion Lake, and the Vermilion River to Sand Point Lake, where it joined the Grand Portage route. His father had recuperated at the fort and joined Samuel in surveying part of the St. Marys River in September. After returning to New York City, Barclay promptly informed the Foreign Office of the gratifying results of the expedition, and Tiarks started writing his report for the commission.[53]

Tiarks also prepared his "Remarks on the Seventh Article of the Treaty of Ghent" for the Foreign Office. The northwest point was no longer in contention, he stated, because he had proved it was in Angle Inlet. In his comments, he hinted at future difficulties adjusting the boundary through the Neebish Channels in the St. Marys River and in the area from Lake Superior to Lac la Croix. He also correctly presumed that if the British claimed the St. Louis River line the Americans would claim the Kaministikwia, but the country between the two, he reported, was "of very little value."[54]

At their November, 1825, meeting in Albany, Barclay

and Porter accomplished little. After conducting some routine business, they postponed adjusting their accounts, then agreed to adjourn and reconvene in New York on May 22, 1826. On the basis of his informal discussions with the British, Porter emerged from the conference believing an "amicable adjustment" of the boundary would soon be achieved. He had presumed Barclay and Tiarks had gone west to explore the feasibility of a St. Louis River line, but when the British commissioner remained silent on that point as well as on his Lake of the Woods expedition, Porter concluded that the possibility of a British claim to a route south of Grand Portage would be abandoned. In this hope he was to be disappointed during the year that followed.[55]

CHAPTER 6

Disagreements Unresolved, 1826–27

AFTER FOUR SEASONS of field work west of Lake Superior, Barclay and Porter thought they had laid the foundation for a boundary settlement in 1826, but the goal which seemed nearly in hand proved to be elusive. For a variety of personal and diplomatic reasons, the commissioners were forced into irreconcilable positions, and their opportunity to settle the Article 7 boundary slipped away.

As the two men prepared for their 1826 meeting in New York, their problems were further complicated by Foreign Secretary Canning. Once satisfied that the northwest point of Lake of the Woods was indisputable, Canning, anticipating an odd boundary configuration, instructed Barclay on March 8, 1826, to survey the due-south line prescribed by the Convention of 1818 from that point to the 49th parallel. Barclay in turn suggested to Porter that they formally consider the matter at the upcoming meeting scheduled for May. Realizing that consideration of the due-south line was not covered by Porter's commission, which only authorized work under Articles 6 and 7 of the Treaty of Ghent, Barclay invited the American to obtain his government's permission to do the additional surveying.[1]

Although Porter was not enthusiastic about the idea, he relayed Barclay's letter to Secretary of State Henry Clay with a request for an official reaction. His inquiry lay unanswered over the summer of 1826. Clay and President John Quincy Adams saw no need for haste because the May meeting of the boundary commissioners had been postponed until fall; they also had misgivings about the proposal and were understandably reluctant to prolong the commission.[2]

Impatient with the delay, Barclay asked Charles R. Vaughan, British minister to the United States, to approach Clay about the matter. Clay and President Adams acted on the question after receiving Vaughan's inquiry and a reminder from Porter, who was being hounded by Barclay. At last Clay notified Porter that the president acceded to the proposal "not only from a disposition to conform, in this respect, to the wishes of Great Britain, but from the considerations that much harmony has hitherto happily prevailed between Mr. Barclay and yourself, in the discharge of your arduous duties, and that you already possess materials, which may enable you to execute what is proposed, and from the persuasion that no time will be unnecessarily wasted by you."[3] While the degree of harmony still existing between Porter and Barclay was not so great as the president appeared to believe, Adams and Clay seemingly hoped that by thus accommodating the British it would be easier to resolve the several

anticipated points of contention under Article 7. Such was the status of the due-south line proposal as Barclay and Porter approached the New York meeting.

The conference had been postponed until October, 1826, to allow more time for the laborious task of readying some three dozen maps in quadruplicate and the continuing searches by Delafield and Hale for more information to substantiate their claims. As the agents sorted through their data, they became increasingly concerned about the three Neebish Channels in the St. Marys River, where there was certain to be a dispute over the ownership of large Sugar Island. The difficulty in the Neebish Channels seems not to have been fully comprehended until after the 1825 surveys were completed and Ferguson and Thompson began intensive work on their maps.[4]

Basically the question involved which of the three waterways the boundary should follow. If it were drawn through either the Western Neebish Channel, which followed along the United States shore to Lake Nicolet, or the Middle Channel between St. Joseph and Neebish islands, then Sugar Island would belong to Great Britain, and the United States would be denied access to the Eastern Neebish Channel and Lake George, which was the deepest passage and the only one Great Lakes schooners could navigate. The United States wanted control of the deep channel in order to ship supplies to Fort Brady, the American military post on the south bank of the St. Marys River. The British claim to Sugar Island was linked both to a desire for American recognition of the St. Louis River boundary line and to Barclay's irritation over the Canadian reaction to his surrender of Barnhart Island in the St. Lawrence River as part of the settlement of the boundary under Article 6. In negotiating that compromise in 1822, Barclay and Porter had awarded Grand (now Wolfe) Island to Britain and the Long Sault Islands, including Barnhart, to the United States. As a result the United States received the only navigable channel around that island. This time Barclay would hold out for a compromise more to his liking.[5]

The commissioners, agents, and surveyors met in New York City for seven days between October 4 and 17, again on October 23, and finally on November 10. The expected British and American differences were voiced soon after the meeting got under way. To no one's surprise, Hale claimed the Middle Neebish Channel in the St. Marys River and the St. Louis River west of Lake Superior for the boundary line, and Delafield countered with claims to the Eastern Neebish Channel and the Kaministikwia River route.[6]

50

Hale maintained the Middle Channel offered the most direct route between Lakes Huron and Superior and an impartial division of territory would be effected by assigning Sugar Island to Great Britain and others nearby to the United States. Concerning the area west of Lake Superior, Hale remained confirmed in his opinion, first delivered to the commissioners in October, 1824, that "nothing like a Long Lake is to be found between the west end of Isle Royale and the discharge of the River St. Louis." As evidence he referred to the maps of the boundary surveyors and to information from the late William McGillivray that the St. Louis was the water line intended by the 1783 treaty.

Delafield urged the acceptance of a boundary through the Eastern Neebish Channel, arguing that the United States had a right to Sugar Island under the principle that it was to follow either the middle or the greatest depth of water. The line through Lake Superior, declared Delafield, should be an exception, since the treaty makers had said it must run north of Isle Royale, thereby eschewing any intention of keeping to the middle of the lake. The mandated line north of Isle Royale, he continued, pointed directly to the Kaministikwia River as the intended Long Lake of the 1783 commissioners. To his persuasive argument he added additional information on the Kaministikwia's historic use and the fact that it was depicted on various old maps as leading to a body of water named Long Lake.

During the week following their opening presentations, the British and American agents offered further claims and counter claims. Hale described in some detail his proposed line through the St. Louis River to its junction with the Embarrass River, which would be ascended to the divide separating it from the Lake of the Woods watershed. Beyond the divide the boundary would descend the Pike and Vermilion rivers into Sand Point Lake, where it would join the old Grand Portage route and follow it to the northwest point of Lake of the Woods as determined by Tiarks. The British agent accompanied these claims with Samuel Thompson's sworn statement that the St. Louis River route was the most direct way to Lake Superior and with Tiarks' report on Lake of the Woods.[7]

Although Delafield and Porter had learned the true purpose of Tiarks' mission some time before the New York meeting, they seemingly had not seen his results until Hale presented them. Delafield seems to have been particularly upset by the submission of Tiarks' report and Hale's claim to the most northwest point in Angle Inlet. He argued that the report should not be accepted as evidence because Tiarks' work had not been jointly authorized by the commissioners and because his conclusions were at variance with those of commission surveyor David Thompson. The agent also charged that Tiarks' report was both unverified and inaccurate.

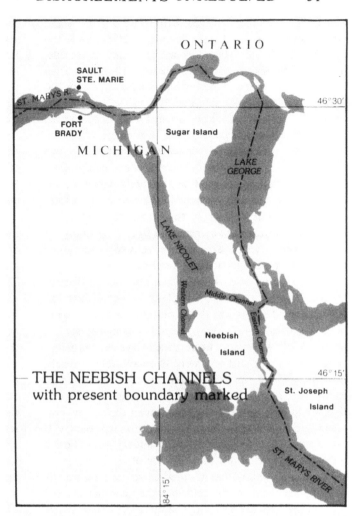

THE NEEBISH CHANNELS with present boundary marked

After a six-day recess, the meeting reconvened on October 23. Barclay and Porter haggled at some length about procedures. Finally they decided to review the sectional maps and record all their points of agreement and disagreement on the entire Article 7 boundary from Lake Huron to Lake of the Woods.[8]

During their surveys and while preparing their maps, the surveyors and draftsmen had been guided by certain principles carried over from the Article 6 work. In 1817 Porter and Ogilvy had at first interpreted the 1783 treaty's provision calling for a middle line by water to mean one equidistant from both shores. They immediately recognized, however, that an equidistant line would not always be possible because of irregularly shaped lakes and crooked water courses; in addition, such a line would have divided islands. Therefore they had decided that whenever an island was split by the equidistant line, it would be surveyed and granted to the country that had the greater share; the acreage of the lesser share would be credited to the loser and applied the next time the line intersected an island. For example, if Great Britain were given island No. 1 because the equidistant line placed 200 acres on the British side and only 100 acres on the United States side, the United States would have a credit of 100 acres. Then if island No. 2 were divided by the boundary line with 200 acres on the American side and 100 on the British side, the American credit would be applied in order to give the entire island to the United States. In practice, of course, the acreages were never so convenient, and at times it was necessary to apply the credits piecemeal and compromise when the statistics could not be absolutely balanced. But the intention was clear enough—the two countries desired an equitable division of the islands touched by the boundary. Those obviously removed from the equidistant line were not surveyed, except in the sense of determining by eye their proximity to the shoreline.[9]

The Article 6 commissioners had also agreed that adjustments in the general principle of an equidistant line would be made to assure the advantages of navigation to both countries. If only one navigable channel existed, it would be followed without reference to its size or proximity to either shore. If there were two navigable channels, the one carrying the greater amount of water would be followed. But if there were three or more channels, the line would pass through the one nearest the center, provided a good navigable channel was left to each country. If no navigable channel existed, the boundary would be run only with reference to a fair division of territory.

Porter and Ogilvy had adopted these rules informally and applied them in the field, but they had not entered them in the Article 6 journal. The surveyors under Article 7 had carried over the same rules for their work, even though Barclay and Porter had never formally invoked them. The understanding of the commissioners concerning surveying methods was therefore tacit rather than formal. Porter charged that Barclay "had been governed by the spirit of most or all" of the rules, but when formal adoption of them was suggested, he had "evaded the subject, and evinced a manifest unwillingness thus to commit himself."

After reviewing the maps, the commissioners entered their differences over the boundary around Sugar Island in the journal of October 23. They then agreed that the rest of the St. Marys River boundary would run from the middle of the river about a mile above the island to Lake Superior. It would continue across the lake, passing about 100 yards north of Chapeau Island off the northeast tip of Isle Royale.[10]

From there on the commissioners disagreed about the line all the way west to the first island in Rainy Lake. Porter claimed the border should run to the mouth of the Kaministikwia by passing north of Pie Island in Thunder Bay, adding, at Delafield's suggestion, that the cluster of islands, of which Pie was the largest, was really the long-sought Isle Phelipeaux. The Americans' proposed boundary then followed the Kaministikwia to Dog Lake, which Porter and Delafield assumed "to be the same water which is called in the Treaty of 1783 Long Lake." It passed through Dog Lake and crossed the divide along the "Old Road of the French." West of the Height of Land the route followed the Savanne River, Lac des Mille Lacs, Baril, Windigoostigwan, Pickerel, and Sturgeon lakes, and the Maligne River to Lac la Croix. From the middle of Lac la Croix it continued via the Namakan River to Namakan Lake, emerging at the foot of Kettle Falls at the entrance to Rainy Lake.

Barclay proposed that from the Chapeau Island area, the boundary should pass just north of Isle Royale and run directly to the mouth of the St. Louis River. In describing its passage up the middle of that stream, Barclay identified 52 islands, arbitrarily numbered sequentially from east to west. Seven more were similarly identified in the Embarrass River. The proposed boundary then continued over the divide to the Pike River via a series of portages, through Vermilion Lake and Vermilion River to Crane Lake, intersecting the old Grand Portage route in Sand Point Lake and following it from there to the first island in Rainy Lake. The passage of the line through the middle of the lakes and rivers was very carefully described with reference to all the adjacent numbered islands.

From Island No. 1, just below Kettle Falls in Rainy Lake, to Lake of the Woods, the commissioners had no difficulty in determining the boundary, recognizing there was no alternative to a middle passage through Rainy Lake and its outlet. Between Kettle Falls and Lake of the Woods, the surveyors had mapped 38 islands situated near the line, and like islands in the other lakes these were referred to simply by number rather than by name.

In locating the border through Lake of the Woods, Porter and Delafield finally accepted Tiarks' conclusions, although they remained disgruntled by his secret mission. The northwest point was decreed to be at the head of Angle Inlet at 49° 23' 55″ north latitude and 95° 14' 38″ west longitude. Once they had concurred in this, the commissioners were readily able to trace the boundary through the southern and western portions of Lake of the Woods by using the middle-of-the-waters principle. The line, which took into account the need for mutual navigation rights, was drawn by referring to 11 islands numbered from southeast to northwest.

Barclay and Porter were cognizant of the provision in the Treaty of Ghent which allowed Great Britain and the United States to refer unresolved boundary problems to the arbitration of a neutral power, whose tendency would be to compromise. If the commissioners had broken off their talks after presenting their most extreme claims, there would have been virtually no chance that an arbitrator, or for that matter any British or American statesmen in the future, would agree that the boundary west of Lake Superior should follow either the Kaministikwia or the St. Louis routes. Delafield had discerned this long before he made his argument for the Kaministikwia, a move he regarded simply as a counterploy rather than as a demand for valuable additional land.[11]

For their part the British had several reasons to be interested in the St. Louis River boundary. One of them was to regain Grand Portage in order to satisfy the old traders who were still unhappy about being forced out. The only way to accomplish this, Barclay believed, was to claim the first natural boundary to the south, which happened to be the St. Louis River. But this motive was insignificant compared to his interest in gaining Sugar Island in the Neebish Channels and obtaining a reconsideration of the 1822 Barnhart Island settlement in the St. Lawrence River.[12]

Once their extreme proposals had been made, the commissioners agreed to submit modifications. Porter offered as the boundary west of Lake Superior a line up the Pigeon River and along the most continuous water passage, which deviated from the old Grand Portage route at Arrow River, Hunter Island, and the Namakan River. Barclay countered by proposing that the United States could enjoy free navigation of the Eastern Neebish Channel in exchange for similar British privileges on the American side of Barnhart Island and the islands at the head of Lake St. Clair, the waterway connecting Lakes Huron and Erie. From Chapeau Island to Rainy Lake Barclay offered a line to Grand Portage and over its trail to the Pigeon River and the site of Fort Charlotte. From there the boundary was to follow the old trade route used historically rather than the most continuous water route suggested by the Americans.[13]

As another possibility Barclay proposed a line along the Pigeon River and the old trade route, provided Porter would agree that all portages, including the Grand Portage Trail, would be free and open to use by both countries. Such a border would still be part land and part water. Since Porter adhered to a strict interpretation of the Treaty of 1783 for a water boundary, he answered that he did not have the authority to accept Barclay's proposition.[14]

The commissioners also talked about the determination of the due-south line from the northwest point of Lake of the Woods to the 49th parallel, which had been authorized by both governments. They agreed that to obtain the information necessary to trace the line the surveyors would have to be sent back to Lake of the Woods in 1827. As long as additional field work had to be done, Barclay suggested, why not extend it westward to include determining and marking key places on the 49th parallel from the due-south line to the Red River?[15]

The 49th parallel had already been determined and marked at the Red River by Major Stephen H. Long

during his government-sponsored expedition in 1823. The commissioners were aware of this from the published report of Long's trip, but Barclay was skeptical of the explorer's conclusion that the settlement of Pembina (now in extreme northeastern North Dakota) was really south of the border. He understood it was only several hundred yards south, a difference he thought "so small . . . as to require accurate observations to determine" it. Persuaded by Barclay that Long's observations were "taken probably in haste and with imperfect instruments," Porter concurred in the need to extend the work. He quickly obtained President Adams' consent to mark the 49th on the west shore of Lake of the Woods and at the Red River.[16]

Even before the agreements and disagreements were officially recorded on October 23, it seemed obvious that the work of the Article 7 commission would not be concluded at the New York meeting. Once Porter had offered his compromise line, Barclay responded that he would have to consult his government, necessitating a delay of several months to allow for an exchange of correspondence. Clay and Adams were displeased by this development, but rather than abort the commission, they decided to allow it to continue, "under the hope that it may lead to an agreement . . . and prevent an appeal to a third power, the necessity of which would be much regretted."

Barclay, however, was not satisfied to wait patiently for instructions from London. After leaving the meeting on October 23, he asked Charles Vaughan to intercede by contacting Secretary of State Clay. In briefing Vaughan, the commissioner indicated his willingness to accept Porter's water line, because he thought it would be the compromise recommended by any arbitrator. It was in the Neebish Channels and the Barnhart Island areas, Barclay emphasized, that he needed Vaughan's assistance in protecting Britain's vital interests.[17]

With Vaughan's intercession under way, Barclay's only remaining business with Porter was the formal closing of the New York meeting. Conferring on November 10, the commissioners agreed to report their differences to their respective governments, assuming directives would be forthcoming which would allow them to reconvene on March 1, 1827. The preparation of their final reports was delayed in the hope that differences would be reconciled and the entire Article 7 boundary would be agreed upon.[18]

Barclay's involvement of Vaughan not only failed to bring immediate and favorable results, it contributed to a hardening of both American and British views. Clay was not at all inclined to consider a privy deal, so he referred Vaughan's missive to Porter, who became yet more wary. The commissioner feared that although his claim to the Eastern Neebish Channel was "clearly and unequivocally indicated by the principles" upon which he "had uniformly acted," Clay might surrender Sugar Island to strike a compromise with the British. He appealed to the secretary not to cede the 40-mile-square island, which he described as "large and valuable, and in point of soil and timber as well as local situation much superior to the *adjoining mainlands*," especially as a source of building material for the nearby fort. Porter also considered it vital for the United States to have at least a share of the navigation rights in the Eastern Neebish Channel. The use of this deep passage, he told Clay, would ensure "good sloop navigation from Niagara River to every part of Lake Superior, with the exception of about a mile in the St. Mary's River around which there is already a boat canal that will doubtless soon be enlarged by the government into a passage for Lake vessels."[19]

Clay discussed the Neebish Channels matter with President Adams, who concurred with Porter's opinion. The secretary of state then bluntly informed Vaughan that the president regarded the Barnhart Island question as settled under the Article 6 agreement, and that it could not be linked to the Neebish Channel question unless it became part of a broad diplomatic negotiation. The United States government would not intercede in the negotiations, he added, because they were still pending in the hands of the boundary commissioners. Adams had decided that if the commissioners failed to agree, the problems would have to be resolved at some future date in another way.[20]

While preparing their response to Vaughan, Adams and Clay also considered a request from Porter for their reaction to Barclay's proposed compromise line up the Pigeon River and along the old voyageur route with all portages "free and open" to citizens of both countries. To their way of thinking, this idea should be rejected as nothing more than a lever to exercise British will in the Neebish Channels. But rather than rule on the merits of the proposal itself, they decreed that Porter did not have the authority to consider it, nor could he contract for any "new Engagements in behalf of the United States." The authority to enter new engagements, Clay informed the commissioner, could be granted by President Adams only to someone who had "a diplomatic character," which Porter did not possess. It was an extraordinary decision for officials who had only recently readily consented to surveys beyond the northwest point of Lake of the Woods clearly not authorized by the Treaty of Ghent.[21]

After receiving the Adams-Clay ruling, Porter became pessimistic about resolving his differences with Barclay. The administration's decisions on the line west of Lake Superior and the Neebish Channels were actually in keeping with his own thinking. If he had acted independently he probably would have reached the same conclusions. It was not the decisions per se that made Porter less optimistic, but rather their uncompromising tone. He seems to

have been particularly worried by Clay's insultingly abrupt letter to Vaughan, suspecting the administration might be laying the groundwork to use the boundary as a *cause célèbre* to underscore its other differences with Great Britain.[22]

Porter seems to have genuinely wanted a boundary settlement. He can hardly be faulted for representing his country's interests strongly, nor for being upset when external circumstances threatened to abort years of effort. As a man who had political ambitions, Porter also feared he would be blamed if the boundary remained in controversy. There was much truth, he had to acknowledge, in the comments of his friend and former surveyor William A. Bird: "I was sorry to learn that you found it necessary to differ on the Settlement of the Boundary," Bird wrote, "for altho you may show the Government that you are in the right, others will think that you ought, after spending so much time with the subject, to have closed it. The people do not investigate such matters."[23]

With each passing day Porter realized the chances for a settlement of the Article 7 boundary were rapidly deteriorating in the general decline of Anglo-American relations. The United States and Great Britain had gotten along comparatively well during the early years of the boundary commission. For countries that had recently been at war, they had taken a major step toward resolving their differences with the Convention of 1818. Settling the Article 6 boundary without great contention had contributed further to good relations. By 1826, however, a number of old problems that had been only temporarily assuaged once again became issues. The two countries had not settled the Maine boundary, the agreement not to draw a boundary in Oregon was about to expire, and there was a need for a new commercial treaty. Moreover things were about to get worse.

With these issues on hand the Adams administration sent Albert Gallatin to London to assist Rufus King, who was again serving as United States minister to Great Britain. While Gallatin was crossing the Atlantic, the British cabinet seriously exacerbated matters by issuing an Order in Council forbidding United States ships to trade with Great Britain's colonies in the West Indies and South America. The order, which caused an immediate crisis in Anglo-American relations, was Canning's reversal of British policy under which the United States had enjoyed most-favored-nation status in the British West Indies trade.[24]

Gallatin was coldly received by Canning and made little progress for many months after the opening talks in August, 1826. Canning's recalcitrance strengthened the resolve of Adams and Clay not to compromise on any of the

MEMBERS of the American mission negotiating the peace treaty ending the Revolutionary War were John Jay, John Adams, Benjamin Franklin, and Henry Laurens. They are pictured with William Temple Franklin (standing at right), Franklin's son and secretary to the delegation, in a painting by Benjamin West. The work was left unfinished because the British negotiators refused to pose. Courtesy the Henry Francis du Pont Winterthur Museum.

GRAND PORTAGE, being restored in this 1974 photograph, was a major British fur trade post from the mid-18th century until about 1804. Control of this important depot, located at the beginning of the Grand Portage Trail that bypassed the unnavigable lower Pigeon River, was considered vital to traders in the central and western regions of Canada. Photo by Kenneth Carley.

THE HIGH FALLS of the Pigeon River are one of the natural impediments to canoe travel that made the Grand Portage Trail necessary to fur traders. Such rugged terrain along the lower river also slowed surveyors in 1908–18, when the boundary there was finally measured and marked.

FORT WILLIAM, the successor to Grand Portage, was built by the British North West Company about 1803 at the beginning of the Kaministikwia River route to the interior. In the 1820s the post, then operated by the Hudson's Bay Company, served as an outfitting point for American and British boundary commissions. The site of the post, shown here as it looked in 1812, is at Thunder Bay, Ontario. Courtesy Lieutenant-Colonel S.A. Heward, Hudson's Bay Company Collection, Winnipeg.

PETER B. PORTER, American boundary commissioner under Articles 6 and 7 of the Treaty of Ghent from 1816 to 1827, ultimately failed to reach agreements with British commissioner Anthony Barclay over the controversial northwest point of Lake of the Woods and the boundary through the Neebish Channels in the St. Marys River. Courtesy Buffalo and Erie County Historical Society, Buffalo, N.Y.

JOSEPH DELAFIELD, agent to Commissioner Peter B. Porter, competently supervised the work of the United States boundary commission between Lake Huron and Lake of the Woods in the 1820s. From Robert McElroy and Thomas Riggs, eds., *The Unfortified Boundary* (1943).

BOUNDARY SURVEYORS in the 1820s passed through Lac la Croix, one of several border lakes whose numerous islands made it extremely difficult to establish a mid-water line. From John J. Bigsby, *The Shoe and Canoe* (1850); courtesy Public Archives of Canada, Ottawa.

DANIEL WEBSTER (far left), United States secretary of state, and LORD ASHBURTON (near left), special envoy for Great Britain, wrote a treaty in 1842 that resolved two major boundary controversies — the line between Maine and New Brunswick and the border from Lake Huron to Lake of the Woods, including Minnesota's northern border. Ashburton mezzotint courtesy Public Archives of Canada.

HENRY H. SIBLEY (far left), fur trade agent and Minnesota political figure, was among the first to promote the development of a lucrative trade between the Red River borderland and St. Paul.

NORMAN W. KITTSON (near left) established a trading post in 1844 at Pembina near the border to attract the patronage of Canada's métis population and lure free traders away from the Hudson's Bay Company.

ALEXANDER RAMSEY (far left), first governor of Minnesota Territory, sought aid from the United States government to improve trade routes and acquire Indian land in the northern Red River Valley. In the 1860s he represented Minnesota expansionists in the United States Senate.

JAMES WICKES TAYLOR (near left), who moved to St. Paul from Ohio in 1856, became the most outspoken advocate of Minnesota expansion into the Red River region of Canada.

THE 49th PARALLEL marker near Pembina, first erected in 1823 by Major Stephen H. Long and replaced in 1849 by Major Samuel Woods, was depicted as the "International Boundary Post" in the October, 1860, issue of *Harper's New Monthly Magazine*.

THE MÉTIS of the lower Red River Valley in the 1850s and 1860s regularly organized massive buffalo hunts into American territory. Painting by Paul Kane; courtesy Royal Ontario Museum, Toronto.

A PERTINENT QUESTION

MRS. BRITANNIA.—"IS IT POSSIBLE, MY DEAR, THAT YOU HAVE EVER
GIVEN YOUR COUSIN JONATHAN ANY ENCOURAGEMENT?"

MISS CANADA.—"ENCOURAGEMENT! CERTAINLY NOT, MAMMA. I
HAVE TOLD HIM WE CAN NEVER BE UNITED."

A CARTOON published in the
Canadian publication, *Diogenes,*
for June 18, 1869, reflected the
sentiments of Canadians on
the subject of annexation to the
United States.

LOUIS RIEL (center) is pictured
in 1869 with other leaders of the
métis rebellion against the takeover of Rupert's Land by the
Dominion government of Canada. William B. O'Donoghue, an
officer in Riel's provisional government and leader of the so-
called Fenian Invasion of the
Red River Settlement in 1871, is
seated on Riel's left.

outstanding issues. Thus, when they received the inquiries from Vaughan and Porter concerning the Article 7 survey, they were not disposed to be conciliatory.[25]

Only two weeks later, when Clay answered Vaughan in mid-November, 1826, the administration had probably concluded there was no longer a possibility of settling the Article 7 boundary. After that Adams and Clay considered no alternatives and gave no instructions to Porter to do so. Annoyed by Barclay's complaint that Porter was dallying in paying the balance due Great Britain under the moeity arrangement, they ordered Porter to adjust the commission's expenses to Barclay's satisfaction, because they did not want to give "just ground for the smallest complaint on the part of the British Government."[26]

By late November Porter was aware of Adams' unwillingness to compromise on the boundary, but he did not bother to inform Barclay about it until the following April.[27] As was his custom, Barclay was wintering in Savannah and could very easily have been reached by letter. But Porter, perhaps clinging to the faint hope that the Foreign Office would initiate a compromise, did not want to foreclose any such possibility with news of the decisions. The American commissioner, who was not optimistic, must have anticipated that the Foreign Office would be as unbending as the State Department. By delaying his announcement of the United States position, he may have wished it to appear that Great Britain's refusal to compromise had caused the failure of the commission.

Canning never seriously considered working out a compromise on the Article 7 boundary. Like Clay and Adams, he reasoned that greater issues were at stake, and he could not afford to comply with American desires on a comparatively insignificant matter. The boundary from Lake Huron to Lake of the Woods was not a pressing question. The region was virtually unoccupied, so there were no fears that rival groups of settlers would war over the border. If the land remained unsettled, the status quo would be extended and, since British traders dominated Lake Superior and the area to the west, they would not be hurt by the lack of a boundary agreement. Canning realized that Great Britain had little to lose. The differences between the proposed compromise lines were slight. Therefore he could afford to think that the Article 7 boundary should either be resolved on British terms or not at all. Like Porter, however, he wanted the other side to be blamed if the commission failed. Consequently the Foreign Office too bided its time without making any clear decision.

In response to Barclay's report of October 28 on the commission's stalemate, Canning early in 1827 instructed him to forego the surveys beyond the most northwest point of Lake of the Woods and to concentrate on Article 7. Because of the slow mail service from London to Savannah to New York, as well as some tardiness on Barclay's part, Porter did not learn of Canning's decision until

April, 1827, well after the March 1 date on which the commissioners had hoped to meet. He was informed by Delafield, who heard about it from Barclay's father. The Americans had been tentatively planning to send Ferguson and Whistler to Lake of the Woods during the summer, and the Adams administration had requested a congressional appropriation to survey the due-south line and the designated points on the 49th parallel to the Red River. Once Porter knew the Foreign Office had rejected further surveys, he concluded that the only work to be done was to close the commission, adjust expenses, and exchange final reports. He was disappointed, for he would have welcomed another opportunity to try to acquire Sugar Island.[28]

Relinquishing the British claim to that island was the one thing Barclay was not free to do. In January, 1827, when Canning ordered the abandonment of the additional surveys, he authorized Barclay to work out a compromise on the area west of Lake Superior. He also ordered him to close the commission and make a report on the disputed Neebish Channels that could be referred to a third power for arbitration. Barclay never broached this possibility to Porter, because he realized the American commissioner would not agree to any line west of Lake Superior without the accompanying British concession of Sugar Island. Besides, there were matters of principle and tactics; before approaching Porter he wanted to know what the United States had decided regarding the proposed compromises discussed at their last meeting. Anticipating further conferences with Porter, Barclay wanted more room to bargain. On April 4, 1827, he asked the Foreign Office if Great Britain would be willing to agree on a boundary through the Eastern Neebish Channel, thereby giving up Sugar Island, if the United States would agree to a boundary west of Lake Superior that followed the old commercial route from the Pigeon River. If this compromise were rejected, he asked, should he proceed to close the commission?[29]

Any hope Barclay entertained for compromise was soon shattered by the news that the United States had rejected the settlement proposed at New York and that Porter had withheld this information from him for five months. Angrily the British commissioner again turned to the Foreign Office for instructions. Viscount Dudley, Canning's successor, who had delayed his response to Barclay's suggested compromise, was deeply offended by the American decision. Without issuing an opinion on the compromise, he ordered Barclay "to close your commission with as little further delay as possible and to make your report."[30]

Porter and Barclay, who had already reduced their staffs, agreed to close the commission in October, 1827. Before doing so, they exchanged bombastic attacks, quibbling over the merits of their positions on the boundary line west of Lake Superior. The immoderate language of their letters was hardly that of compromisers, but both understood their polemics were merely smokescreens hiding the one really crucial issue—Sugar Island. Porter had never been greatly concerned about the area west of Lake Superior, which to the end of his commission service he believed was "a section of country uninhabited, and I might perhaps add, uninhabitable; and therefore not likely to be a cause of future collision." If they could have agreed on Sugar Island, Porter thought he and Barclay would have had "no serious difficulty in reconciling our other differences which were of minor importance." The American was convinced that the British government's insistence on obtaining Sugar Island was part of a secret plan to abort the Article 7 work, thereby throwing the boundary into turmoil and making possible a reconsideration of the Article 6 settlement.[31]

In reality the two commissioners disagreed because the various boundary problems were interrelated. In all probability Porter was right in thinking that, had it not been for the Neebish Channels dispute, they could easily have settled on the line west of Lake Superior. But it was Porter who insisted that any compromise on the Pigeon River line had to be linked with the British concession of Sugar Island. Barclay was not as dogmatic as Porter about the island, but he was interested in rectifying some aspects of the Article 6 agreement. He regarded his rejection of Porter's claim to the Eastern Neebish Channel as a way of accomplishing this aim. Given time and encouragement from their governments, the commissioners quite probably would have been able to work out all of the outstanding questions. But before they could do so, they became entangled in the broader web of diplomatic intrigues. In 1827 Great Britain and the United States signed treaties extending the recognition of each other's rights in Oregon and submitting the Maine boundary dispute to arbitration. Both agreements, however, were completed without good will. In effecting them, Gallatin's long, sometimes acrimonious conferences with British diplomats served only to confirm the mutual feeling that there was no need to continue work on the Article 7 survey.[32]

Given these circumstances, Barclay and Porter's last meeting, held in New York City on October 22 through 27, 1827, was perfunctory. During the six days the commissioners, assisted by their remaining staff members—David Thompson and secretary-physician Richard Williams for Great Britain and Joseph Delafield and Donald Fraser for the United States—completed the filing of all the Article 7 boundary maps, adjusted their expense accounts, and agreed to exchange their final reports.[33]

Thirty-four maps, including all of those completed after the 1826 meeting, were officially filed in quadruplicate with two copies assigned to each commissioner. Some showed the proposed line from Lake Huron to the northwest point of Lake of the Woods along what had been assumed in 1822 to be the boundary through the Pigeon River and the old commercial route. Others showed important deviations—the St. Louis River route and the three areas where the most continuous water line lay north of the old commercial track.[34]

In the final adjustment of their accounts, Porter and Barclay determined that the moeity expenses of their commission under Articles 6 and 7 for the ten years from 1817 through 1827 amounted to $93,316.31 for Great Britain and $84,786.19 ½ for the United States. To equalize expenditures the United States was to pay Great Britain $4,265.06 or half of the excess of the British expenses, so the actual cost to each country totaled $89,051.25. Although these figures were published in the official journal of the last meeting as the complete expenses of the boundary survey, they do not include the salaries of the commissioners and agents nor the cash paid by the agents for sundry items.[35]

With the expenditures balanced, the commissioners had only to end their commission formally. Delafield and Porter needed time to complete the United States report, so the commissioners agreed to exchange their final reports in New York City in December, 1827. Then, the journal states, "it appearing that there remains no further need for the continuance of this Board, the commissioners now declare it to be adjourned *sine die*."

Because the Article 7 commission ended inconclusively, each commissioner recognized the heightened significance of his final report. Government officials, diplomats, legislators, and anyone else interested in the boundary would in years to come rely on these reports as principal sources of information. Thus they had to be prepared with a new audience in mind, one that included those who would determine the boundary in the future.

Although the two reports dealt with the same topics, they were dissimilar in organization, format, and tone. Barclay compiled an elaborate tome of 255 pages—195 of text and 60 of appendixes. It was divided into parts and subdivided into sections, each fitting into the whole like a piece of disputation in logic. In every part he advanced a contention, presented claims, reasons, and evidence, and drew conclusions. His language was sharp, often adversely critical, and in places contemptuous of the American commissioner and agent. The text of Porter's final report, written as a continuous narrative without numbered sections, ran to only 46 pages plus some 35 pages of appendixes. It seems to have been composed with the goal of concisely presenting conclusions rather than arguments. After seeing the British report, Porter and Delafield may have thought they erred in preparing such a short United States summary.[36]

Actually these final reports offered little new information to anyone familiar with the history of the commission's work. The commissioners for the most part reviewed only the main points covered in their joint meetings. Barclay stressed that the British claim to Sugar Island was supported by the conclusions of the Article 6 commission, under which the United States had received Barnhart Island. In writing of the area west of Lake Superior, he presented a lengthy and largely contrived case for the St. Louis River line. Then, perhaps because of a fear that the Kaministikwia might become the future boundary, he undercut his claim to the St. Louis River by including his ultimate compromise proposal—a line up the Pigeon River and along the old commercial route with all portages free and open to both nations. Barclay should have known future diplomats would be likely to seize upon such a suggestion as a reasonable solution.[37]

In his report Porter set down his opinion that an application of the principles used in the Article 6 survey would result in Sugar Island's assignment to the United States. He supported his obligatory claim to the Kaministikwia River by attaching the arguments Delafield had advanced at the 1826 meeting and a series of nine maps, some showing Pie Island as Isle Phelipeaux and others depicting Long Lake on the Kaministikwia.[38]

Cognizant of the weaknesses in his Kaministikwia claim, Porter went on to describe carefully the various compromises he had discussed with the British commissioner. He had rejected Barclay's idea of running the boundary over the portages, he said, because it was not a water line; he had refused his modified proposal, with its condition that all portages be free and open to both nations, because "such a stipulation would involve the exercise of powers not confided to him [Porter] by his Commission." Although he stopped short of recommending any of the compromise routes, he left the impression that he would not be dissatisfied if the boundary were drawn along one of them.

The final reports were exchanged shortly after Christmas, 1827, and copies of each were duly filed with the British Foreign Office and the United States Department of State. There was no noticeable immediate reaction to them, and it is doubtful that they were even read carefully by officials of either government. Neither the United States nor Great Britain wanted to submit the Article 7 differences to arbitration by a third power, so the survey conclusions were quietly shelved. They would not be revived until 1838, when the northeastern border controversy awakened interest in all aspects of the unresolved boundary.[39]

CHAPTER 7

The Webster-Ashburton Treaty

IN 1842 DANIEL WEBSTER, United States secretary of state, and Lord Ashburton, special envoy for Great Britain, clarified the last troublesome aspects of the Canada-United States boundary as initially defined in the Treaty of 1783.[1] Determined to prevent another Anglo-American war, they quietly resolved the explosive Maine-New Brunswick boundary controversy and in the process fixed what became the northern Minnesota border, which had been left unsettled by the commissioners under Article 7 of the Treaty of Ghent. Had it not been for the critical Anglo-American dispute over the northeastern boundary, the Lake Huron to Lake of the Woods segment would doubtless have remained unresolved for many more years.

The northeastern boundary controversy stemmed from another ambiguity in the 1783 treaty. The negotiators in Paris had agreed on a line running north from the head of the St. Croix River to the "highlands" dividing the watershed of the St. Lawrence River and the Atlantic Ocean and westward along the highlands to the Connecticut River. American and British commissioners appointed under Articles 4 and 5 of the Treaty of Ghent attempted to identify that boundary, but found no area north of the St. Croix's source that could be accurately described as highlands.[2]

The American commissioner claimed the divide separating the watersheds of the St. Lawrence and Atlantic should be regarded as the highlands. This contention, although logical, was challenged by the British commissioner, for such a line would leave Canada only a narrow belt of land between northern Maine and the St. Lawrence River. It also threatened to separate Lower Canada from the maritime provinces of New Brunswick and Nova Scotia. Since the War of 1812, when American invaders had exposed the defensive vulnerabilities of Lower Canada, the British had feared that in the event of another Anglo-American war, Quebec and the rest of Lower Canada would be isolated from Atlantic ports. Supplying Lower Canada was especially critical during the winter, when the lower St. Lawrence was blocked by ice. Consequently the British regarded a military road from the major port of Halifax, Nova Scotia, to Quebec as vital to the defense of Lower Canada. A portion of the best route, by way of Fredericton, New Brunswick, to Rivière du Loup on the St. Lawrence below Quebec, lay through land claimed by Maine. The British did not want the American boundary pressing against that route, and they steadfastly refused to *recognize the northernmost claim of the United States.*[3]

Instead the British held that Mars Hill, about 100 miles

south of the divide sought as the boundary by the United States, best met the definition of highlands and should be the starting point for a line drawn to the head of the Connecticut River. The total disputed area between the lines preferred by Great Britain and the United States amounted to about 12,000 square miles. With such a substantial difference the American and British commissioners, after nearly a decade of field work and consultation, reached an impasse on the Maine-New Brunswick boundary. In 1827 the two countries, fearing clashes between rival land claimants who were pushing toward the borderland, agreed to submit the problem to arbitration by King William of the Netherlands.[4]

William's task was to determine the border described by the 1783 peace treaty, but he concluded that a natural division following "highlands" was impossible. In his award announced on January 10, 1831, the monarch recommended a compromised division of the disputed territory. By his judgment the United States would have been granted 7,908 square miles, while Canada would have received 4,119 square miles. Great Britain favored the

THE DOTTED LINE on this map indicates where King William's recommended boundary differed from the line established by the Webster-Ashburton Treaty of 1842.

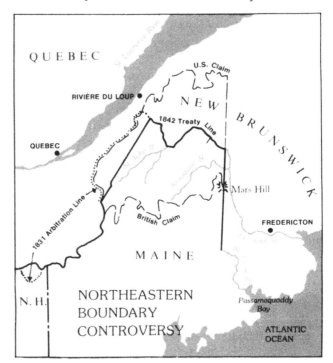

NORTHEASTERN BOUNDARY CONTROVERSY

decision because its Canadian award, although smaller in area than that of the United States, would have provided a direct route for the long-sought military road.[5]

The first American reaction to the king's decision came from William Pitt Preble, the United States minister to the Netherlands. Without waiting for instructions from his government, Preble, a former Maine judge and champion of the state's expansion at the expense of New Brunswick, denounced William's award, charging that the king had exceeded his authority. An arbitrator, he contended, could only define the treaty line, not determine a completely different one. He and his supporters argued vehemently that the highlands mentioned in the Treaty of 1783 did exist and Maine's territorial claims along the St. Lawrence-Atlantic divide followed them.[6]

President Andrew Jackson was privately inclined to accept the king's recommendation, but he recognized the political hazards. Consequently he sought the advice and consent of the Senate. After prolonged consideration and debate in 1832, the senators advised that the award be rejected and negotiations between the United States and Great Britain be renewed.

Martin Van Buren, Jackson's successor, and his secretary of state, John Forsyth, considered trying to compromise the northeastern boundary with Great Britain, but they, too, faced opposition in both the Maine legislature and Congress. The state's contention that the boundary should strictly follow a literal interpretation of the Paris peace treaty line was supported in the United States House of Representatives by Caleb Cushing of Massachusetts, whose commonwealth still held title to some lands in Maine.[7]

At the same time he was championing Maine's cause, Cushing revived the dormant question of the old Article 7 boundary from Lake Huron to the northwest corner of Lake of the Woods. On May 28, 1838, he introduced a resolution, which was readily approved by the House of Representatives, calling on President Van Buren to send to the House the reports of the Article 7 commissioners, all related correspondence between the United States and Great Britain, and "any other information in possession of the Executive on the same subject." Cushing's terse resolution offered no explanation, but it is likely he hoped to broaden the boundary question to include all disputes with the ultimate view of trading claims in various sections. Certainly Maine's prospects would have been improved if Great Britain had eagerly desired some area west of Lake Huron which the United States might concede in exchange for the disputed Maine territory.

If these were his intentions, Cushing must have been disappointed when he read Barclay's and Porter's final reports. Duly submitted on July 2, 1838, by Van Buren and Forsyth, the reports with all their appendixes were published by the House and became public information for the first time. They of course recorded the slight differences that had remained between the boundary commissioners and spelled out their suggested compromises.[8]

After the House had reopened the question of the Article 7 boundary, Forsyth attempted to include it with the more pressing northeast segment in a general settlement with Great Britain. He talked and corresponded with Henry S. Fox, British minister to the United States, about creating another joint commission, but the two men could not agree on particulars for its organization and duties. Forsyth also introduced the subject of the line west of Lake Huron, suggesting that the countries submit the disputed points of the Article 7 boundary to "some friendly Sovereign or State for final decision" while they were "still free from many of the painful embarrassments which have attended the efforts of the Parties to fix other portions of the line."[9]

The diplomatic overtures of Forsyth and Fox were overwhelmed, however, by events that precipitated a new crisis on the Maine-New Brunswick frontier. By 1838 rival land claimants, emboldened by the militancy of their state and provincial governments, intensified their activities in the disputed region. Maine rushed a reported 10,000 militiamen to the frontier, where they were soon faced by British troops. Fortunately an outbreak of hostilities was averted by General Winfield S. Scott, commander of the United States Army, who was sent to the seething frontier to arrange a truce. He allayed the war threat considerably by negotiating the withdrawal of the military forces to opposite sides of a temporary compromise line. Although this calmed tensions somewhat, it did not reconcile any of the major issues that had caused a great wave of Anglophobia to ripple throughout the United States.[10]

During the Jackson and Van Buren administrations, American and British relations had deteriorated with respect to so many questions that virtually every section of the United States had some grievance against John Bull. Taken together, these dissatisfactions helped to create a massive national sympathy for Maine. Particularly in such western states as Missouri, United States interest in obtaining Oregon was stirred during the 1830s by the activities of American missionaries and explorers in the Pacific Northwest. British interest in perpetuating the independence of the Republic of Texas further offended westerners and southerners, who generally desired its annexation.

Southern opposition was also spurred by the seeming British threat to slavery. After that institution was abolished in the British Empire in 1833, Great Britain assumed the role of an international policeman in controlling the African slave trade. The British tried to suppress it by stopping and searching slave ships, a practice euphemistically called the "right of visit." Southerners, who were also being buffeted by abolitionists in the United States, found support in the federal government, which held that any American consent to the right of visit had to be accompanied by a formal British renunciation of impressment.

These far-flung differences were aggravated by American sympathy for Canadian dissidents during the abortive rebellion of 1837 in Lower and Upper Canada. When Canadian rebels took up arms to win more power for popularly elected assemblies at the expense of appointed governors and councils, they received backing from the northern borderland of the United States. Americans helped supply the insurgents and provided havens for them within striking distance of Canada. Support for the rebel cause was stimulated both by the belief that the rebellion, like the American Revolution, struck a blow against British tyranny and by the rampant Anglophobia in the United States.[11]

American zeal caused Canadian authorities to strike back. Some New Yorkers employed a small ship named the "Caroline" to ferry supplies to the rebels across the Niagara River above the falls. In December, 1837, a group of loyal Canadians crossed the river and seized and destroyed the "Caroline" after a skirmish in which one American was killed. The United States charged Great Britain with violating American territorial rights, but the British maintained the Canadian loyalists were acting under orders during a national emergency. The "Caroline" affair, the single most explosive event growing out of the Canadian rebellion, lingered as a sore point. Its effects were exacerbated a year later by the celebrated case of Alexander McLeod. A Canadian deputy sheriff at the time of the "Caroline" affair, McLeod was arrested and imprisoned in New York in November, 1840, charged with involvement in the seizure and destruction of the ship. When a New York grand jury indicted him on arson and murder charges, Lord Palmerston, the British foreign secretary, warned that Great Britain would declare war on the United States if McLeod were convicted and executed.[12]

While the McLeod case was pending and feelings of ill will were escalating, governmental changes in both the United States and Great Britain brought about improved relations. Van Buren and Forsyth had wished to conciliate Great Britain, but troublesome incidents and the anti-British tradition of the Democratic party undercut them. Van Buren's defeat in 1840 by William Henry Harrison not only removed an executive who was closely associated with an era of ill feeling, but replaced him with a president from the more pro-British Whig party. Harrison's willingness to improve relations was signaled almost at once when he named two New Englanders with Anglophile leanings—Daniel Webster and Edward Everett—to key diplomatic posts. Webster, as secretary of state, and his good friend Everett, as minister to Great Britain, formed the team that undertook to resolve major differences between the two countries.[13]

Nearly 60 years old when he became secretary of state in 1841, Webster was one of the best-known figures in the United States. A lawyer by profession, he had distinguished himself in Congress as an eloquent spokesman for New England in a public career spanning nearly 30 years. Although widely considered the likely Whig nominee for president in 1840, he was passed over in favor of Indian-war hero Harrison of Ohio. Fearing the loss of his Senate seat, Webster campaigned hard for Harrison and was rewarded with a key cabinet position. When Harrison died after only a month in office, Webster continued as secretary of state under President John Tyler.[14]

The new secretary had long been familiar with the Maine boundary dispute, both as a senator from Massachusetts and as a popular visitor in England in 1839. When he became secretary of state, he gave it a high priority. During the summer of 1841, with Tyler's approval, he informed the British minister to the United States that he was willing to discuss the northeast boundary problem and other issues. He then assigned Everett the delicate task of broaching the subject to the British prime minister and the foreign secretary.[15]

Webster's diplomatic overture coincided with changes in the British government that made Sir Robert Peel prime minister and the conciliatory Lord Aberdeen his secretary of state for foreign affairs. The new secretary replaced Lord Palmerston, a flag-waving nationalist, whose stridency had offended the United States and most other major nations. Although Peel and Aberdeen desired improved relations with the United States, they, like Palmerston, regarded the possible conviction and execution of McLeod as a serious provocation. The diplomatic climate improved immensely when McLeod was found innocent by a New York jury in October, 1841.[16]

Shortly after the McLeod verdict, Aberdeen expressed his willingness to negotiate the Maine-New Brunswick boundary. As his special envoy for this task he selected Lord Ashburton and sent him to Washington, D.C., to meet with Webster. The 67-year-old Ashburton, who was Alexander Baring before attaining his peerage, was a member of the famous Baring banking house. As a young man he had represented the concern in the United States and had married the daughter of a Pennsylvania senator. During his long career as a financier and a member of Parliament, Ashburton consistently advocated good relations with the United States as one of Britain's foreign policy goals. His friendly disposition toward America and Webster's pleasure at his appointment augured well for fruitful talks.[17]

As Ashburton readied for his Washington trip in February, 1842, Aberdeen prepared a résumé of major issues and broad instructions authorizing the envoy to negotiate "for the settlement of the different matters in discussion between Her Majesty and the United States." In contemplating the northeast boundary, which he regarded as the paramount issue, Aberdeen saw at once that Great Britain's earlier approval of the arbitrator's award placed it in an awkward negotiating position. King William's compromise line, rather than the southernmost British claim, would be the logical starting point for any discussions. In his instructions of February 8, 1842, Aberdeen expressed a desire to obtain land south of the Netherlands award line, but added he would settle for the king's compromise. His tone throughout indicated a willingness to be reasonable, and it is apparent he did not believe either country should obtain its most extreme claim.[18]

Aberdeen also covered the Oregon and Article 7 boundary questions. He did not think the Oregon matter was as politically explosive as that in the northeast, but he felt it should be settled to avoid future collisions. Interestingly the foreign secretary was much more insistent on British territorial rights in Oregon than in Maine-New Brunswick. He instructed Ashburton to work for a Columbia River demarcation and to refuse any American proposal to extend the 49th parallel from the continental divide to the Pacific. As Ashburton soon learned, Aberdeen had not reckoned with the ardor of American expansionists to gain land north of the Columbia.[19]

Almost casually the foreign secretary touched on the Article 7 boundary as "a third question of disputed territory, which although of less importance than either of those upon which I have just addressed you, has nevertheless given rise to much discussion and negotiation." Aberdeen had obviously studied the reports of Barclay and Porter, for he accurately identified the commissioners' differences and suggested compromises. Without explaining or justifying Barclay's claim to the St. Louis River line, he stated merely that the boundary should be compromised and that a reasonable settlement would be Barclay's proposal of 1826, which would have granted Sugar Island to Great Britain and drawn the boundary west of Lake Superior along the Grand Portage Trail to the Pigeon River and then along the traditional voyageur route to the northwest corner of Lake of the Woods. The minister instructed, however, that if this proposal proved to be "impracticable, or attended with great difficulty," Ashburton could yield Sugar Island to the United States in exchange for an "equivalent advantage" in Oregon or elsewhere along the border.

Although Aberdeen's instructions dealt largely with the three boundary questions, he also reviewed other issues—the "Caroline" affair, for which the United States was still seeking an apology; the McLeod case, which, despite the accused's acquittal, concerned British officials because a Canadian national had been tried in a state

court; and the right of visit. Armed with these lengthy instructions, as well as a dossier of memorials and maps mostly relating to the Maine-New Brunswick boundary, Ashburton sailed for the United States.[20]

But as the envoy was crossing the Atlantic, his instructions were revised when other cabinet members, once informed of them, refused to settle for the Dutch award as the northeast boundary. In a long dispatch to Ashburton on March 31, Aberdeen explained that the cabinet feared a boundary based on the arbitration award would place the essential winter road skirting the line in an indefensible position in the event of war with the United States. He ordered Ashburton to make every effort to improve on the king's recommended compromise. To do so, the minister implied, would call for some British concessions.[21]

Aberdeen proposed that Great Britain relinquish its claim to two disputed areas—a tract of some 150 square miles near the headwaters of the Connecticut River, and a narrow strip about three-fourths of a mile wide stretching some 160 miles from the Connecticut to the St. Lawrence. Since 1818, when the Article 5 commission had corrected the line of the 45th parallel, placed too far north by surveyors in 1774, the strip had been a potential trouble spot. Aberdeen believed the two concessions would be a fair exchange for the roughly two million acres of "unoccupied pine swamp" the British wanted south of the Netherlands award line. But if the United States balked, Britain was prepared to indemnify Maine for the land.[22]

Soon after Ashburton arrived in Washington on April 4, 1842, he began informal meetings with Webster. Moderate in both temperament and diplomatic goals, he brought to the talks a long perspective of Anglo-American relations. Both men were of the Revolutionary War generation, and both had personally witnessed the disastrous effects of the War of 1812, which Webster had vigorously opposed as a young congressman. Neither had experience as a professional diplomat, which may have been an advantage. With little concern for either protocol or past differences, they discussed the outstanding issues between their countries. Compromise and conciliation were the hallmarks of their numerous talks, which sometimes continued into social occasions. By diplomatic standards, their methods were unorthodox. They first talked privately about issues in a preliminary way without keeping records of their conversations. After they had reached a general consensus, one or the other would set down a written proposition, which was then further deliberated and refined.[23]

After only a few weeks the compatible Ashburton and Webster were optimistic about amicably compromising all the most troublesome issues except one—the boundary. Both men worried over the increasing militancy of Americans, especially in the northeast. In their support of

Maine's extreme claim, Webster reported to Everett, the "people of the United States" had a too simple answer for a very complex problem. When the Tyler administration decided to involve commissioners from Maine and Massachusetts in the boundary negotiations, both Webster and Ashburton were irritated. This plan and the need for Webster to mollify the two states' leaders in person interrupted their talks for about a month.[24]

Meanwhile Aberdeen studied the first extensive report he had received from Ashburton. On April 25 when the envoy wrote it, he believed he would be able to settle the Oregon boundary at the Columbia River line. He did not mention the Article 7 boundary, indicating the subject had not yet come up in his talks with Webster. As for the northeast boundary, Ashburton emphasized that Great Britain should not appear to be greedy, for the United States, that "jealous, arrogant, democratic Body," would be sorely offended if Britain asked for more territory than had been awarded by King William. While he would try for more land, he advised that the Netherlands award line would be better than no agreement at all. Taking his emissary's views into consideration, Aberdeen on May 26 set down further guidelines for the negotiations, giving Ashburton unprecedented latitude. He reiterated that Canada needed a strip of land south of the Netherlands award. In return Great Britan would be willing to cede a tract at the source of the Connecticut, renounce its claim to the narrow strip between the old and new 45th parallels, and permit United States citizens to float their timber and produce down the St. John River. The prime minister regarded the latter as a major concession, for the St. John flowed mainly through New Brunswick on its way to the sea. But following Ashburton's counsel, Aberdeen concluded that if these proposals were unacceptable to the United States, he would settle for the Netherlands award line. The foreign minister did not mention either the Oregon or Lake Superior area boundaries.[25]

Ashburton found Aberdeen's final instructions "perfectly sufficient" for his purposes. They gave him the flexibility he desired as the negotiations resumed. The Maine and Massachusetts commissioners arrived, and Ashburton found their presence a test of both his tact and his patience. After his first meeting with them, he was relieved on at least one score, for he concluded that Great Britain would not be asked to indemnify the two states. He presumed, correctly as it turned out, that the United States instead would be obliged to reimburse them.[26]

At Webster's request Ashburton put into writing a formal proposition on the Maine-New Brunswick boundary on June 21. By that time the two statesmen had apparently reached an informal accord and their principal remaining task lay in convincing the commissioners from Maine and Massachusetts. Ashburton's opening remarks carried a strong call for compromise. Concentrate on the present needs of both countries, he urged, and avoid quibbling over the geographic details of the Revolutionary War peace treaty. Using the Netherlands award as a starting point, Ashburton asked that Great Britain be granted a tract south of the part of the award line lying between the St. John and St. Lawrence rivers. This area, he noted, was occupied by Canadians, who should be left under British jurisdiction. In return for this concession, he offered the United States the small contested tract near the source of the Connecticut River and the strip between the old and new 45th parallels, both of which had been granted to Great Britain by King William. Beyond these proposed territorial swaps, the envoy expressed his willingness to negotiate American commercial use of the St. John River. The latter was calculated partially to appease Maine, for the St. John afforded the most convenient trade route for farmers and lumbermen in the northern part of the state.[27]

In his proposition Ashburton limited all territorial exchanges to those considered in the Netherlands award. His strategy in making the trade-offs acceptable was to offer land granted by King William to Great Britain in exchange for territory awarded to the United States. Throughout the negotiations Aberdeen, Ashburton, and Webster avoided any linking of the northeast, the Lake Superior area, and the Oregon boundary issues. All three seem to have been content to consider the unique aspects in each region on their own merits.

By the time he proposed a specific northeast settlement, Ashburton had written off any hope of resolving the Oregon boundary. His earlier optimism about obtaining a Columbia River line was dimmed by Webster's unwillingness to challenge American expansionists in the face of the enhanced national interest in the Pacific Northwest caused by the reports of a naval expedition led by Lieutenant Charles Wilkes. Without a basis for compromising their disparate views, the negotiators dropped the subject from further consideration.[28]

For a troubled time in early July, the tiresome proceedings and the hawkishness of the Maine and Massachusetts commissioners depressed Ashburton. On July 13 he reported to Aberdeen that his favorable expectations of late June had been fraught with "delay and difficulties," most of which he blamed on the state commissioners. Webster, also fearing that the agreement might be lost, connived to convince the commissioners that the British proposition on the northeast boundary should be accepted. His success was abetted by the timely discovery of a map, purportedly marked with a red line by Benjamin Franklin in 1782, which showed the boundary lying even farther south than Great Britain's extreme claim. In addition, the Tyler administration agreed to reimburse Maine and Massachusetts for lands lost by a compromise line. These payments helped make the northeast boundary agreement acceptable to the states, even though it left Maine with almost 900 square miles of territory less than it would have received under the Netherlands award.[29]

Throughout their talks, Webster and Ashburton continued to intermingle deliberations on the key northeast issue with conversations about other questions, including the line from Lake Huron to the northwest point of Lake of the Woods. Its adjustment was not formally proposed, however, until after they had concluded the Maine-New Brunswick settlement with the state commissioners. In a letter of July 16 Ashburton introduced it as a "further question of disputed boundary . . . about which we have had some conferences." The extent and precise nature of those talks are not known, but related records suggest that neither Ashburton nor Webster saw the northwest boundary as a major issue and that they were never in fundamental disagreement over it.[30]

Ashburton's disinterest in the northwest boundary merely reflected the posture of the Foreign Office. After covering it in his original instructions, Aberdeen did not mention it again. Ashburton was likewise silent on the subject, first mentioning it casually in his dispatch of July 28. At that time he remarked only that he had "at last settled the terms of the Convention of Boundaries from the River St. Croix to the Lake of the Woods." Not until August 9, the very day he signed the treaty with Webster, did Ashburton report any details of the northwest boundary agreement to Aberdeen.[31]

Webster's records show his aim was to compromise a line that might be troublesome in the future. The secretary of state made no concerted effort to become well informed about the northwest boundary until after Ashburton's formal proposal concerning it on July 16, 1842. Until then he had sought firsthand data from only one person who had some information about Sugar Island.[32]

Ashburton, on the other hand, had made a thorough study of the nature of the boundary problems west of Lake Huron. Anthony Barclay, who was then living in New York City, made available the final reports as well as "a set of very perfect Charts of the Country." The envoy also learned from Barclay about the Canadian desire for navigation rights through the American channels by the islands of Long Sault and Barnhart in the St. Lawrence, and he secured more information on that matter from an emissary sent to Washington by Canada's Governor-general Charles Bagot. Ashburton, who acknowledged to Aberdeen that he had "received much useful advice and assistance from Mr. Barclay," certainly had the opportunity to talk candidly with the former commissioner about his near-compromise with Porter and the worthlessness of the wilderness west of Lake Superior.

The British proposal for the northwest boundary was concise and unambiguous. Without harking back to past differences, Ashburton offered Sugar Island to the United States. It was, he observed, "the only object of any real value in this controversy." As for "the wild country between Lake Superior and the Lake of the Woods," he commented, "it really appears of little importance to either party how the line be determined." In keeping with his instructions and Barclay's compromise plan, Ashburton thought the boundary should follow the Grand Portage Trail to the Pigeon River and continue along the old commercial route to Rainy Lake, where it would merge with the line to Lake of the Woods agreed upon by Barclay and Porter. In exchange for Sugar Island he asked for the British right of navigation on the United States side of islands in the St. Clair River and around Barnhart and Long Sault islands.[33]

Webster delayed responding to Ashburton for 11 days in order to continue his research. He had already solicited the opinion of Robert Stuart, the former trader at Mackinac, who attested to the excellent soil and bountiful maple trees of Sugar Island, on which local American settlers depended for annual revenue. Joseph Delafield substantiated the island's agricultural value and added his opinion that the "mountainous, rocky, and barren" country west of Lake Superior could sustain only fur traders and fishermen. James Ferguson called the region "one waste of rock and water" producing only pine timber. Both Delafield and Ferguson insisted that the mouth of the Pigeon River was the Long Lake intended by the 1783 treaty.[34]

Given this information, Webster agreed to Ashburton's proposal concerning Sugar Island and to the common use of the navigable channels in the St. Lawrence and St. Clair rivers. He asked only for reciprocity with respect to the channel on the Canadian side of Bois Blanc Island in the Detroit River and for a slight alteration west of Lake Superior. He proposed that the boundary run through the mouth of the Pigeon River and along the old commercial route to Rainy Lake, because "It is desirable to follow the description and the exact line of the original treaty as far as practicable." To satisfy Ashburton, however, he agreed that all waterways and portages along the boundary line should be used freely by both nations.[35]

Ashburton pronounced Webster's reply to be "the final result of the many conferences we have had on this subject." He thought it was "substantially correct in all its parts, and we may now proceed without further delay to draw up the treaty." Their delineation of the border from Lake Huron to the northwest point of Lake of the Woods was embodied in Article 2 of the agreement signed on August 9, 1842. The boundary through the Eastern Neebish Channel was carefully specified to place Sugar Island in the United States. Then from the mouth of the St.

Marys River to a point "one hundred yards to the north and east of i[s]le Chapeau," just northeast of Isle Royale, it followed the line agreed upon by Barclay and Porter.[36]

From the point off Isle Chapeau, Ashburton and Webster traced the boundary southwesterly by a mid-water line to the mouth of the Pigeon River, then up that stream and along the old fur trade route to Angle Inlet in Lake of the Woods. From the lake's northwesternmost point, specifically identified as 49° 23′ 55″ north latitude and 95° 14′ 38″ west longitude, they agreed on a due-south line to the 49th parallel, which was followed to the Rocky Mountains. The treaty also specified that "all the water-communications, and all the usual portages along the line from Lake Superior to the Lake of the Woods; and also Grand Portage, from the shore of Lake Superior to the Pigeon river, as now actually used, shall be free and open to the use of the citizens and subjects of both countries."

Ashburton and Webster only generally described the boundary from Isle Royale to the northwest point of Lake of the Woods because they intended to mark it on the maps prepared by Barclay's and Porter's men. Ashburton had pronounced those maps to be "excellent" and had suggested using them to save both countries the expense of a new survey. The line traced on them ran between the numbered islands along the approximate middle of each lake. The diplomats knew that, with the exception of David Thompson's monument "No. 1" near the northwest point of Lake of the Woods, the boundary was not marked on the ground. They did not think this would cause any inconvenience in the near future, since the adjacent lands were not attractive to settlers.

The Webster-Ashburton Treaty has been generally regarded as the instrument that blunted the threat of a third Anglo-American war, primarily because the two statesmen were able to compromise the northeastern boundary. As it turned out, the agreement also settled the northern boundary of what was soon to be Minnesota Territory, fixing it largely according to the drastically narrowed possibilities dictated by the Article 7 commissioners. Besides defining the northeast and northwest boundaries, the pact included articles providing for American commercial use of the St. John River, mutual extradition of criminals, an agreement to enforce laws banning the slave trade, and a stipulation that both countries would maintain naval patrols off the coast of Africa to discourage that trade. During negotiations Ashburton had also made a quasi apology for Canadian involvement in the "Caroline" affair.[37]

While the treaty accomplished its main purpose of fixing the northeast boundary, Webster knew it would not satisfy diehard western and southern Anglophobes who were in a dither about the British in Oregon, the "Creole"

incident, and impressment. Assuming there would be vocal opposition in the Senate from some southern and western Democrats, he used secret funds placed at his disposal by President Tyler for launching a clandestine campaign to manipulate public opinion. Mainly through ghost-written articles and editorials printed during the period of negotiations in sympathetic New England and eastern newspapers, Webster presented a highly favorable impression of the treaty. The planted editorials appeared to be an authentic portrayal of local sentiments. Not only were Maine and Massachusetts pleased with the suggested northeast boundary settlement, according to the editorials, but the agreement promised to resolve the other major issues that concerned various sections of the nation. By overemphasizing the satisfaction of the citizens in the two states most affected by it, Webster's ploy created widespread national support for the treaty.[38]

His propaganda was so effective that, by the time the pact was submitted to the Senate, American citizens generally were not aware of its narrow scope. Consequently antitreaty senators, such as Thomas Hart Benton of Missouri, fought an uphill battle with public opinion as well as with the prestigious Webster, who extended his opinion-molding campaign to the Senate. The president's message transmitting the treaty to the Senate was written by Webster in Tyler's name. It stressed the pleasure of the Maine and Massachusetts commissioners with the document, implying that the nation, which had previously anguished over the plight of these states, should now join them in embracing the treaty. Then for the senators' edification he revealed some supposedly fresh and important information about the northwest boundary and the area west of Lake Superior.[39]

Downplaying the compromise efforts of the Article 7 commissioners, Webster implied that Barclay had made a hard claim to the St. Louis River boundary. By failing to mention Ashburton's compromise proposal, he deliberately gave the impression that the British diplomat had supported Barclay's claim. According to the story Webster told the Senate, he had prevailed in this "matter of difference" and had thereby acquired for the United States the area between the St. Louis and Pigeon rivers, "a territory of four millions of acres, northward of the claim set up by the British commissioner under the treaty of Ghent."

It was a skillfully worded misrepresentation that served Webster's purpose well. Not only did it convince senators, but later historians too have assumed the secretary of state won a major concession of land that Ashburton had coveted.[40] That assumption, however, is no more valid than the argument that Webster conceded the land between the Pigeon and Kaministikwia rivers, for both would have to be based on the false notion that the negotiations had as their basis Porter's and Barclay's extreme claims. In fact Webster and Ashburton took as their starting point the commissioners' proposed compromises. Ashburton did not seek to retain the land between the Pigeon and St. Louis rivers, so it cannot be said that he conceded it. It is true that within the limitations of the compromise plans, both negotiators conceded something. Ashburton surrendered Barclay's claim to Sugar Island, and Webster gave up Porter's claim to the most continuous water line, thereby leaving to Great Britain three tracts, including Hunter Island.

Not only was Webster's acquisition west of Lake Superior vast, he advised the Senate, but it was also "considered valuable as a mineral region." This claim was apparently intended to placate westerners who were upset by his failure to acquire Oregon. The secretary did not name specific minerals, nor did he offer any authority for his statement.[41]

Because extensive iron ore deposits were later found in northeastern Minnesota, some historians have fallaciously assumed that the secretary of state was referring to iron ore when he mentioned the area's value "as a mineral region." A second related and equally undocumented supposition has held that knowledge of minerals was extant at the time of the 1783 peace treaty, and that Benjamin Franklin knew about valuable deposits in the Lake Superior area. Both men have received credit for their foresight in securing the region for the United States.[42] Despite Webster's claim, neither he nor Ashburton—nor for that matter anyone else at the time—was aware that northeastern Minnesota was a likely iron-mining region. But as Webster undoubtedly knew, there were a number of factors that would make claims concerning the area's mineral wealth plausible.

During the mid-1800s the United States was actively seeking minerals on the frontier. Government explorations normally included a mineralogist, and there was a persistent hope, if not an expectation, that minerals would be discovered in unsettled regions. This belief was supported by the finding of lead deposits in Wisconsin, Iowa, and Missouri, as well as by information on the copper of the upper Michigan peninsula, which had been known to Indian, French, and British people before the United States acquired the area. Finds along the Ontonagon River and the favorable report of the Michigan state geologist in February, 1842, intensified public demands for private prospecting and mining in the region. Although the United States government had obtained mineral rights to Indian lands in upper Michigan and northern Wisconsin in 1826, pressure from copper miners in 1842 led to a new treaty by which the land itself was purchased. The upper Michigan copper fever, which occurred while Webster was negotiating with Ashburton, was widely reported.[43]

The cagey Webster was wise enough to know that promoters were not expected to provide hard proof of their claims. The temper of the times was such that his general reference to minerals would cause many to think that copper also existed west of Lake Superior. Actually the presence of iron ore in northeastern Minnesota was not confirmed until the geological reconnaissance of Joseph G. Norwood in 1848-50. His discovery of "thin layers" of ore near Gunflint Lake was made public when the report of his supervisor, David Dale Owen, appeared in 1852, but it created no excitement. Besides, all the factors necessary for a mineral rush, including advertising and capital, did not then exist. Numerous samples of iron ore were extracted during the Vermilion Lake gold rush of 1865-66, but the area that was to become the Vermilion Range was not extensively reconnoitered until 1875-80, when expeditions sponsored by eastern capitalists revealed quantities of hard iron ore.[44]

If Webster hoped his touted acquisition of the land between the Pigeon and St. Louis rivers would spare the treaty from criticism, he was badly mistaken. The very people it was intended to soothe were the least fooled by it. The northwest boundary stipulation was bitterly attacked by Thomas Hart Benton, who spoke "against this treaty not so much for the Senate as for the country." The senator castigated both the pact's provisions and its omissions, including the failure to acquire Oregon. While he attacked each provision at length, Benton hit hardest at the international line set in the area west of Lake Superior, where Webster had "sacrificed an important boundary" by surrendering Porter's claim to the most continuous water route from the Pigeon River to Rainy Lake. Not only had the secretary relinquished a legitimate American claim, Benton contended, but he had made "the President sign a statement which leads the country to believe that he has made an acquisition of four millions of acres of fine mineral land. The detection of this fallacy, and the exposure of this subserviency, are not only necessary to save us from gross error about these four millions of acres; but also to show us the spirit in which the treaty was made." Benton's main objection to the northwest boundary was that Webster had given up what the senator thought was the only thing of any real value in the entire area—exclusive American use of the Grand Portage Trail, which, he observed, the British had voluntarily abandoned years before.[45]

The vitriolic oratory of Benton and other critics who attracted attention, both then and later, belied the overwhelming support for Webster and his treaty in the Senate. Only nine days after receiving it, the senators approved the document by a vote of 39 to 9. The pact was similarly raked over the coals in Parliament, where Ashburton was accused of having surrendered to the United States, but these attacks too were more bombast than substance. The two countries exchanged ratifications in

London on October 13, 1842, thereby agreeing on an international boundary from the Atlantic coast to the continental divide in the Rocky Mountains. Four years later, when the United States and Great Britain extended the boundary along the 49th parallel from the Rockies to the Strait of Georgia north of Puget Sound, an ocean-to-ocean line had been achieved on paper. Although no one gave it much thought, the northern limits of Minnesota, Wisconsin, and Michigan had been defined while settlement was still concentrated in their southern sections.[46]

CHAPTER 8

Minnesota Expansionism and the Unmarked Boundary

FOR NEARLY 30 YEARS following the Webster-Ashburton Treaty, the boundary from Lake of the Woods to the Rocky Mountains remained unmarked and virtually forgotten while activity focused on the line in the Northeast and far Northwest. In that interval Minnesota Territory was established in 1849, the state entered the Union in 1858, and the Civil War was fought. Not until the late 1860s did international interest shift to the border between Canada and Minnesota. It was sparked by a crisis in American-Canadian relations in which northward-looking Minnesotans figured prominently. As a result the United States and Great Britain established a joint commission to survey the segment between Lake of the Woods and the Rockies in 1872-76.

Soon after the 1842 treaty was concluded, the two countries co-operated in surveying and marking the northeast boundary. Then the movement of American settlers into the Pacific Northwest and the influx of a small number of British subjects into the Vancouver and Victoria areas of British Columbia prompted the measuring of the land boundary from the Strait of Georgia eastward to the continental divide between 1857 and 1861. Crossing over 400 miles along the 49th parallel, this work was conducted without serious incident or disagreement, but the exchange of final reports was not accomplished until 1869, primarily because of strained relations between the two countries during the American Civil War and early Reconstruction Era.[1]

The survey went almost unnoticed as public attention turned to the acrimonious dispute over the water boundary and the San Juan Islands lying between the Georgia and Juan de Fuca straits. Once again extreme differences caused both the United States and Great Britain to hint that only war would settle the matter. The question was not so much ownership of the islands as it was control over ship passages around them. Eventually the two nations agreed to arbitration of the dispute by a neutral party— Kaiser Wilhelm I of Germany. In 1872, 13 years after the controversy began, the Kaiser ruled in favor of the American claim, thereby quieting the most contentious problem to arise along the United States-Canada boundary since the Maine-New Brunswick crisis.

At the time field work was in progress along the 49th parallel in the Pacific Northwest, there was also a flash of congressional interest in marking the line from Lake of the Woods to the Rockies. On March 26, 1860, during consideration of appropriations for the Oregon boundary survey, Senator Jefferson Davis of Mississippi proposed an amendment that made available any balance of funds from the western work for use in marking the 49th parallel east of the Rockies. Davis urged that it would be cheaper to proceed eastward with the current survey crews than to begin a new project in the future. He also pointed to the settlements in the northern Red River Valley which made boundary determination desirable. Although Davis' amendment passed easily, the long delay in closing the Oregon commission prevented any work east of the Rocky Mountains.[2]

Nearly a decade went by before the section of unsurveyed boundary west of Lake of the Woods again came to public attention. Then the events leading to its joint survey in 1872-76 were a culmination of the convergence over half a century of two frontiers—one American, thrusting northwest from the Great Lakes, and the other Canadian, isolated in the northern Red River Valley. The meeting of these frontiers was characterized by aggressiveness on the part of Americans, particularly Minnesotans, who by the late 1860s were working vigorously to bring about United States annexation of sizable portions of western Canada.

The Americans' desire to annex parts of Canada was a natural outgrowth of the clash between the two frontiers. From its start in 1812, Lord Selkirk's Red River Colony was beset by difficulties stemming from poor planning, inadequate financing, and constant harassment by the North West Company and its mixed-blood employees, who deeply resented the incursion of agricultural activities into their customary hunting domain. The merger of the North West and Hudson's Bay companies in 1821 ended the threat of armed hostiles, but the straggling settlement was then devastated by drought, floods, and locusts.[3]

Following these natural disasters, an estimated 500 Selkirkers fled from the Red River Colony in the 1820s and 1830s. They took the easiest exit—the route south up the Red River—which led them into the United States and then east across Minnesota to Fort Snelling at the junction of the Minnesota and Mississippi rivers. Some remained at the fort, but most eventually made their way down the Mississippi to settle in Illinois, Indiana, and Missouri. These emigrants and the government expedition headed in 1823 by Stephen Long were among the earliest contacts between the Red River and the upper Mississippi.

The most significant conduit between the two frontiers, however, was provided by the fur trade, which dominated the early American movement into Minnesota. The Americanization of the area began in 1816, when the American Fur Company of John Jacob Astor assumed control of the North West Company's posts. Alarmed at the lingering influence of British traders, Astor and his chief lieutenants convinced the federal government to extend its military frontier to the upper Mississippi. The presence of a garrisoned post, they reasoned, would not only discourage British traders but would help keep the Dakota and Ojibway tribes at peace. In 1819 the War Department sent troops of the Fifth Regiment of Infantry to the junction of the Mississippi and Minnesota rivers, where during the next year they began construction of the post that became Fort Snelling. For nearly three decades it was the northwesternmost military fortification in the United States. Because of its location at the head of navigation on the Mississippi, it assumed a broad significance as a rendezvous for traders, Indians, missionaries, explorers, settlers, and occasional travelers.[4]

As long as the fur trade held sway, Minnesota's population growth was slow. The situation changed, however, with Indian land cessions in 1837. The formation of Wisconsin Territory in 1836, along with the decline of the fur trade and the increasing plight of the Indians on the upper Mississippi, caused the federal government to negotiate with the indigenous Dakota and Ojibway people for the cession of a triangle of land between the St. Croix and Mississippi rivers. The opening of this delta area in 1838 attracted New England lumbermen and a number of townsite planners. Within a few years the towns that became the centers of population in early Minnesota—St. Paul, St. Anthony, and Stillwater—had been founded, and the region began to emerge from fur trade dominance.[5]

Some traders continued to operate, however, where Indians who were indebted to them had not ceded their lands. Among them was Henry Hastings Sibley, the last agent of the American Fur Company at Mendota near Fort Snelling. Faced with the declining trade in his region, Sibley became interested in a new field—the borderland along the Red River. His associate in this venture was young Norman W. Kittson, a Canadian whom he had met when both worked for Robert Stuart at Mackinac in the early 1830s. Kittson went northwest to assess the trade possibilities in the lower Red River Valley. Seeing a potential market in the cluster of métis and Indians near the mouth of the Pembina River and in the bands of free traders north of the boundary, Kittson moved his base from Big Stone Lake to Pembina in 1844.[6]

Although he was a fur trader, Kittson's real purpose in moving to Pembina was to curry the patronage of discontented settlers north of the border. Living near the Hudson's Bay Company's major post of Fort Garry on the present site of Winnipeg, they had long been unhappy with the firm's restrictive policies. Incidental free trading as well as some local participation in community affairs

were permitted by the fur company, but until Kittson's arrival at Pembina the several thousand inhabitants of the Fort Garry area were forced to rely almost exclusively on the company to meet all their needs. Since its primary concern was the fur trade, the Hudson's Bay Company was not interested in stimulating the commercial and agricultural development of the region. This attitude, along with the length and difficulty of the route from England through Hudson Bay and then to Fort Garry, meant that consumer goods were very expensive and in short supply. The economic isolation of the colony also reinforced the fur company's political control over the settlers.[7]

Kittson's presence and his energetic popularization of the Red River Trails to carry goods and furs between St. Paul and the settlements on the lower Red were welcomed by those who sought some relief from company practices. Consequently from the start he attracted rebellious free traders to Pembina, placing him at odds with the Hudson's Bay Company. In its initial response to Kittson's challenge, the firm closed York Factory on Hudson Bay to importers, whom it suspected of supplying the illicit free fur trade. The move was a blunder, for it drove more of Fort Garry's independent traders into Kittson's waiting arms. The company soon countered, however, by undercutting the American at a series of border posts. It also underscored its determination to dominate the area's business by persuading the British government to station a contingent of troops near the boundary for a two-year period in the late 1840s. Unfazed, Kittson extended his operations along the border, so that by the early 1850s his realm stretched from Rainy Lake on the east to the Souris or Mouse River, in present north-central North Dakota, on the west. While he was willing to engage the Hudson's Bay Company in a trade war, he saw it as an unequal contest in which he was outmanned, outfinanced, and lacking in government support. Kittson and his Minnesota political allies therefore undertook to interest federal officials in the Red River Valley, in the hope that the effort would result in trade benefits for St. Paul and newly created Minnesota Territory.[8]

The political entity of Minnesota Territory came into being largely because several thousand inhabitants of the area between the St. Croix and Mississippi rivers made it clear they did not wish to be included within the new state of Wisconsin. As lumbermen and old traders, they had little in common with the farmers and lead miners there. An uninhabited region of nearly 300 miles separating them and the settled portion of Wisconsin enhanced their solidarity and isolation. By actively participating in the new state's two constitutional conventions, these would-be Minnesotans succeeded in being excluded when Wisconsin was admitted to the Union in the spring of 1848. After a brief, awkward period as a legal no-man's land, the delta west of the St. Croix became part of Minnesota Territory, which was established in March, 1849.[9]

As created by Congress, the territory was very large— nearly twice the size of the present state. It stretched from the St. Croix west to the Missouri and White Earth rivers in what is now South and North Dakota. Almost all the land within it remained in Indian hands. Minnesota boosters, led by Kittson's friend Sibley, its first territorial delegate to Congress, and Alexander Ramsey, its first territorial governor, realized that settlers and everything that went with them—railroads, cities, banks, schools, and "progress"—could be attained only after the cession of most of the Indian land. To these promoters the most coveted area was the "Suland," the holdings of the Dakota in southern Minnesota. But their expansionist desires also reached to the north, so that the Red River Valley was caught up in their plans.[10]

During the territory's first summer, when an effort to treat with the Dakota failed, the United States War Department sent a military expedition to the Red River Valley led by Major Samuel Woods, commandant of Fort Snelling. Several prominent men, including Thomas Ewing, secretary of the interior, William Medill, commissioner of Indian affairs, Jonathan E. Fletcher, agent to the Winnebago Indians at Long Prairie, and veteran Minnesota trader Henry M. Rice, had called for such an expedition, charging that Hudson's Bay Company agents were crossing the international boundary with impunity to trade with the Indians. Officials in the Indian service also complained that American buffalo were being wantonly destroyed by Canadian métis hunters, who sold much of the meat to the British trading company. The wholesale slaughter of these animals, they said, threatened the well-being of Indians south of the border. These incursions were not new; they had been of long-standing concern to the War Department, which feared the negative influence of the northerners on the Dakota Indians as well as on the American fur trade.[11]

The Woods expedition was ordered "to make a military examination" of the Red River to determine the feasibility of establishing a military post there. The prospect of such a post was welcomed by Kittson, Sibley, and Ramsey, who saw it as an aid in developing the territory. Woods was further ordered to explore the Red River as far north as the boundary and to report on the Indians and activities of the Hudson's Bay Company in that region.[12]

The expedition reached distant Pembina after nearly two months of difficult travel during the rainy summer of 1849. The major, who had heard much about the settlement, expected to find a village and was openly disappointed when he saw Kittson's "trading establishment" standing alone on the left bank of the Pembina River near its junction with the Red. About a mile down the Red stood the home and Roman Catholic chapel of Georges-Antoine Belcourt, a French-Canadian missionary who had spent 17 years in Rupert's Land, as the Hudson's Bay Company's western land holdings were known, before moving south of the border in 1848. The mixed-blood population, which Woods reported numbered 1,026, lived in huts and cabins randomly scattered nearby.[13]

Woods and Captain John Pope, a topographical engineer assigned to the expedition, visited the site where Long's party had marked the 49th parallel just north of the Pembina in 1823. Woods noted: "The post set up by Major Long had rotted away, but the place is still preserved by a stake that is firmly driven in the ground. I placed a post there and merely marked on it '*August* 14, 1849.' There is a small house belonging to a half-breed, built on the English side, within a few feet of the line. The English [*Hudson's Bay*] Fur Company's trading post is about *two hundred* yards from the line on their territory, consisting of a 'small shanty,' but they now have under erection very extensive buildings. The post marking the line is thought not to be accurately on the 49th parallel, but some two or three hundred yards within our territory. This impression arises from statements said to have been made by Major Long, as well as English observers, and the cautiousness they exhibit in settling near the marked line. I did not attempt to confirm or correct the position of the post placed by Major Long, for fear of leading to greater errors." Pope began to talk with the Hudson's Bay Company factor about the boundary line, but Woods, not wishing to create a fuss, forbade "him as an officer of the expedition" to pursue "that subject with any official from the other side of the line."[14]

Pope never had the satisfaction of measuring the 49th parallel, but on August 21 and 22, through astronomical observations taken at seven different hours, he confirmed that Pembina was slightly south of the boundary. He and Woods, who evidently had many differences during the expedition, wrote separate reports in which they disagreed completely on the need for a military post near the border. Pope was disturbed by the British trespassers and recommended the government establish a fort as a way of supporting Kittson, who, he suggested, stood alone against the challenge of the more powerful foreigners. Woods saw no need for a fortification, however, suggesting that it would benefit only certain special interests.[15]

Woods's stand was not popular with Minnesota expansionists. Governor Ramsey, in his first message to the territorial legislature in September, 1849, called for federal aid to improve the Red River Trails to Pembina; two months later he urged the establishment of a military post there. His interest was buttressed by Belcourt, who sought United States aid as a way of checking liquor peddling by Hudson's Bay Company employees. The missionary also believed that the presence of a military post at Pembina would have the salutary effect of increasing the population there by luring residents from across the border into the United States.[16]

Despite the urgings of Ramsey, Belcourt, and officials in the Indian service, the War Department chose not to fortify Pembina. But ever resourceful, Ramsey and Sibley tried a new tack. In the course of skillfully steering the preparations for treaties with the Dakota through the federal bureaucracy, Sibley managed to secure an appropriation of $10,000 for the purpose of negotiating a land cession with the Ojibway of the Red River Valley. After obtaining the Suland during the summer of 1851, Ramsey set out to negotiate an Ojibway treaty at Pembina. There he, the official party, and a military escort were met by Kittson on September 11. The trader, who had tired of extending credit to the Ojibway, was said to have been "a strong factor in persuading the Indians to accept the governor's offer." By the treaty they signed on September 20, the assembled chiefs surrendered most of their claims to the Red River Valley—some five million acres—and seemingly opened the way for the movement of settlers who would develop its rich agricultural potential.[17]

Dealing with the Ojibway proved to be far easier than getting the treaties approved by the United States Senate. Some senators were disturbed by charges of fraud and deceit in the negotiation of the Dakota cessions. These voiced concerns, however, seem to have been a pretext for certain southern senators who viewed the two treaties with the Dakota and that with the Ojibway as the opening drive for statehood of an area that would be unalterably opposed to the slavery interests of the South. The acrimonious debate alarmed Sibley, who feared all three treaties would be lost. Realizing compromise was in order, he decided to sacrifice the Ojibway cession so those of the Dakota, which were more vital to territorial growth, would be accepted.[18]

The Senate's rejection of the Ojibway treaty was a serious setback for the would-be Minnesota developers of the Red River Valley, and their aspirations lay dormant for several years. While Kittson and his successors continued to trade in the Pembina area, the rest of Minnesota Territory entered a boom period after passage of the Dakota treaties and the placement of Dakota people on reservations in 1853. The rush of settlers into the Suland exceeded even the wildest expectations of the leaders. From less than 5,000 people in 1849, the territory leaped to approximately 40,000 inhabitants by the summer of 1853. Three years later there were 150,000. Since statehood was predicated on a population requirement, the flood of settlers enabled Henry Rice, Sibley's successor as territorial delegate in Congress, to propose to the House of Representatives late in 1856 a bill authorizing Minnesotans to take the first legal steps toward becoming a state.[19]

During the ensuing discussion of the shape and extent of the future commonwealth, the question of expansion to the northwest came into clearer focus. There were some in Minnesota, mainly farmers and railroad promoters in the region south of St. Paul, who wanted an east-west state stretching from Wisconsin to the Missouri River, with a northern boundary starting on the St. Croix not far upstream from Stillwater. These borders, they proclaimed, would ensure agricultural development and railroad construction. But many influential Minnesotans, including all the old advocates of expansion into the Red River Valley, pressed for a north-south state encompassing both prairie and forests to assure economic diversity. If an east-west one were formed, they feared St. Paul might lose its designation as the capital and with it the political dominance the city then enjoyed. But more important they saw a north-south shape as giving Minnesota a part of the international boundary. Proximity to Canada was a prime consideration of the schemers and dreamers who envisioned St. Paul as the metropolis for the vast region reaching across the Red River Valley and into western Canada.[20]

To James Wickes Taylor, a newcomer to St. Paul who helped advocates of a north-south state prevail, Canada's proximity was the most important consideration. Taylor, who had spent most of his adult life in Ohio as a lawyer, journalist, and librarian, was well prepared to speak and write on St. Paul and the area to the northwest even before moving to Minnesota in 1856. As state librarian of Ohio from 1852 to 1856, he had read avidly about Minnesota and western Canada. He prophesied that "Central British America," as he called western Canada, was "apparently destined by Nature, at least as far as the Rocky Mountains, to be closely associated with the future of St. Paul." After moving to his adopted home, according to a biographer, Taylor's interest in railroads and their political and economic role in its development "became for him almost a religion." With his breadth of information, eloquence in both speaking and writing, and boundless energy and zeal, Taylor soon emerged as the strongest proponent of the new wave of Minnesota expansionism.[21]

Impending statehood stirred speculative interest in the future of the area's northwestern reaches. That interest was reflected in the 1857 sessions of the legislature, where a remarkable number of acts benefiting the Red River area were passed. Among the 49 towns incorporated during the extra session alone, seven were located in the valley. One of them, St. Vincent, was situated on the Red River just south of the international border. For it the legislature chartered a ferry and authorized the construction of a branch railroad as well as telegraph lines to terminate there. Although it was located on land that still belonged to the Ojibway, a St. Paul firm sent Charles W.

Iddings to St. Vincent in the summer of 1857 to survey the new townsite along with that of Pembina on the opposite shore of the Red. By February, 1858, the two towns had been platted with streets named for well-known fur traders and legislators.[22]

Minnesota interest in the border country and the inviting expanse beyond quickened the desire of many Canadians to occupy their own West. Amid increasing nationalism, there was considerable sentiment in Canada to annex the Hudson's Bay Company's vast domain and open it to settlement. But before a specific plan could be formulated, more information was needed about the nature of the country. To collect that data, British and Canadian officials in 1857 dispatched two major exploring expeditions. The British party was headed by Captain John Palliser, while the Canadian study was done principally by geologist Henry Youle Hind and surveyor Simon J. Dawson. In 1857-58 the groups studied the geography, agricultural potential, and overland routes of the vast plains region between the Red River and the Rockies. Their observations and optimistic reports on soil fertility and desirable railroad routes stimulated both Canadian and American interest in central and western Canada. About the same time the Canadian prairies took on new importance with the discovery of gold along the headwaters of the Fraser River in British Columbia. In the spring of 1858 news of the strike spread quickly as Minnesota was entering the Union. Caught in the throes of a disastrous financial panic that had burst the territorial boom, Minnesotans clamored for information about the new El Dorado. Reports of thousands of Californians rushing to the new mines sharpened excitement among St. Paulites, who believed their city was the logical outfitting point for gold-seeking Minnesotans and easterners.[23]

Taylor led the way in organizing the so-called Fraser River Convention, a group of men eager to establish an overland route to the gold mines. The convention, which met in St. Paul in July, 1858, gave Taylor an opportunity to promote his ideas for transcontinental railroads that would run from the city to the Pacific along his favorite course — northwest to the Red River, down the Red to the Saskatchewan River, and along it westward to the base of the Rockies. In spite of the lack of developed trails, some Minnesotans and other American argonauts made their way overland to the gold strikes. The Fraser River Convention loudly ballyhooed the rush, hoping to gain state and federal support for route improvement. But state aid was not forthcoming, nor did the federal government share St. Paul's interest in the Fort Garry trade.[24]

Circumstances dictated that St. Paulites assume the responsibility for promoting their own schemes. During the Fraser River rush interest in the Fort Garry area had rekindled for another reason. In 1857 the Hudson's Bay Company completed arrangements to ship its goods to the fort through the United States. This decision, which virtually ended shipments by way of Hudson Bay, benefited St. Paul, the terminus of the Red River Trails and a supply point for the settlements to the north. Once Hudson's Bay Company supplies began flowing through St. Paul in 1858, some of the city's promoters urged closer commercial ties with Fort Garry, a move they believed would also increase interest in the Fraser River region. With both Fort Garry and the remote gold fields in mind, St. Paul boosters, working through the city's chamber of commerce, sent steamboat captain Russell Blakeley to investigate the navigation potential of the Red River. Blakeley's favorable report led the chamber to raise some $2,000 as a prize for the individual who first placed a steamboat on the Red. The challenge was met by Anson Northup, who, after disassembling his boat and hauling it overland by wagon from the Crow Wing River, launched the "Anson Northup" on the Red late in May, 1859. The small steamer, which was enthusiastically greeted at Fort Garry on June 9, cemented St. Paul's ties with its northern neighbors and made the city the nearly exclusive supplier of the Red River settlements.[25]

Taylor, meanwhile, did not allow the lack of federal support for northwestern railroads to dismay him. Fully convinced that commerce between St. Paul and western Canada was on the upswing, he prevailed upon the United States Treasury Department in 1859 to appoint him as a special agent to study trade and transportation links between the United States and Canada west of Lake Superior. In this capacity Taylor optimistically predicted in 1862 a popular movement in the Red River Colony for either "independence or annexation to the United States."[26]

Like other publicists of Minnesota's Manifest Destiny, Taylor overstated his case. He was emboldened by the existence at Fort Garry of a small, active, American party, whose members preached the inevitability of annexation by the United States. He tended to overlook the influence of the larger Canadian party, which wanted Hudson's Bay Company rule replaced by a union with Canada. Reporting in 1862, Taylor could not yet appreciate the detrimental effects on the annexation movement of either Minnesota's war with the Dakota Indians or the Civil War. But it soon became apparent that the Indian offensive, which raged for a short time in August, 1862, would discourage northwestern expansion for some years, as Minnesotans took refuge behind a defensive line of hastily constructed settlers' forts. The effects of the Civil War were to be even more far-reaching.[27]

Minnesotans quickly felt the impact of the Civil War's heavy demands on manpower and its drain on government funds for supporting internal improvements—both of which stalemated real growth in the state. Although Minnesota's population more than doubled during the 1860s, its desperate economic plight resulting from the acute Panic of 1857 was not greatly improved until the conflict ended. In a broad sense, the war also damaged the expansionist movement, because it created poor relations between the governments in Washington, D.C., and Great Britain, which supported the Confederacy. Some nationalistic-minded Canadians even believed that Britain's prosouthern stance might provoke the Union to invade Canada in order to compensate for possible territorial losses in the South. Others were convinced that, should the Union win, invasion would still occur because southern opposition to northern expansion would be removed. These concerns, along with a growing fear of American economic imperialism, spurred Canada's plans for the creation of a dominion government.[28]

Despite their apprehensions about an American threat, Canadians had little to fear from an annexation movement during the Civil War. No really strong sentiment for it existed in the United States. Even in Minnesota it was economic co-operation rather than acquisition of Canadian land that initially motivated Taylor and his supporters. But by late 1865, Minnesota expansionists became increasingly wary of a growing movement by American protectionists and Anglophobes to end the reciprocity agreement between the United States and Canada. To Taylor and other like-thinking men, the Reciprocity Treaty of 1854 was vital to any hope of future economic union with Canada. Consequently, when the United States abrogated the treaty in March, 1866, many Minnesotans were converted to the doctrine of annexation.[29]

It was Taylor who led the most overt effort to achieve Minnesota's expansionist destiny. After the repeal of reciprocity he was again asked by the Treasury Department to prepare a report on trade relations with Canada. He used the opportunity to propose a union of the two countries. To do so, he drafted a bill entitled "An act for the admission of the states of Nova Scotia, New Brunswick, Canada East, and Canada West, and for the organization of the territories of Selkirk, Saskatchewan, and Columbia." It provided that the eastern Canadian provinces would enter the United States as states, and the western regions would become territories. Widely discussed in the newspapers, the proposal attracted a great deal of attention both north and south of the border. But there was very little real enthusiasm for it in Canada and not much more in the United States. The scheme apparently had an impact north of the border, where Canada and Great Britain hastened to complete the formation of the Dominion in 1867. Under the British North America Act, Canada received an unprecedented degree of self-government and the authority to bring the western land holdings of the Hudson's Bay Company into the Dominion. The act, which became effective on July 1, 1867, stimulated Canadian nationalism, but it also increased the fervor of annexationists in Rupert's Land who opposed the transfer of their region.[30]

Minnesota expansionists did not give up. They were well represented in Congress by Senator Alexander Ramsey, former governor of the territory and later of the state, who entered the Senate in 1863. "Bluff Alec," the recognized leader of Minnesota's Republican party, had long been interested in the commercial destiny of St. Paul, and he was not reluctant to support unpopular causes. Fully aware that the administration of President Andrew Johnson had little interest in expansion into Canada, he nonetheless entered the fray. In December, 1867, Ramsey introduced a bill in the Senate calling for Canada to cede to the United States all of its land west of the 90th meridian (near present Thunder Bay, Ontario) in return for restoration of reciprocity. The bill failed to pass, but it had the effect of hastening the addition of Rupert's Land to the Dominion.[31]

Hoping to arouse public opinion, Ramsey and Taylor turned to the Minnesota legislature. There was considerable interest among Minnesotans in a transcontinental railroad that might reach into Canada, as well as notable resentment of the Alaska Purchase Act, which was then awaiting congressional appropriations. Taylor drafted a resolution, which the state legislature approved on March 6, 1868, endorsing the Alaska Purchase but making it obvious the lawmakers' first choice of added territory was western Canada rather than Alaska. The resolution fell on deaf ears. Nevertheless, several months later Ramsey reintroduced in the Senate a revision of Taylor's 1866 plan of union. This time he called on the United States to consider a treaty with Great Britain to acquire Canada west of the 90th meridian. The Senate approved, but the action was only perfunctory; there was little national interest in what appeared to be an effort to promote the economy of St. Paul.[32]

In spite of their failure to win federal support, the annexationists persisted. Freedom for western Canada, they said, would be achieved only when it became part of American democracy. Refusing to recognize the profound changes wrought by the Dominion Act, they told themselves the Canadian confederation would not work because the people of the West would not accept it. It was only a matter of time before a new opportunity for annexation would appear; they stood ready to grasp it.[33]

Ramsey and Taylor saw the inauguration on March 4, 1869, of President-elect Ulysses S. Grant as that opportunity. The former Union Army commander was known to be interested in the annexation of Canada, as was his secretary of state, Hamilton Fish. Annexationist sentiment in the Senate was led by Charles Sumner, a key figure among the Radical Republicans and chairman of the Committee on Foreign Relations. Sumner, in fact, suggested that Great Britain should cede Canada to the United States as compensation for the indirect costs of damages caused by the Confederate cruiser "Alabama," which had been built in England with the knowledge of the British government. Fish was sufficiently intrigued by this idea to propose it to Edward Thornton, British ambassador to the United States. Thornton responded politely that Great Britain would relinquish Canada if and when the Canadians desired it. His answer plus some vocal opposition from congressmen and the American press were enough to discourage Fish. While he, Grant, and Sumner were interested in acquiring Canada, they would not be aggressive about it. Because the administration had no justifiable rationale to push for annexation, they were careful to avoid any action that could be construed as interference in Canada's internal affairs.[34]

Meanwhile the Canadian government acted decisively, completing arrangements to purchase Rupert's Land from the Hudson's Bay Company in 1868. Its decisiveness had strong repercussions in the Red River Valley among the local métis, who had not been included in the negotiations. Ignored by the government in Ottawa, they distrusted it and feared domination by outside officials. Moreover rumors were rife that when Rupert's Land was transferred to the Dominion, Canada would not recognize the squatters' claims they held under the Hudson's Bay Company's aegis.[35]

A series of incidents in 1868–69 so threatened their way of life that the métis felt forced to take matters into their own hands. When a Canadian expedition began building the Dawson Road from St. Boniface, near present Winnipeg, to Northwest Angle Inlet on Lake of the Woods in 1868, the métis became apprehensive. Their fears escalated the following spring, when some members of the road crew began staking claims to land east of the Red River at Ste. Anne des Chênes or Oak Point. In October, 1869, Canadians who had been sent to make a preliminary survey of Rupert's Land were stopped by a group of métis under the leadership of Louis Riel. This act of defiance led to additional misunderstandings and finally to the capture by Riel and his followers of Fort Garry on November 2, 1869. The métis leader established a provisional government for Rupert's Land with the hope of freeing it from both Canada and the Hudson's Bay Company. While he wished to avoid Canadian control, he did not necessarily intend to join forces with the American party in the Red River settlements which favored annexation by the United States. Nonetheless Taylor and other Minnesota expansionists looked upon Riel as a potential ally and seized on the rebellion he led as yet another possible chance to annex some of western Canada.[36]

The American intriguers set to work. Late in 1869 Taylor received a secret commission from Hamilton Fish to supply the State Department with information about the attitude of the Red River inhabitants toward the United States and about commercial prospects in western Canada. His pro-annexationist reports were reinforced by men such as Oscar Malmros, the United States consul at Fort Garry, Enos Stutsman, a lawyer and customs official at Pembina, and Joseph A. Wheelock, editor of the *St. Paul Daily Press*. Malmros, a Ramsey crony who had received his position with the help of the senator, wrote to Fish offering to raise a force and seize the lower Red River area. The secretary of state promptly vetoed this wild idea and reprimanded the consul. Stutsman, a former Dakota Territory legislator, was well known as the leader of the American intriguers at Pembina. On the very day Riel captured Fort Garry, he wrote President Grant that the majority of the Red River settlers favored annexation by the United States. Wheelock, who had long believed in the inevitability of the annexation of western Canada, enthusiastically publicized the cause. These men in combination with Taylor were so active, articulate, and persuasive, and so successful in obtaining newspaper coverage, that their goals appeared to have broad public support. In truth, their militancy proved to be an embarrassment to the Grant administration, forcing it to back away from any annexationist desires it may have had.[37]

Although the annexation movement was primarily inspired by a comparatively few Minnesotans and constituted no real threat to Canada, Dominion officials at the time did not take it lightly. New and untried, Canada's government was distrustful of the neighboring nation to the south; it also had yet to prove its strength to its own people. Quick action seemed necessary to save the Red River settlements from the United States. The government immediately organized the province of Manitoba, the first to be added to the confederation. Its newly appointed governor and an expeditionary force were already on their way to Fort Garry when the Manitoba Act was proclaimed on July 15, 1870. The occupation of the fort on August 24 by British and Canadian troops, led by Colonel Garnet J. Wolseley, toppled the Riel government and served notice that Canada would control its own West.[38]

The old dream died hard for the Minnesota annexationists. After Riel and his officials fled to the United States, they were befriended by Ramsey, Taylor, and their cohorts. Ramsey in fact escorted William B. O'Donoghue, the former treasurer of Riel's provisional government, around Washington, D.C. He even arranged an audience for him with Grant, who was told of O'Donoghue's mission to liberate the Red River area from Canadian "tyranny." The president commented only that the United States would be interested if a majority of the Red River inhabitants showed a clear desire for annexation.

O'Donoghue then turned to the Fenian Brotherhood, which several years earlier had made raids into Canada from New York to publicize the cause of Irish independence from Great Britain. Although the brotherhood officially chose not to help him, a few of its members resigned from the organization in order to do so. Contemporary newspapers, however, publicized O'Donoghue's men as Fenians, and the erroneous belief persisted that the Irishman led a Fenian raid into Canada.[39]

Actually O'Donoghue recruited only about 35 men, including two "generals" and a "colonel." On October 5, 1871, this "expedition" moved north from Pembina and seized the Hudson's Bay Company post just north of the boundary as marked by Long. Troops at the nearby American military post of Fort Pembina, which had at last been established by the United States War Department the year before, quickly apprehended the invaders and turned them over to American civil authorities. In the ensuing trials, all charges were dismissed for lack of evidence that the raiders had committed a crime against the United States.

For those who needed further proof, the O'Donoghue affair should have settled the question of whether the Dominion or the United States would control western Canada. After confederation Canada had asserted itself in the West, whereas the American interest was largely Minnesota-inspired and Minnesota-led without any real backing from the federal government. Ramsey conceded the cause, but Taylor, who had been appointed United States consul at Fort Garry in 1870, hoped to use his position to bring about an eventual union of the two countries.[40]

Although Minnesota's Manifest Destiny to expand to the northwest was checked at the boundary laid down in London in 1818, the annexation movement nonetheless affected development on both sides of the border. The opening of the Red River frontier south of the 49th parallel was led by Minnesota promoters, and the rapid Canadian organization of the area to the north was in part a reaction to Minnesota's threat. The boundary, which had seemed so free during Kittson's days and so impermanent at the height of Minnesota's Manifest Destiny movement in the late 1860s, became more concrete with the creation of Manitoba and Canadian occupation of the Red River area.

By 1870 the line along the 49th parallel westward across the Great Plains had long been legally established on paper, but it was still not officially marked on the ground. At Pembina the Long-Woods marker was generally accepted as the boundary demarcation, but there was some question as to the accuracy of its placement, due largely to later surveys that had been done in the area. In fact, at least three other spots in addition to the Long-Woods post had been identified as the 49th.

The first of these was ascertained in 1857 at the instigation of Captain John Palliser, who visited Pembina as part of his reconnaissance of the area west of the Red River for the British Colonial Office. With the assistance of Minnesota surveyor Charles Iddings, Palliser and his men determined that the Long-Woods monument was at 48° 59′ 49″, or about 370 yards south of what they calculated to be the 49th. The Englishman preferred to accept the earlier marker as the boundary, however, because it was more advantageous to Great Britain. He cautiously obtained Iddings' assent to its acceptance, thinking it "may perhaps be the means of avoiding unpleasant disputes by-&-bye."[41]

About three years later Pembina residents, offended by a whisky peddler who had set up shop just inside British territory, marked a second spot as the 49th parallel, probably without benefit of astronomical observations. Their "Whiskey post" was erected about a mile north of the Long-Woods monument. It was apparently ignored in 1867 by Moses K. Armstrong, a deputy surveyor for Dakota Territory, who completed a rectangular survey in the Pembina area, extending the parallel line westward from the Long-Woods marker for 36 miles. Canadian surveyors headed by Lieutenant-Colonel John S. Dennis determined yet another boundary point at Pembina in 1869, calculating it to be 204 feet north of the Long-Woods marker. Dennis based a rectangular land survey on his point and measured and marked the 49th for some distance west of it. His line, however, was not compatible with that of Armstrong, which Dennis noted wandered into Canada about ten miles west of the Red River.[42]

Thus in 1870, when preparations for the construction of the American Fort Pembina were under way, no one was quite sure where the boundary really ran. Because the new post was to be located only about two miles south of the international boundary, it was necessary to establish the 49th parallel accurately in order to mark out the military reservation. The survey was done by Captain David P. Heap over a five-day period in May.[43]

After completing his measurements for latitude, Heap selected "six observations which I believed to be the most accurate and reliable, and which most closely agreed with each other." He concluded that Long's marker was 4,763 feet south of the 49th parallel, and the Hudson's Bay Company trading post was in the United States. Heap marked his site, the fifth possible one in the area, with an oak post at the edge of the woods on the west side of the Red River. From it he measured and marked the parallel 35 miles to the west, which carried him nearly to the foot of Pembina Mountain. At one-mile intervals he erected "stout stakes," each inscribed "U.S." on the south side and "B.P." (British Possessions) on the north side, as a warning that the army intended to control the flow of trespassers across the border.

Heap's efforts soon created an uproar. The resurveyed boundary not only promised to take some land from Canada, but it also presented another opportunity for American plotters. John C. Stoever, the United States collector of customs at Pembina, was quick to react. He ordered an inventory of the entire stock of goods at the Hudson's Bay Company post, which Heap's marker indicated was in the United States. But realizing that the new border line was not necessarily official, he asked George S. Boutwell, secretary of the treasury, whether he should regard Long's post or Heap's marker as the true boundary. If the latter was recognized, Stoever wrote, he would have to levy customs on the goods of the Hudson's Bay Company post.[44]

Boutwell referred the question and Stoever's letter to Secretary of State Fish, asking whether Heap's line "has been established by competent authority binding upon the two governments of Great Britain and the United States." The State Department, which by then had abandoned any thought of annexing western Canada and did not wish to offend either Canada or Great Britain, opted for the traditional Long-Woods boundary marker. The Treasury Department was told there had been no official joint boundary survey, and it was asked to do nothing that would "disturb the existing conditions of things on the border."[45]

In the meantime Fish informed Britain's Ambassador Thornton of Heap's survey and suggested the two nations organize a joint boundary commission. But Fish, according to Thornton, also wondered if Canada might want to appoint someone to verify the new line. During the course of several weeks all necessary parties, including the United States ambassador to Great Britain, were notified. The consensus was that the nations should prepare for a joint survey of the boundary segment from Lake of the Woods to the Rockies. Pending the results they would regard the Long-Woods marker as the boundary at the Red River. None of the diplomats involved insisted the post was accurately located; they merely adopted it as expedient because it had customarily been accepted and its use for the time being would assure tranquility in the Red River Valley. Although the Grant administration was sincere in its desire to co-operate in marking the boundary, some Manitobans feared American aggression. As a precaution, Lieutenant-Governor Adams G. Archibald arranged to have a company of troops rushed into camp only a half mile from the Hudson's Bay Company's Pembina post, imperiled by Heap's survey.[46]

The Grant administration, thinking in terms of launching the survey in 1871, asked General Andrew A. Humphreys, chief of the United States Army Corps of Engineers, to prepare an estimate of its expenses. Humphreys' report, which became the authority for the size, organization, and cost of the subsequent survey, pointed up the immensity of the task. Stressing that the line to be surveyed and marked was about 860 miles long and that the working season in that climate was brief, Humphreys was sure the project "would have to run through two seasons at least, if not longer." The party, totaling an estimated 71 persons, would be organized as a headquarters unit headed by a boundary commissioner, with a secretary, two astronomical crews, and two surveying groups. Yearly field expenses, said Humphreys, would be about $102,000. Allowing a year for office work in preparing maps and reports after the measurements were completed, he thought the total cost to the United States would be approximately $325,000.[47] Great Britain and Canada were expected to supply a similar work force and budget.

With Humphreys' estimate in hand, President Grant recommended the project to Congress in his annual message on December 5, 1870. Despite his urging, Congress refused to be rushed. The House of Representatives, which received background information from the State Department in January, 1871, passed a resolution in February endorsing the principle of the survey. But its members were not persuaded that $100,000 annually was needed, and, according to Edward Thornton, some insinuated that the survey was not necessary, because "it was not improbable" that Canada north of the unmarked line would be given to the United States in payment for the "Alabama" claims. The House refused to approve the requested appropriation, and any hope of beginning the survey in 1871 disappeared.[48]

When the 42nd Congress assembled for its second session in December, 1871, the Grant administration renewed its request. This time the House approved, but only after reducing appropriations for the first year by half to $50,000. The Senate accepted the House bill, and the special act authorizing United States participation in a joint survey of the boundary line from Lake of the Woods to the Rockies was approved on March 19, 1872, 64 years after the Convention of 1818 had set down its course.[49]

CHAPTER 9

The Red River—Lake of the Woods Survey, 1872–73

DURING THEIR FIRST SEASON in the field in 1872, the British and American survey parties worked along the 49th parallel between Pembina on the Red River and the west shore of Lake of the Woods, as well as from the northwest point of the lake southward to the 49th. The difficulties of surveying in swampy terrain hampered their progress. Differences between the two commissioners in temperament, experience, age, and attitude gave rise to disagreements that prevented them from meeting the principal objectives of the season's work. Other issues, too, began to take shape which would exacerbate the antagonism between the commissioners and linger on into 1875.

Unlike the American Congress, the British Foreign Office and the Canadian government had no doubts about the need for the survey. The Foreign Office endorsed it, and the exchequer's only reservation was that Canada should agree to "bear a share of the expenditure." Canadian officials, no doubt welcoming the opportunity to assert their young country's influence on the frontier, readily agreed to pay half the costs, but expected to have a voice in the organization of the commission, whose work, they anticipated, should be of benefit to Canada.[1]

In its planning the British government was inclined to follow precedents set by the Oregon survey and to use men who had participated in it. For its estimates of expenses the War Office turned to Colonel John S. Hawkins, commissioner of the Oregon project, who was asked to prepare a detailed report incorporating accurate information about the area to be surveyed. His recommendations, presented in February, 1871, ranged over a variety of subjects—the size and organization of the commission, its routes of travel from England to the Red River Valley, the starting point of its work, its winter quarters on the frontier, and the need for military escorts. Hawkins, who may have been influenced by Humphreys' estimate, explained his endorsement of a large and costly British commission. The working season, he reminded the War Office, began in May, when the grass was long enough to feed animals, and lasted only until October, when "the snow begins to fall"; in addition, it was known that some Indians in the boundary area were hostile to the Americans and possibly also to the British. "The inference to be drawn from these two considerations," he stated, "is that the working parties should be as numerous as possible, to take advantage of the short season, and strong enough to protect themselves."[2]

Hawkins' report, which became the basis for many subsequent actions of the British commission, was printed for the use of the Foreign Office in March, 1871. Several months later certain tensions became evident between Great Britain and Canada that would persist throughout the survey. Canadian officials, while not challenging Hawkins directly, evidently believed the British estimates did not measure up to those of the United States, and they urged the British to organize the commission on a scale comparable to Humphreys' outline for the American party. The exchange was an early indication that, to the dismay of British officials, Canadian authorities would not be averse to increasing the costs of the project.[3]

Canada's determination to have its way became more pronounced during the selection of the British commissioner. Both Lord Granville, British foreign secretary, and Lord Kimberley, colonial secretary, preferred a veteran of the Oregon survey. They undoubtedly had in mind such men as Charles W. Wilson and Samuel Anderson, both Royal Engineers with extensive practical field experience who understood the necessary mathematical and astronomical principles. The Canadians' choice was Donald R. Cameron.[4]

The 37-year-old Cameron had no particular professional qualifications for the post. Of Scottish Highland stock, he was trained in French military schools before earning a commission in the Royal Artillery. He later served with the British army in India and Canada, and while in Halifax in 1869 he married the daughter of Dr. Charles Tupper, a cabinet officer in Sir John A. Macdonald's government and former premier of Nova Scotia.[5]

Although British officials were not impressed with Cameron's credentials, they were reluctant to reject him for fear of insulting the Dominion government, which was to pay half the commission's expenses. Granville was not pleased at the prospect of supervising the work of a man who apparently lacked any theoretical or practical knowledge of surveying. But believing it vital that the Canadians be satisfied, he voiced no opinion officially; neither did he express approval of what he regarded as a patronage arrangement. The reluctant Granville delayed a decision as long as possible, with the excuse that there was no point in naming a British commissioner until after the United States had appropriated survey funds. Cameron, understandably anxious, was held off with the terse explanation that his appointment would be made at the "proper time."[6]

Once Congress had provided funding for the United States commission, the British had to move rapidly to assure that some field work could be done in 1872. Guided by the Oregon survey, the Foreign Office assumed the

British staff should be dominated by Royal Engineers on active duty. Granville accordingly asked Edward Cardwell, secretary of the War Office, to appoint engineers as secretary, astronomer, and assistant astronomers. Cardwell would have preferred to have an engineer officer as commissioner, too, but in June, 1872, Granville forwarded Cameron's appointment to Queen Victoria.[7]

By then the War Office had named the other key officers of the British commission. Arthur C. Ward, who was recommended by Cameron, was appointed secretary. Albany Featherstonhaugh, the son of Anglo-American geologist, explorer, and surveyor George W. Featherstonhaugh, was assigned as ranking assistant astronomer, and William J. Galwey was nominated as the second assistant. The position of chief astronomer went to Samuel Anderson, who, like Featherstonhaugh, was a teacher at the Chatham Engineering School. The 33-year-old Anderson had impressive credentials. He had worked on the Oregon survey for three years, had served as that commission's last secretary, and undoubtedly had the support of such officers of the Royal Engineers as Hawkins and Wilson. Far from being a Cameron minion, he shared the engineers' disdain for the artillery officer who headed the commission and was often critical of his scientific deficiencies during the boundary work.[8]

In line with Hawkins' recommendations, the Foreign Office arranged for a military escort of 44 Royal Engineers. This detachment, which was the envy of the Americans throughout the survey, not only provided the British commission with a certain security, but also assured it of men with engineering training and military discipline. In addition most of the enlisted men in the unit had other useful skills, such as photography, shoemaking, tailoring, and blacksmithing.[9]

On June 6 Cameron was ordered by the Foreign Office to make immediate preparations for a trip to Washington, D.C., and a preliminary meeting with the American commissioner. The following week he received his formal commission. With it came explicit directions to begin the survey at the northwest point of Lake of the Woods and to determine the latitude at Pembina with great care and accuracy. Granville provided the commissioner with a copy of Hawkins' memorandum along with instructions that his mission was simply to survey and mark a line that had been fixed by diplomatic negotiation.[10]

As soon as Congress acted, the Grant administration appointed Archibald Campbell as its commissioner. Only three years before, the 59-year-old West Point graduate had completed his work as commissioner of the Oregon boundary land survey. His background also included brief service as an engineer in the frontier army, eight years as a civil engineer in private life, and office experience as the chief clerk in the War Department. He was the logical choice to head the American boundary commission.[11]

The State Department, like the Foreign Office, was influenced by the Oregon survey in its organization of the American party. It was to be headed by West Point officers, most of whom were military engineers. Named chief astronomer was Francis U. Farquhar, class of 1861, who after gallant service with the Union Army was brevetted a lieutenant colonel. His ranking assistant astronomer was William J. Twining, a graduate of 1863 who had served with Union forces in Tennessee and Georgia. The position of second assistant astronomer went to James F. Gregory, a native of New York City who had received a commission in the army engineers a year after finishing at West Point in 1865. Francis V. Greene, a West Point graduate of 1870 and a distant relative of General Nathaniel Greene of Revolutionary War fame, was transferred from the artillery to the engineers in June, 1872, so he could assume the post of junior astronomer.[12]

On July 21, 1872, Campbell and Farquhar met in Washington with Cameron and Ward. The commissioners confirmed their countries' intentions to start the work at the east end of the boundary line and to establish their first astronomical station near Pembina. Although the meeting was amiable, Cameron seems to have been perturbed upon learning that Campbell and Farquhar were ahead of him in gathering information about the Lake of the Woods area.[13]

Cameron had already received certified copies of the maps of Lake of the Woods prepared by the surveyors in the 1820s, printed copies of the Webster-Ashburton Treaty and part of the Article 7 journal as published in the *British and Foreign State Papers*, and extracts from Barclay's and Porter's final reports as published by the United States House of Representatives. Nevertheless he left the Washington meeting convinced that he needed still more information about the boundary history of the Northwest Angle. He immediately asked Granville to get in touch with Anthony Barclay, then a British pensioner living in Connecticut, and inquire about the location and appearance of the monument at the northwest point of Lake of the Woods. He also asked that Barclay supply any data and private memoranda he might have concerning the determination of that critical point.

After the Washington meeting Cameron and Ward went to Ottawa to complete arrangements with Canadian officials. The Dominion government and the British Foreign Office had agreed that Canada would name such survey officials as the surgeon, veterinarian, commissary officer, and geologist, and select the necessary civilian manual laborers.[14]

During his month in Ottawa, Cameron came to realize just how active the Dominion government intended to be in the survey. He had little opportunity to consult with

Canadian officials about the men to be added to the commission, and he was not privy to their selection. He was simply assured, as the Foreign Office had been earlier, that they would be "well-qualified Canadians." Faced with an effort to add more assistant astronomers than he believed were needed, Cameron pleaded with Dominion officials, to no avail, that he did not have the authority to hire them. On the last day of August he was presented with a list of 23 Canadian officers and specialists.[15]

Most of the Canadians were easterners, hailing principally from Ottawa, Kingston, and Toronto. They included Dr. T. J. W. Burgess as surgeon, William G. Boswell as veterinarian, Lawrence W. Herchmer as commissary officer, A. G. Forrest and Alexander L. Russell as surveyors, and as assistant astronomers George F. Burpee, William A. Ashe, George C. Coster, and William F. King.[16]

While Cameron and Ward were looking after affairs in Ottawa, Featherstonhaugh and Galwey were receiving special training from Sir George B. Airy, the royal astronomer. The Foreign Office had readily accepted Hawkins' suggestion that the men be given instruction in the astronomical methods of marking a boundary. The lessons were undoubtedly beneficial, but unfortunately Cameron was not included among the students.[17]

Chief astronomer Anderson led the astronomical party and the detachment of Royal Engineers from England via steamship and Great Lakes steamer to Duluth, and by Northern Pacific Railroad to Moorhead, newly established as a major station in the Red River Valley. They continued northward by Red River carts as far as Frog Point, near the mouth of the Goose River, which was the head of navigation on the shallow Red for most of that year. From there they were taken aboard Kittson's rickety little steamer, the "Dakota," to Pembina, where on September 18 they joined Cameron and Ward, who had arrived from Ottawa by way of Thunder Bay, the Dawson Road, and Fort Garry or Winnipeg, as it was then becoming known. The assembled British party made camp a short distance north of the Hudson's Bay Company's post near the border.[18]

Although he did not have Cameron's logistical problems, Campbell's preparations and travel were also complicated. He remained in Washington as long as possible to co-ordinate activities and to remind Fish that the niggardly congressional appropriation would barely carry him through a shortened season. In a flurry of activity in June and July, the commissioner arranged to borrow astronomical and surveying instruments from the army engineers and guns and ammunition from the army arsenal at Rock Island, Illinois. He also secured a military escort from the garrison at Fort Pembina and sent Farquhar to St. Paul late in July to purchase supplies and have them forwarded by civilian contractors.[19]

At last late in August, Campbell, Farquhar, and most of the American party headed for the boundary. They traveled by rail from St. Paul to Breckenridge, the Red River Valley station of the St. Paul and Pacific Railroad, and then moved overland from nearby Fort Abercrombie to Fort Pembina, where they arrived on the evening of September 5. At this straggling, two-company infantry post they joined Francis Greene and assistant astronomer Lewis Boss, who had arrived nearly three weeks earlier. Greene and Boss had transported all the surveying instruments, traveling from New York City to Buffalo, then by lake steamer to Duluth, and from there by rail and steamboat to Pembina. There was little they could do in the border area until the main American party arrived, but they had begun taking observations with sextants and chronometers to establish the approximate latitude and longitude at Pembina.[20]

Campbell immediately put his assembled party to work. Time was short. He wanted to be out of the region by November 1, because he had neither the funds nor the inclination to spend winters along the boundary. From the start the commissioner, his crew members, and the government assumed that most of their work would be seasonal.

With an escort commanded by Captain Abram A. Harbach, the American commission moved north on September 6 and set up its camp near the site of the Long-Woods boundary post. The party had clear nights for its initial observations, and the cool night air discouraged the mosquitoes. "While they are in a state of torpor," Campbell noted optimistically, "we may be able to complete the work in the neighborhood of Lake of the Woods, as it is said to be absolutely impossible to carry on a survey in that region during the mosquito season." As events transpired he need not have been concerned. Soon after the arrival of the British party, an early, four-day snowstorm swept the area, not only killing off the mosquitoes, but introducing the men to the rigors of winter in the north land.[21]

Sleepy Pembina was awakened by the arrival of the two commissions, whose members added substantially to the settlement's meager population. British and Americans alike were fascinated and frustrated by the frontier about which they had heard so much. The men had some foreknowledge of the heat, the cold, and the mosquitoes, but they seem not to have expected the smallness of Pembina. Few of them had ever been in such a virtually unoccupied area. Pembina proper consisted of three stores, 15 houses, a Catholic church, a post office, a land office, a customs house, and a steam-powered mill. The tiny settlement of St. Vincent lay across the Red River. Fort Pembina, the white-painted American military post with its neat picket fence, stood about a mile and a half north on the west bank of the Red and south of the Pembina River.

North of the boundary as marked by the Long-Woods post, but south of it according to Heap's survey, was *North Pembina*—a scattering of huts built around a British customs house and the Hudson's Bay Company's stockaded fur post. The fort served as the headquarters of the company of soldiers Lieutenant-Governor Archibald of Manitoba had arranged to have stationed near the boundary pending the arrival of the surveyors.

Even before reaching the border area, Cameron had selected North Pembina as the site of his commission's permanent camp for the duration of the survey. Since the Foreign Office had deemed it impractical for the British commission to return each year to eastern Canada or England, the camp would also serve as its winter quarters. From North Pembina the British could conveniently work east and west along the 49th parallel, and supplies could easily be brought by rail and steamboat from St. Paul. In addition it was close to the Americans' camp a quarter of a mile to the south. Construction of the winter quarters, which were named for Lord Dufferin, governor-general of Canada, was accomplished by a civilian contractor with imported labor and materials.[22]

Anxious to start surveying, both parties worked feverishly unpacking and sorting supplies, setting up tents, obtaining animals and wagons, and readying instruments for their first astronomical station. In contrast to the number of workers on the Article 7 boundary survey west of Lake Superior in the 1820s, the joint commission of the 1870s was massive. Since its purpose was to survey and mark a diplomatically known boundary rather than reconnoiter various possible lines, it required well-staffed astronomical and surveying parties. The terrain itself seemed to dictate the need for many men. Not only were considerable distances involved, but the intimidating muskeg swamps west of Lake of the Woods made the commission's planners cautious. They were skeptical of their ability to move rapidly, and they tended to magnify the ferocity of winter, which they correctly assumed would curtail most of their activities. As a result they wanted as many men as possible in order to use their working seasons effectively.

Cameron's party during the fall operations in 1872 included 4 officers and 44 enlisted men of the Royal Engineers, 40 civilians, and a number of temporary employees. The group was divided into a headquarters unit of 21 men, 3 astronomical parties of 10 men each, 2 surveying parties of 9 members each, with the remainder assigned to depot units or surveying teams as circumstances dictated.[23]

The American commission was almost entirely a civilian force. Only Campbell and four of the astronomers were army engineers. The party was neither as flexible nor as skilled as the British, because it had no well-trained core unit comparable to the versatile Royal Engineers. Most of the men hired in Minnesota were described only as laborers or teamsters. On October 4, 1872, Campbell enumerated 56 men in his group, including a wagonmaster and 20 teamsters. The escort company of infantrymen from Fort Pembina was not considered part of the commission. Including the soldiers and temporary employees, the American group during the fall of 1872 probably comprised about 100 men.

On September 18, the same day Anderson and the British astronomical party arrived at Pembina, the commissioners arranged a joint staff meeting. Cameron was pleased to learn that preliminary American calculations had placed the 49th parallel well to the south of the Hudson's Bay Company's post and quite close to the Long-Woods marker. Then the commissioners and astronomers plotted the season's work. Their broad goal was to complete the survey from the Red River to the northwest point of Lake of the Woods, but five sites were to receive special attention: Pembina, the northwest point of Lake of the Woods, the 49th parallel on the west shore of the lake, and two astronomical stations on the 49th between Lake of the Woods and the Red River. Because much of the terrain in those areas was swampy, they hoped to complete the surveying soon enough to allow the British to begin clearing a strip along the boundary during the winter when the ground was frozen. Before much surveying was done, the commissioners and astronomers agreed that if there were a difference in calculations of 50 feet or less, they would simply accept the mean.[24]

The uncertainty over the latitude of Pembina was easily settled. The British, like the Americans, found the true 49th parallel was south of the Hudson's Bay Company's store. Since their surveys differed by only 32 feet, the commissioners accepted the mean as the boundary and acknowledged that the line would fall about 250 yards south of the Hudson's Bay Company post and about the same distance north of the Long-Woods marker.[25] Although this calculation put an end to the significance of the old Long post, the surveyors must have noticed that it was considerably closer to the true 49th parallel than was Heap's marker. The commissioners could not yet formally mark the location of the Pembina boundary, because the new calculations had to be rechecked in office studies. The result of their work was virtually certain to be confirmed, however, and it immediately quieted the anxieties of the United States customs collectors.

With the Pembina determination completed by early October, the British and Americans dispersed to work elsewhere. Their destinations had been reconnoitered by Russell, the Canadian surveyor who with several men had traveled to Pembina by way of Angle Inlet and the general course of the boundary west of Lake of the Woods. He had spent two hours at the head of Angle Inlet futilely looking

THE UNITED STATES BOUNDARY COMMISSION headed by Archibald Campbell from 1871 to 1876 was photographed at Pembina. Standing in back are James E. Bangs, secretary; William J. Twining, first assistant astronomer; Francis V. Greene, junior astronomer, and four unidentified members of the military escort. Seated are James F. Gregory, second assistant astronomer; Francis U. Farquhar, chief astronomer; Commissioner Campbell; and two officers of the escort. Courtesy Provincial Archives of Manitoba, Winnipeg.

THE BRITISH BOUNDARY COMMISSION during the 1870s included (standing, left to right) George F. Burpee, William F. King, and George C. Coster, assistant astronomers; Lawrence W. Herchmer, commissary officer; Samuel Anderson, chief astronomer; George M. Dawson, geologist; William A. Ashe, assistant astronomer; and Alexander L. Russell, surveyor. Seated are William J. Galwey, second assistant astronomer; Arthur C. Ward, secretary; Donald R. Cameron, commissioner; Albany Featherstonhaugh, first assistant astronomer; Dr. T. J. W. Burgess, medical officer; and Dr. William G. Boswell, veterinarian. Courtesy Provincial Archives of Manitoba.

FORT PEMBINA, the American military post established just south of the border in 1870, was garrisoned by two companies of infantry when the United States boundary commission arrived there in 1872. Soldiers from this post provided a military escort for the commission as it worked along the border between the Red River and Lake of the Woods. Courtesy Provincial Archives of Manitoba.

THIS TELESCOPE was used by British astronomers to determine latitude along the boundary in the 1870s. Courtesy Provincial Archives of Manitoba.

MEMBERS of the American commission established a base camp near the 49th parallel and the Red River in September, 1872. A temporary facility, it was used only until they left the boundary area in November of that year. Courtesy Provincial Archives of Manitoba.

THE STEAMBOAT LANDING at Harrison Creek in the Northwest Angle on Lake of the Woods, shown here in the early 1870s, was used by immigrants traveling the Dawson Road from Port Arthur and Fort William on Lake Superior to Winnipeg on the Red River. Courtesy Public Archives of Canada.

IN 1872 this segment of a charred oak log was said by Indians at Angle Inlet to be part of the monument David Thompson erected in 1824 to mark the most northwestern point of Lake of the Woods. British commissioner Cameron refused to accept it as evidence, however, prolonging the controversy over the lake's northwest point. Courtesy Public Archives of Canada.

THE SITE of David Thompson's 1824 marker at Angle Inlet was indicated by this reconstructed log monument in 1872. Canadian geologist George M. Dawson, a member of the British boundary commission, is shown in this photograph. Courtesy Provincial Archives of Manitoba.

MEMBERS of the American boundary commission built this tower of logs in 1872 at their survey station on Lake of the Woods. It is probably the same structure discovered in a dilapidated condition in 1912 by surveyors at Angle Inlet. Records showed James F. Gregory erected the 36-foot tower "on the spit of land immediately to the west of the assumed N.W. Point" of the lake. Courtesy Provincial Archives of Manitoba.

SAMUEL ANDERSON, chief astronomer of the British commission, supervised the cutting of this vista along the meridian line between the 49th parallel and the "Indian monument" at the northwest point of Lake of the Woods in October and November, 1872. This photograph of two unidentified workers was taken one and a half miles south of the Dawson Road. Courtesy Provincial Archives of Manitoba.

BRITISH COMMISSIONER Donald R. Cameron, shown climbing into an army ambulance, and American Commissioner Archibald Campbell, seated in the back, were photographed with other members of their joint commission as they prepared to leave the Northwest Angle at Lake of the Woods in 1872. Courtesy Public Archives of Canada.

BRITISH SURVEYORS in 1872 constructed this astronomical station on the 49th parallel at
Pointe d'Orme on the Roseau River 33 miles east of the Red River.
Courtesy Public Archives of Canada.

DURING THE WINTER of 1873–74, American surveyors led by Francis Greene rechecked
calculations and built temporary mound markers along the boundary between the Red River and
Lake of the Woods. Following the advice of Pembina settlers, they dressed in several layers of
clothing to endure blizzards and below-zero temperatures and traveled by mule-drawn sleighs
and dog sleds. Drawing from U.S. Boundary Commission, *Reports . . . Lake of the Woods
to . . . the Rocky Mountains* (1878); courtesy National Archives.

COAT, TROUSERS, CAP, and mittens of fur, a woolen havelock, and several
scarves kept this teamster warm while working for the British boundary
commission during the fierce winters of the 1870s.
Courtesy Public Archives of Canada.

TENTS and a makeshift cooking shack were part of the depot established at the Turtle Mountains of North Dakota by commission members in 1873 as they carried the boundary survey west from the Red River toward the Rocky Mountains. Courtesy Provincial Archives of Manitoba.

WORKMEN called "sappers" built sod mounds 10 to 12 feet in diameter to mark the boundary line on the barren prairies between Pembina and the Rockies in the 1870s. Courtesy Public Archives of Canada.

DISH-SHAPED IRON PLATES with the inscription, "British and United States Boundary Commissions 1872–4, 49° North Latitude," were to be buried at a depth of two feet in each earthen mound marking the boundary line. This plate, one of two known to exist in 1980, hung in the office of the Canadian boundary commissioner in Ottawa. Courtesy Canadian Section, International Boundary Commission, Ottawa.

THE 20-FOOT-WIDE boundary vista ran arrow-straight through the mountains toward monument number 249 east of Gateway, Montana. From International Boundary Commission, *Joint Report . . . Gulf of Georgia to . . . Lake of the Woods* (1937).

for the remains of Thompson's reference monument before canoeing to the 49th parallel on the west shore of the lake.[26]

Anderson and Farquhar led separate parties to Angle Inlet, while Twining and Galwey, operating independently, were sent to the intersection of the 49th with the west shore of Lake of the Woods. Featherstonhaugh and Greene were dispatched with small parties to survey different sections of the parallel line east of the Red River after each had established an astronomical station. Both Cameron and Campbell regarded the northwest point as the key site to be determined, and they planned to join Anderson and Farquhar for a firsthand reconnaissance of Angle Inlet.

Campbell intended to follow instructions to locate an already existing boundary line from the northwestern point of Lake of the Woods south to the 49th parallel, while Cameron hoped there would be some way of gaining the Northwest Angle for Canada. His hopes were based on instructions from Granville, who, on the recommendation of Hawkins, had told Cameron that the small piece of land on the west side of Lake of the Woods formed by the meridian line due south from the northwest point "should, *if possible*, be preserved to the Dominion of Canada." Granville had reminded the commissioner, however, that he could not change the location of the due-south line; he could only measure and mark it as it had been established by treaty.[27]

Canada's special interest in the northwest point was related to its problems with transcontinental transportation. After the formation of the Dominion in 1867, westward expansion seemed assured, and there was an increased effort to provide means of movement to the frontier. A national railroad was thought to be the ultimate solution; until the tracks could be laid, however, other emigration routes would have to be used. But the most often-traveled—the long and slow Kaministkwia route west from Fort William—would not suffice. Therefore the Canadian government in the late 1860s and early 1870s sponsored the improvement of the Dawson Road, a combined land-and-water route from Fort William to Fort Garry or Winnipeg. Because travel by water was preferred wherever possible, a landing for boat passengers leaving Lake of the Woods was built at Angle Inlet, a convenient jumping-off place for the overland journey to Winnipeg. Since the northwest point of the lake and the meridian line were unmarked, surveyors of the Dawson Road made no particular effort to ensure that their landing was within Canadian territory. Instead they placed it at the most accessible point, a small peninsula formed by Harrison Creek on the south and the waters of the inlet on the north (see map on page 92). The dock was on the left bank of Harrison Creek, about midway between its mouth and

what proved to be the meridian line. By the time the Dawson Road opened in 1871, plans were well under way for the boundary survey.[28]

The serious possibility that the survey could imperil Canadian control of the boat landing was no doubt discussed in 1872 by Cameron and the Dominion surveyor general in Ottawa. But in addition to the immediate question of the landing, there was a distinct possibility that the Dawson Road would become the path of the future transcontinental railroad.[29]

Cameron arranged to have Forrest, an experienced surveyor, take an advance party from Ottawa on August 14 to reconnoiter and map Angle Inlet. Forrest's surveyors completed the map, but they could not accurately determine the meridian line because they were not able to fix the most northwest point of the lake. Information in Barclay's and Porter's journals showed that David Thompson's monument, from which the northwest point had been determined by Tiarks, was located on a small spit of land, but Forrest could find no monument there. The surveyor knew the northwest point had to be in a very restricted area near the head of Angle Inlet; from that approximation he easily determined that the due-south line would probably fall about a mile west of the Dawson Road boat landing, placing it in American territory.[30]

But Forrest made another discovery that greatly intrigued Cameron. In tracing the somewhat meandering mid-water boundary line up Angle Inlet, as prescribed by the 1783 treaty, Forrest found that in at least two places it crossed the due-south line specified by the 1818 agreement. This "looped line," as it came to be called, immediately raised the question of conflicting ownership. Cameron concluded that Tiarks' most northwest point had to be completely in British territory, because it was nearly a mile north of the southernmost place where the 1783 and 1818 lines crossed. By his reasoning, Great Britain should own everything north of the 1783 line and everything west of the 1818 line, and it followed that the waters of the small loops would also have to belong to the British.

Although he saw no inherent value in the water areas within the loops, Cameron viewed their existence as a reason to seek a readjustment of the boundary at the northwest point of Lake of the Woods. After acquiring Forrest's information—several weeks before the astronomers attempted to find the northwest point—he informed Granville on September 23 "that the irregularities" of the crossed lines "may afford a convenient opportunity for inviting the government of the United States to reconsider the course of the boundary from its entrance into the Lake of the Woods to its exit therefrom along the 49th parallel of latitude." He had not reported the loops to Campbell. "Should negotiations follow the discovery [of the irregularities] by United States officers," he reasoned, "the

United States government may have less difficulty in agreeing to a readjustment of the boundary line in accordance with the desire of the Canadian Government."

Soon after arriving at Angle Inlet on October 9, Farquhar and Anderson were told that Forrest had not found the northwest point or any trace of the large wooden monument upon which it was based. The main difficulty, the Americans concluded, was caused by high water, which elderly Indians judged to be five to eight feet above the lake's level in the mid-1820s. Because many fires had swept the area, the astronomers thought only the base of the old monument probably remained under water.[31]

A MAP OF ANGLE INLET from the 1878 report of the United States boundary commission shows how the mid-water boundary defined in the Treaty of 1783 looped across the meridian line set by the Convention of 1818. The dock and route of the Dawson Road appear on the bank of Harrison Creek at lower left. Courtesy National Archives.

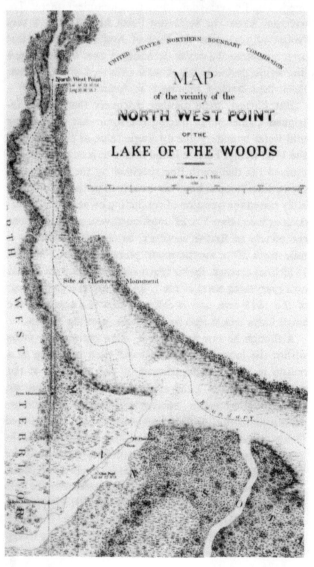

In their search for Thompson's monument, the astronomers asked for assistance from some Indians who, Farquhar reported, "asserted that they could point out the spot as several were still alive who had seen it just after the monument was erected." The price the Indians asked for the desired information, however, was "so exorbitant that their proposals were not entertained." Then, for reasons Farquhar did not explain, two Indians took him to a spot where they claimed the reference monument had stood.

Much of the credit for finding the site of Thompson's marker was given by Gregory to James McKay, a member of the Manitoba Parliament and manager of the Dawson Road. According to Gregory's account, McKay, a mixed-blood who spoke the Ojibway language fluently, enlisted the help of an old chief who led Anderson and Farquhar into some rushes near the shore off a small point of land. There Farquhar, wading in two and a half feet of water, found depressions "where portions of two logs had laid at right angles with each other, and, in the included angle, a cavity such as would have been left by the removal of a log." Later the Indians showed the astronomers two pieces of charred and badly decayed oak that bore ax marks and appeared to have lain at right angles to each other. Evidently the central post had been removed somewhat earlier by the Indians who had attempted to sell information to Forrest.[32]

Anderson, Farquhar, and Campbell were willing to accept the "Indian monument" site. While there was a possibility that it might not be precisely on the spot of Thompson's marker, even though the evidence indicated that it was, the difference between the two sites could not be great. Any alternative to the Indian monument would be a quibble, because it could change the location of the most northwest point and the meridian line by only a matter of feet.[33]

Cameron conceded that the Indian monument had to be quite close to, if not on, the site of the Thompson monument, but he professed to be bothered by some miscalculations on the part of Tiarks. Because Webster and Ashburton had written Tiarks' most northwest point into their treaty, the American and British astronomers sought to locate it on the ground. Anderson and Farquhar agreed that the latitude recorded in the treaty (49° 23' 55" north) made it seem to be nearly 500 feet to the north of where it actually was, and the longitude cited in the document (95° 14' 38" west) made it seem to be nearly five miles west of where it proved to be. Neither man, however, was particularly concerned by Tiarks' miscalculations. In fact Anderson thought the German astronomer had performed well with the instruments available to him. Cameron saw Tiarks' errors as yet another opportunity to debate the location of the northwest point and the boundary line itself, and he would not agree to Campbell's request that the Indian monument be the base for fixing the northwest point. Although it took him months to communicate to the Foreign Office his precise alternative, Cameron evidently wanted a northwest point based on the ground location of the measurements given in the Webster-Ashburton Treaty.[34]

Although Cameron would not accept the Indian monument, he agreed that the northwest point as calculated from it would become the basis of a preliminary meridian line to be cleared by the British during the winter. Campbell, recognizing that once the line was a reality it would be more difficult to alter it later, assented to the United States paying half the expense of the work. The American was clearly disgruntled by the young artillery officer's attitude, and he reminded him that their assignment was to mark the boundary, not to seek alternatives. Throughout the survey, Campbell remained convinced that Cameron wanted to win the Northwest Angle for Canada. The British commissioner seems to have ignored the American's pique, preferring to think of himself as a successful diplomat who had the opposition on the defensive.[35]

Despite the stalemate at Angle Inlet, the three American parties accomplished a great deal during the first season. While Farquhar and Gregory worked with Anderson and Forrest at the inlet, Twining and Galwey located the 49th parallel on the shore of Muskeg Bay. Proceeding by boat from Angle Inlet, they marked the spot in the water where the due-south line struck the 49th parallel, established a station on land due west of it, and by October 24 fixed the starting point of the westward boundary. Meanwhile Greene's party spent some five weeks measuring 33 miles of the line east from the Red River as far as the Roseau River. In addition to establishing an astronomical station, the men were to survey a belt of land five miles wide on the American side of the boundary. Their progress was hampered by the swampy terrain, which was perhaps the greatest impediment throughout the survey.[36]

Featherstonhaugh, who was working to the east of Greene's party, had even more trouble with the bogs. "These muskegs," he reported, "are four or five feet deep in many places; they have on the surface a skin of sod which scarcely supports the weight of a man, and when it is pierced the muddy water rises in the hole nearly to the top. A person breaking through goes down to his middle, and has some trouble getting out again."[37] As Featherstonhaugh looked ahead to a winter in the field, he must have envied the Americans who were scurrying like ducks before the certainty of a storm.

Campbell and his men returned to Pembina early in November, but their departure was delayed for a week while the commissioner completed a number of miscellaneous chores. He had already decided on winter quarters for the astronomers and their assistants at Detroit, Michigan, *having rejected St. Paul as too cold and too costly.* Farquhar, Twining, Gregory, Greene, and Boss would

spend the winter recalculating their observations and working further on fixing star locations that would provide data in measuring latitude the following season. Campbell would lobby the State Department and Congress in Washington for upgraded salaries and equipment more comparable to those of the British commission. Before leaving the border region, the commissioner remanded the infantry escort to Fort Pembina and arranged to put horses, provisions, supplies, and equipment into storage at both Forts Pembina and Abercrombie. When wagon transportation from Pembina to Abercrombie was secured, Campbell and Farquhar moved out ahead of the main party. Reassembled at Fort Abercrombie on the upper Red on November 19, the two groups departed at once for the railroad at Breckenridge, leaving the British, the boundary, and the winter behind them.[38]

Cameron had received only short notice of Campbell's departure, and he was upset that the American would leave before formally agreeing on the latitude at Pembina. Campbell no doubt thought that, in view of his counterpart's attitude toward the boundary at the Northwest Angle, it would be wise not to concede a possible bargaining point. Consequently the commissioners parted without meeting these two principal objectives they had set for their first season's efforts.[39]

During most of the winter of 1872–73 the British kept three astronomical parties in the field. Anderson supervised the clearing of the bog-ridden meridian line for 16 miles southward from Angle Inlet in late October and November. The job was done by Indian laborers, who preferred to work only in the mornings. Despite these labor problems a narrow trace was cut, which Anderson hoped would not have to be changed because of Cameron's cavil about the most northwest point. After clearing the meridian line, Anderson worked with Lindsay A. Russell, Canada's deputy surveyor general, to fix the longitude of Pembina by exchanging telegraph signals between there and the Chicago Observatory.[40]

Having finished his work on the west shore of Lake of the Woods, Galwey returned briefly to Dufferin for supplies and instructions before undertaking his winter assignment along the 49th parallel. His party was to cover the western end of the line near Pembina, while Featherstonhaugh continued eastward from Roseau Lake to Lake of the Woods.

By April, 1873, the British had established five astronomical stations including those at Pembina, Angle Inlet, and the west shore of Lake of the Woods; traced a line for 88½ miles along the 49th parallel from the Red River to Lake of the Woods; and surveyed over 500 square miles of land adjacent to that boundary. In addition all their magnetic and astronomical observations had been recorded, so the work could be rechecked later.[41]

Campbell's major concern during the winter of 1872–73 was to convince the State Department and certain congressmen—who understood neither the necessity nor the nature of the boundary survey—that his commission required $125,000 for 1873, two and a half times the amount appropriated for 1872. For a brief time Campbell feared some adverse publicity appearing in the *St. Paul*

Daily Press would undo his lobbying effort. But not only did Congress appropriate the requested sum, it acted promptly enough so the parties could get into the field early in May, 1873. The commissioner justified the increase on two grounds: the Americans would be working for a full season, and a larger party was required to take the survey through Dakota Indian lands.[42]

CHAPTER 10

West to the Continental Divide, 1873–76

WITH THE SURVEYING between Lake of the Woods and the Red River practically completed, the joint commission in 1873 turned its attention to the boundary stretching 765 miles westward to the Rockies. The remaining work of surveying and monumenting the long border, much of it through Indian-held lands, required three seasons. During that time the two major problems that marred the co-operative effort—Canada's attempts to acquire the Northwest Angle and a disagreement over the method used to measure lines of latitude along the 49th parallel—were solved to the satisfaction of the British and American governments and the disappointment of the British commissioner. When the last party left the field in the autumn of 1875, 853 miles of the 49th parallel boundary from Lake of the Woods to the continental divide in Montana had been measured and marked.

The Dakota Indians on the northern plains were not actively warring against the government in 1873, but past events made hostilities seem likely. The volatile Dakota War of 1862 in Minnesota was still fresh in the memories of both Indians and frontier soldiers. Its bitter aftermath, which included army expeditions into Dakota Territory in 1863, 1864, and 1865 and the establishment of a military frontier in the eastern region of the territory, had not ended. Most of the Santee Dakota who had fled from Minnesota had been placed on reservations; hundreds more had escaped into Canada. In reaction to the expeditions dispatched to control the renegade Santee, as well as a gold rush in Montana, the Yanktonai band had warred against the troops and attacked Missouri River travelers in 1865 and 1866. Shortly thereafter some Teton Dakota led by Red Cloud successfully opposed the opening of the Bozeman Trail in Wyoming. An uneasy truce was brought about by the Laramie Treaty of 1868, but it was fragile and might be upset by the appearance of a large expedition of white men.[1]

Concerned about leading his party into Dakota lands, Campbell arranged for an escort commanded by Major Marcus Reno of the United States Seventh Cavalry—the unit which was to win enduring fame three years later at the Battle of the Little Big Horn. Although Canada had experienced no particular difficulty with the Dakota, Cameron could not be sure the Indians would always be able to distinguish between American and British surveyors. He therefore arranged to hire 30 mounted mixed-bloods to reconnoiter the country in advance of the astronomers. These men, when added to the increased numbers

of teamsters, herders, and couriers necessary to operate the enlarged transportation system, brought the size of each commission to about 270 members.[2]

Although the first British party of surveyors left Dufferin in mid-May, most other members of the two commissions did not head west until June. Both groups had undergone some reorganization made necessary by additions and resignations. The most significant change was the Americans' loss of Farquhar, who resigned for personal reasons. Twining was promoted to chief astronomer, a position he held for the remainder of the commission's work. Like Farquhar, he enjoyed a good professional relationship with Samuel Anderson. Moreover, as chief engineer of the Department of Dakota in 1869, he had explored much of the territory to be covered in 1873 and 1874.[3]

The men of both commissions were in the field early in July when Campbell and Cameron met at Pembina. In their discussions they talked about their differences over how to measure a line of latitude. Both knew it was necessary to reach a settlement, for the line could not be accurately determined until the problem was reconciled. With every mile the work progressed westward, the possibility that it would have to be redone became more burdensome.[4]

Theoretically a line of latitude is parallel to the equator, and like the equator it has to be slightly curved. Without practical experience to guide him, Cameron insisted the 49th parallel from Lake of the Woods to the Rockies should be exactly parallel to the equator. Ignoring the advice of his chief astronomer, he contended that this curved line or mean parallel, as it came to be called, was mandated by the Convention of 1818. Campbell readily conceded that, in the abstract sense, a line of latitude was parallel to the equator and that it was physically possible to determine it. But not one to waste time on abstractions, he quickly raised the practical question of how to mark such a curved line on the ground, attacking the idea as wasteful both in terms of time and money. To trace such a curved line, would require first to determine the latitude at designated astronomical stations placed probably no farther than 20 miles apart. When this had been done along the entire 800-mile boundary, and all calculations were rechecked under laboratory conditions, surveyors would have to retrace the entire route and adjust the slightly curved line from each of the astronomical stations. This resurvey, Campbell claimed, would add a full year to the field work. And for what good purpose? he asked. True, the curved line would dip slightly to the south, but it would not add an appreciable amount of territory to Canada. Thus the American counterproposed that they fix the latitude as expeditiously as possible.[5]

Campbell preferred the astronomical method of measuring latitude, used in the Oregon survey, by which the two parties fixed the 49th parallel at selected sites and connected the points by straight lines. Such a boundary was not truly on the 49th; in places it might be either slightly north or south of the true parallel. This inconsistency was unavoidable, because it was not always possible to locate the 49th parallel at exactly the same distance from the equator. Variations from station to station, such as hills and valleys, magnetic attraction, and even the thickness of the earth's crust, could mean that the 49th parallel as determined in one spot might be somewhat north or south of a neighboring one.[6]

Campbell believed that every astronomical station along the line of latitude had to be calculated with great care and that American and British differences had to be within the 50-foot limit. Once the stations were established, however, he would have no patience with petty squabbling over whether the line was abstractly pure. The American commissioner had an additional argument for his case. Suspecting the work of the 1870s survey would be refined in the future, he pointed out that a mean line would be much more difficult to recover should the boundary monuments be obliterated, while the astronomical line could be easily reconstructed from the readings of the astronomical stations. Despite his experience and eminent common sense, Campbell could not sway Cameron in his insistence that the most accurate line of latitude would have to be parallel to the equator.[7]

After a slow start the 1873 survey moved rapidly. Along the route the workers were plagued by mosquitoes, shortages of forage, water, and fuel, threatening prairie fires, and even a September blizzard. Despite these obstacles the surveying and astronomical parties accomplished their season's goal. In early October they halted the survey 408 miles west of the Red River.[8]

The success of the 1873 season was clouded by the failure of the commissioners to agree on any points of difference. Although they periodically exchanged views on the method of determining latitude, they merely restated their positions in somewhat different language. Campbell also held to his stand that the most northwest point of Lake of the Woods should be calculated from the Indian monument, while Cameron insisted it should be measured according to the intersection of the mid-water line of the 1783 treaty and the latitude and longitude given in the Webster-Ashburton Treaty. The British commissioner thought his position was strengthened by information provided by Anthony Barclay, who had responded to a series of questions forwarded to him by Foreign Secretary Granville.[9]

Barclay reminded Granville that nearly half a century had passed since he and Tiarks had gone to Angle Inlet. His memories had faded, he said, and his personal records had been carried away from his home near Savannah, Georgia, by Union soldiers in December, 1864. He went on to describe Thompson's monument quite accurately, but he could not recall Tiarks' equipment or his methods. He said, however, that the astronomer had spent a long time at Lake of the Woods and had been satisfied with his findings. Since Barclay's information did not prove conclusively that the Indian monument was Thompson's marker, Cameron seemed to think Campbell would have to accept his alternate method of determining the most northwest point. He sent a copy of Barclay's letter to Campbell, but the American commissioner did not regard the information as particularly significant.

Campbell also refused to deal with the Angle Inlet looped line as a formal issue. The loops were located south of the northwest point of the lake, which as far as the American was concerned was inviolable. He balked at Cameron's suggestion that the crossing of the 1783 and 1818 lines be mentioned as a specific problem in the 1872 journal concerning Lake of the Woods, and the two commissioners, too vain to compromise, became embroiled in the minutiae of the journal's wording. Both men, however, recognized the larger question. To Campbell, caution was the key word, for the United States had something to lose but little to gain. Therefore he insisted that the joint commission existed only to survey and mark the boundary, not to alter it. Cameron, hoping that one small change could lead to a major shift in the boundary at Lake of the Woods, continued to look for an issue to be negotiated, be it the northwest point or the looped line.[10]

Relations between the commissioners were further strained by Campbell's tendency to take offense easily. Perhaps he saw some tactical advantage in these flare-ups, but he also seems to have regarded Cameron as too young, too rash, and too disrespectful of experience. Cameron's knack for choosing exactly the wrong words added to the tension. When he referred to Campbell's astronomical parallel as "patchy," the American took the word in the most derogatory sense, whereupon Cameron explained that he meant only a line "composed of pieces independent and irregular in their directions," in contrast to his "uniform and continuous" curved line.[11]

Satisfied that they could easily complete the work to the continental divide during the next season, Campbell and Cameron ordered their parties out of the field in mid-October, 1873. The British commission retraced its route eastward along the boundary line to make ready for a second winter at Dufferin. The American party marched southeastward from its depot at the second crossing of the Souris River to Fort Totten at Devils Lake in Dakota Territory. At that point the group divided. Most of them continued to the Northern Pacific Railroad at Jamestown and from there to St. Paul, where they were discharged. Twining went on to winter quarters at Detroit. Greene and a smaller party spent the winter working on the line east of the Red River, in order to satisfy Campbell that this portion of the boundary had been jointly surveyed.[12]

While Greene was in the field and Campbell had assumed a wait-and-see attitude toward reaching agreements with Cameron, the British commissioner seized the initiative and enlisted the support of the Canadian government. Soon after returning to the Red River camp, Cameron journeyed to Ottawa, where he visited with such officials as Governor-General Dufferin. He also engaged in considerable correspondence regarding the method of determining the boundary. In memoranda and letters Cameron candidly reviewed for the governor-general the advantages and disadvantages of his mean parallel and Campbell's astronomical parallel. Perhaps because of assurances he received in Ottawa, Cameron regarded the Dominion government as an ally in his campaign for a mean line of latitude. His strategy seems to have been to win Canadian endorsement before presenting his proposal to the British Foreign Office, which would then be more likely to accept a plan that prolonged the survey and added to its costs. On December 14, soon after returning to Camp Dufferin, the commissioner again pressed Dominion officials for a decision. He had just learned, he wrote anxiously, that Greene's men intended to cut the permanent boundary line west of Lake of the Woods during the winter. Before this could be done, he pointed out, the line of latitude had to be defined.[13]

Early in February Cameron received a telegram from Ottawa advising that a committee of the Dominion Privy Council favored measuring the 49th parallel as a continuous curved line — the commissioner's first preference. On February 4 he wrote to Granville asking for instructions on the method of determining latitude. In his letter he took a firm approach, pointing out only the advantages of the mean parallel and none of the possible benefits of the astronomical line. As only a man of deep conviction could, Cameron made the extraordinary observation that the estimated £50,000 needed to run the mean parallel line "does not bear upon the merits of the question . . . and appears to be beyond my province to consider."[14]

Governor-General Dufferin approved the Privy Council recommendation on February 23, enabling Cameron to inform Granville of the Canadians' choice. The commissioner added the advice that Dominion officials "regard the question of cost as a matter of secondary consideration and recommend the adoption of that course which appears to be most strictly in accordance with the terms of the Treaty of 1818." To this communication Cameron appended a lengthy consideration of various methods of marking latitude written two weeks earlier by Anderson. In his innocuous review the astronomer avoided endorsing either the mean or astronomical line, although he had strong opinions concerning the controversy.

Anderson, who disagreed with Cameron on several other boundary matters, kept his true feelings on the latitude question from the commissioner. He minced no words, however, when writing to his old friend and colleague in the Royal Engineers, Charles Wilson. The decision of the Privy Council was meaningless, he complained, because it had been invited by Cameron, who had "suppressed" Anderson's recommendation of "the demarcation of the astronomical parallel as the most rapid, accurate and effectual way of fulfilling the terms of the treaty." The mean parallel, on the other hand, would require retracing about 500 miles of boundary. The astronomer confided that he was in "perfect accord" with Campbell and Twining, neither of whom wanted to spend another year completing the survey.[15]

Anderson asked Wilson to inform Granville about his position on the mean parallel question. "Surely the Foreign Office would never consent to this most unnecessary waste of public money, merely to move the boundary mounds a few feet north and south," he wrote. Even though the "Canadian government seems anxious to prolong the work as much as possible," he added, "that is no reason why the Foreign Office who bear half the expense should be drawn into this most unnecessary expenditure."

The views Anderson expressed for the benefit of the Foreign Office reminded Granville of the British boundary commission's duality. From the start it had been both Canadian and English and, since the disagreement over Cameron's appointment, had suffered no serious conflicts. Now, however, Granville faced a dilemma because of the commissioner's Canadian support. He preferred to satisfy rather than offend Dominion officials, but not to the point of endorsing the mean line. Prolonging the commission's work and expense was not acceptable to the foreign secretary, yet he did not feel personally qualified to evaluate the merits of astronomical versus mean line determinations. Granville also probably regarded Cameron's influencing of Canadian officials as a disturbing act of duplicity.

Despite some vacillation, Granville handled the situation with considerably more fortitude than he had shown when Cameron was named commissioner. He had little difficulty obtaining adverse reactions to the mean line proposal. Major Charles Wilson saw it as enormously expensive, "of no practical value," and unnecessarily precise. For a third of its distance the boundary ran "through a district which is quite unsuitable to settlement or pasturage," the major wrote; "the members of the Commission have been the first white men to penetrate into this district, and it will probably be rarely visited again from the want of wood, water & grass."[16]

Britain's colonial secretary, the Earl of Carnarvon, also bluntly opposed the mean parallel. He knew the astronomical line was favored by both countries' astronomers and by the American commissioner, and suggested that if the Foreign Office needed additional support it should consult the royal astronomer, George Airy. There was need for a quick decision, Carnarvon stated, not only to avoid the loss of a surveying season, but also because he understood "the Candian Government have given an authority to Captain Cameron to commence the mean line—which seemingly adds a further complication to the question."[17]

Hastily reacting to Carnarvon's inaccurate information about Canadian intentions, Granville telegraphed Cameron on March 27: "Do not take any steps for tracing mean Boundary until you receive further instructions from me." Within hours the colonial secretary sent a telegram to Governor-General Dufferin, saying, " . . . reference will be made to Astronomer Royal as to boundary line. All action on instructions issued to Cameron should be suspended pending decision of Her Majesty's Government." Dufferin was puzzled. He had told Cameron about his approval of the Privy Council committee's recommendation as a matter of information only, not as an order. The governor-general acknowledged the Dominion's preference for a curved line, however, and requested Carnarvon's favorable consideration of it.[18]

George Airy, who had recommended the astronomical method of boundary surveying to the British astronomers in 1872, had the last word. When the framers of the Convention of 1818 set the 49th parallel as the boundary, he wrote, they had not intended to call for the degree of accuracy Cameron wanted. Airy was certain they had used the word "parallel" in the sense of ordinary maps, where slight discrepancies in a true parallel line would not even be noted. It was not feasible to trace a line exactly parallel to the equator because of variations in terrain, he added, for the land, unlike the seas, was not smooth. He advised a series of astronomical stations be determined on the ground and the method of connecting them be left to the commissioners and astronomers. If the decision were his, he would trace a boundary of straight lines between stations, even though "a little would be gained in accuracy" if they were parallel to the equator. The entire controversy seemed to Airy much ado about nothing. The territorial difference between a pure mean line and an astronomical line would "be for the most part less than the breadth of a London square." The Foreign Office accepted Airy's opinion without question. Cameron could not have his mean parallel, but if he wanted to salvage his pride by negotiating curved lines between astronomical stations, the British government would not object.[19]

During this contention Prime Minister William Gladstone's Liberal government was ousted by Benjamin Disraeli's Conservatives, bringing the Earl of Derby into the Foreign Office as Granville's successor. The change in ministries provided no relief for Cameron. He soon learned that the British government, not just Granville, opposed the mean line.

In an attempt to save face, Cameron sent the Foreign Office a long explanation of his fight for a mean line. Until he had received Airy's opinion, he had not understood there were two ways of defining a line of latitude. He had always defined it in the strictest sense, which he assumed was the only way. After reiterating his literal interpretation of the intention of the treaty makers in 1818, the commissioner observed that "recent occurrences confirm my impression that international questions of jurisdiction may and will arise even within tracts no broader than a London square. The occurrence of such difficulties, I thought, might be rendered less frequent by a line of uniform course."[20]

At the time Cameron began to push for the mean line of latitude in February, 1874, he also made an issue of the most northwest point of Lake of the Woods. In a letter to the Foreign Office, the British commissioner finally stated his reservations about the authenticity of the Indian monument. He believed that while Farquhar's discoveries, Barclay's information, and David Thompson's 1824 journal tended to substantiate the monument's accuracy, they did not constitute conclusive proof. The logs and depression Farquhar found might represent nothing more than an abandoned haycock, he suggested, for the Ojibway customarily stacked hay on platforms over swamps. Thompson's work, which should "be more commonly described as a Reconnaissance, than a Survey," was so general no specific spot could be precisely determined from it. In addition, a recalculation of Thompson's survey and Tiarks' observations showed the site of the 1824 marker would be 400 feet northwest of the Indian monument.[21]

Cameron's suggested alternative, which he had already proposed to Campbell in 1872, was to determine the northwest point from the place where the mid-water line touched the latitude mentioned in the Webster-Ashburton Treaty. Once again the commissioner did not have the support of Anderson. The astronomer, who had earlier conducted a survey on this basis, concluded that the alternate reference point would shift the meridian only 106 feet west of a line determined from the Indian monument. Like the Americans, he could see no point in arguing over such a narrow strip of worthless land. Shifting the north-south boundary would not solve any related problems, for it would still cross the mid-water line in several places, and pushing it farther into Canadian territory would only aggravate the problem of relocating the Dawson Road docks. Cameron, professing not to have any larger question in mind, such as Canadian acquisition of the Northwest Angle, claimed his only interest was accuracy.

The Foreign Office handled the problem of the northwest point, as it had the latitude issue, by asking for an expert's opinion. Not coincidentally the question was referred to Wilson. The major favored determining the most northwest point from the site of the Indian reference monument—an opinion, he noted, that "is in agreement with the view expressed by the United States Commissioner." Even though the latitude and longitude of the northwest point as determined in 1825 proved to be inaccurate when Angle Inlet was surveyed in 1872, Wilson believed there was no need to consider an alternate site. He thought Thompson and Tiarks had been as accurate as their equipment allowed, and he saw no reason to doubt that the Indian monument was on or nearly on the Thompson site. He also questioned adding a narrow strip to the United States, especially since it would not solve the problem of the looped line. In addition, the 16-mile meridian line Anderson had already cut south of Angle Inlet would have to be redone. Wilson's solution was to shift the most northwest point southward on the meridian Anderson had surveyed to the southernmost contact of the 1783 and 1818 lines.[22]

The Foreign Office promptly ordered Cameron to cooperate with Campbell in establishing the most northwest point from the Indian reference monument. Probably fearing the commissioner would initiate another maneuver, Derby reminded him that any adjustment of the looped line would have to be left to a future diplomatic arrangement between the United States and Great Britain.[23]

By May, 1874, Cameron had received orders to agree with Campbell on what seemed to him to be American terms. Stripped of his other options, he could negotiate only the method of connecting the astronomical stations, which he wanted to settle before leaving Dufferin for the starting point of the 1874 work. Hoping to meet with Campbell and Twining, he traveled to St. Paul in June, but the American commissioner had not yet arrived. Cameron informally proposed to Twining that the astronomical stations be connected by curved lines, but the chief American astronomer insisted on straight courses. The British commissioner left dourly predicting Campbell would accept Twining's recommendation. He would attempt to reach an agreement before the survey was completed to the continental divide, however, because adjustment of the western boundary could best be made by surveyors returning to Dufferin, rather than by another group sent into the field in 1875.[24]

The commissions had only the full months of July, August, and September to complete the survey. The British sent out 257 men and officers outfitted with 324 draft animals and 179 vehicles. The American commission was probably about the same size with an added complement of military personnel for protection against the Dakota, Blackfeet, and Assiniboin Indians. Each commission established astronomical stations at 40-mile intervals, following the guiding principle that there would be a station approximately every 20 miles. As the parties moved west, the Americans surveyed a belt of land five miles wide south of the boundary, and the British did the same north of it. Benefitting from their experience in 1873, the commissions rapidly covered the last 358 miles of boundary.[25]

While encamped at the Milk River in mid-August, Cameron invited Campbell to settle their accounts, offering to resolve the two major problems. The British commissioner would accept both a northwest point in Angle Inlet derived from the Indian monument and a parallel line drawn from one astronomical station to the next, provided it "shall follow a course having the uniform curvature of a parallel of 49th North Latitude." Recognizing he could not persuade Cameron to agree to straight lines between stations, Campbell accepted the offer, observing that "the work will doubtless now be brought to a close without further difference of views."[26]

As their men carried the survey to the western edge of the plains and into the beautiful, rugged mountains that are now part of Glacier National Park in Montana and Waterton Lakes National Park in Alberta, the two commissioners made final plans to mark the boundary. Iron monuments would be placed at intervals of about one mile from Manitoba's southwestern corner to Lake of the Woods, and up to two miles apart along the 16-mile meridian line. Alternate monuments would be set by each commission. The stark area west of Manitoba, which held no immediate promise to ranchers or farmers, would be marked with cairns set farther apart.[27]

The iron monuments, intended to be permanent, were the same as those placed on the Maine-New Brunswick boundary. They were hollow iron castings, eight feet long, designed so equal lengths would be above and below ground. The top portion, a truncated pyramid eight inches square at its base and four inches square at its top, was set in an octagonal flange and topped by a pyramidal cap. The hollow shafts were filled with seasoned cedar poles cut to form and spiked to the iron castings through precut holes. The monuments had an average weight of about 285 pounds, sufficient to discourage souvenir hunters.[28]

In keeping with precedent, the commissioners had each post inscribed with the authority for the survey. On opposite sides in letters two inches high appeared "Convention of London" and "October 20, 1818." The other two sides were left blank. Apparently visitors to the boundary were expected to have an infallible sense of direction, or no curiosity, for the names of the two countries were not inscribed on the shafts. When the markers were set, the words faced Canada and the date faced the United States.[29]

Since the commissioners had defined latitude before all of the boundary had been surveyed, their crews were able to mark the extreme western portions as they proceeded. Because of the mountainous terrain and the imminent close of the season, the men became casual about the line west of the plains, erecting stone cairns as far as ten miles apart. As the British returned eastward in the fall, they constructed conical mounds of earth and stone at approximately three-mile intervals across the plains as far as the southwestern corner of Manitoba. Most of the monuments measured 10 feet in diameter and 6 feet high, but many were 12 by 6 feet, and a few made of earth were 18 by 8 feet. Because these markers would not likely be permanent, it was intended to bury in each at a depth of two feet an enameled iron tablet inscribed "British and United States Boundary Commissions 1872-4, 49° north latitude." But Cameron became alarmed by visiting Indians, and in his haste to move on, he neglected to have the plates buried for a stretch of 118 miles.[30]

The commissioners parted at the base of the Rockies. At last eager to finish the job rapidly, Cameron had ordered his men to do their half of the monument setting during the fall and winter of 1874-75. Campbell, however, did not intend to complete the American share of the work until the autumn of 1875. Leaving the borderland, the Americans headed southwest to Fort Benton where Twining dispatched his crews. By boat and then rail, Twining, Gregory, Greene, and Campbell continued to Washington to complete their maps and final report.[31]

Disbanding the British commission was more complicated. Cameron had to organize monumenting parties, get started on the maps and final report, and dispose of Dufferin all at the same time. Anderson, Featherstonhaugh, Galwey, and six of the Royal Engineers went immediately to Ottawa to work on the maps. To make the charts uniform, Anderson and Greene exchanged numerous letters and telegrams containing detailed information about tracings, symbols, and scales. Although the maps were not finally completed until after the Americans' monumenting was done and Anderson was back in England, most of the work was finished during a period of seven months.[32]

While Cameron arranged the sale of buildings and supplies at Dufferin, he also co-ordinated the work of three small crews marking the 169 miles from the southwest corner of Manitoba to Lake of the Woods. After proceeding rapidly through the dry, open country where wagon travel was easy and iron monuments were used exclusively, the men reached the marshy area about 55 miles west of Lake of the Woods. At a few sites where the ground was firm, iron monuments were set; for the most part, however, earth and timber mounds had to be constructed in the swamps. This work and marking the 16-mile meridian line was done from October, 1874, to March, 1875, under the supervision of D'Arcy East, the chief British surveyor. Assisted by a civilian contractor, East's men also widened the vista strip. At the starting point of the 49th parallel on the west shore of the lake, East personally supervised the construction of an impressive stone cairn seven and a half feet high and eight feet in diameter.[33]

During the time East was in the field, the permanent existence of the Northwest Angle was ensured. When Cameron was told in 1872 by the Foreign Office that the problem of the looped line in Angle Inlet could only be resolved diplomatically, he had taken the decision with equanimity. Since then the commissioner had kept in mind his original instructions to collect information on the possibility of acquiring the Northwest Angle for Canada—a possibility he now thought might be realized.

Aware of Canada's interest in improving transcontinental transportation, Cameron had investigated the feasibility of a canal connecting Lake of the Woods and the Red River. In August, 1873, he had sent George Dawson, the Canadian geologist of the boundary commission, to reconnoiter a possible route. Dawson and two men had paddled their bark canoe up the Reed River, a small stream emptying into Buffalo Bay of Lake of the Woods, to its headwaters in a muskeg bog. They then worked their way through swamps nearly seven miles southwest to the source of what is now Sprague Creek. Following this stream across the boundary into the United States, they entered the Roseau River, which flows back into Canada before emptying into the Red. Dawson did not consider his trip a great accomplishment, for the route was one customarily used by both Dakota and Ojibway. While he believed small steamboats could probably navigate the lower Roseau River and steam launches might operate in the area about Roseau Lake, he had ruled out travel by large boats on existing waterways from Lake of the Woods to the Red River.[34]

Dawson's expedition was only one phase of Cameron's efforts to discover possible new routes between Lake of the Woods and the Red River. From June through October, 1873, East had surveyed the western and southern portions of Lake of the Woods and investigated waterways between the lake and the Whitemouth River to the west. His work ended in the fall at Whitemouth Lake, from which the Dawson Road could be reached by following the Whitemouth River. There he left supplies, anticipating he would return to complete the survey.[35]

Cameron, whose interest in the project took him to Angle Inlet during the summer of 1873, sent East back to Whitemouth Lake in the dead of winter. In February, 1874, the surveyor and a small crew went by dog sleds from Dufferin to the crossing of the 49th parallel by the Roseau River. Ojibway guides led them northward to Whitemouth Lake, which they surveyed, although stormy weather and drifting snow prevented accurate measurements. "As far as could be ascertained," East reported to Cameron, "the whole country lying between the White Mouth River and the Lake of the Woods on the Western and Eastern sides and the Dawson Road and the 49th Parallel on the Northern and Southern is bad swamp or muskeg with but few exceptions."

After reviewing Dawson's and East's information, Cameron in April, 1874, had ordered Anderson to report on the "feasibility of connecting the Lake of the Woods south of the North-West Angle by canal and roadway— with the Red River." The chief astronomer rejected the 15-mile-long Reed River as a possible canal because it was "tortuous and insignificant." He estimated the rest of the route would be at least 160 miles long, compared to the existing 90-mile overland road from Angle Inlet to Winnipeg. Any canal in that area, he added, would require an elaborate system of locks to cross the divide west of Lake of the Woods. Using excavation and lockage estimates made in 1869 by Simon Dawson, Anderson figured the total cost of a canal by way of the Roseau River at £744,000 or $3,664,980. He also noted that Simon Dawson had estimated the cost of a railroad from Angle Inlet to Winnipeg at only £54,000.[36]

Despite Anderson's negative conclusions, Cameron thought a canal was possible. In a lengthy report to the Foreign Office on May 19, 1874, he weighed the advantages and disadvantages of Canadian acquisition of the Northwest Angle. The land east of the meridian line, estimated at 130 square miles, admittedly had no value for mining, farming, lumbering, or fishing. But he urged its acquisition to facilitate transportation in Manitoba, whose eastern boundary then lay 32 miles west of the meridian. Correctly presuming Manitoba would be extended eastward, he predicted that if the United States retained control of the 130 square miles, Canadian vessels moving from the Rainy River to a canal on the west side of the lake would have to cross American territory. Cameron made another prediction which later caught the interest of Canadian and British officials. Because it was worthless and remote, he believed the Northwest Angle would become a haven for "smugglers and refugees from justice."[37]

Based on his experience in India, Cameron regarded the Angle as a potential "Chandernagore [—] an isolated French settlement near Calcutta—where thieves and refugees from all the surrounding country seek freedom from arrest, and organize illegal proceedings." The United States would never establish a military post in the Angle to control these renegades, he contended, because the terrain was not suited to offensive tactics. Acquisition of the Angle would not only save Canada from lawless

riffraff, but would allow more freedom in planning transportation routes. Cameron concluded that "every interest of Canada would be served" if an easily distinguishable boundary ran from the mouth of the Rainy River along the south shore of Lake of the Woods to the 49th parallel. A less desirable alternative was a mid-water line from the Rainy's mouth to the 49th.

Before the summer of 1874, Foreign Secretary Derby apparently planned to ask the United States to eliminate the looped line by fixing the most northwest point at the southernmost contact of the 1783 and 1818 demarcations. But in July, 1874, the Foreign Office again deferred to Canadian desires and was persuaded to try to acquire the Northwest Angle. Canada's minister of the interior, David Laird, rejected Cameron's proposed canal as too costly, but he agreed that the Angle could become a sanctuary for smugglers. He also felt the boundary should be changed to avoid "an awkward and capricious deviation from the more natural line"—but only if Canada would have to make "a very inconsiderable concession to secure the readjustment." The Canadian Privy Council and Governor-General Dufferin endorsed a boundary following the south shore of Lake of the Woods, agreeing that the cost to Canada should be minimal.[38]

Colonial Secretary Carnarvon favored a boundary shift in keeping with either of Cameron's proposals. He too seemed convinced the isolated Northwest Angle was "likely to be made use of to harbour smugglers and to serve as an asylum for refugees from justice," which "would cause complications between Canada and the U.S." It was the only reason he saw for Canada to acquire an additional 130 square miles of land and 275 square miles of water.[39]

Before proposing the boundary adjustment to the Americans, the British had to determine two things: what would the United States expect in return, and what would Canada be willing to pay? After several months the Canadian Privy Council decided its "very inconsiderable concession" should be limited to $25,000. Although Derby's first thought was to have Ambassador Edward Thornton offer the money outright to Hamilton Fish, he soon decided the United States did not need dollars. Carnarvon suggested Fish be asked to adjust the boundary "on the ground of international convenience, and without any payment being made for it." Because the Americans' intentions were unknown, however, Thornton needed some options, which he received in a telegram from Derby in January, 1875. The ambassador was first to ask the United States to change the boundary as an "international convenience"; if that did not work, he was to determine what compensation the Americans wanted, but he was not to offer $25,000 unless forced to do so. In any case Thornton was to get Fish's agreement on a southward shift of the northwest point.[40]

Even with these options Thornton found it impossible to negotiate with Fish at a meeting on February 4, 1875. The secretary of state "showed great disinclination" to move the most northwest point, because it had already been marked. When the ambassador proposed "unofficially" that the boundary be shifted to the south side of Lake of the Woods, "Mr. Fish evinced even more disinclination. . . . He was convinced he said, that Congress and the people of the United States would never be brought to agree to it, unless Her Majesty's Government were prepared to make very great sacrifices." Fish also observed that the Angle was valuable to Canada because of the Dawson Road. These comments gave Thornton some hope, but rather than press the issue, he invited Fish to reconsider the proposals.[41]

A week later, when the two met again, Fish had not changed his mind. Thornton then played his trump card. Would the United States consider accepting payment for the land? The secretary of state answered, "nothing that Her Majesty's Government would be prepared to offer would be accepted by the United States." Because President Grant and his cabinet supported Fish's views, the ambassador concluded "there is no probability that the United States Government will entertain these proposals, at least for the present."[42]

That Fish seriously entertained the British tenders is inconceivable. He surely recognized the seeming anomaly of the Northwest Angle, and he knew the area had little real or potential economic value. But to relinquish it would have been to contradict both the American tradition of territorial acquisition and the literal interpretation of boundary treaties. Fish and other government leaders at the time, who had matured during the height of the era of Manifest Destiny, believed the greatness of their country was based on vast land holdings. To surrender even a small tract was unthinkable. There was a more practical reason for Fish and Grant not to cede the Angle. Since they had failed to back Minnesota expansionists a few years earlier, it would be a grave political error to relinquish land to Canada now. No doubt the secretary of state had that in mind when he spoke to Thornton of the feelings of Congress and the American people.

Fish's rejection ended Canada's last serious effort to acquire the Northwest Angle. With only a slight alteration of its northern extent made in 1925, the Angle has remained practically unchanged since the meridian line was first surveyed. Instead of becoming infamous as a refuge for criminals, as Cameron and the British had envisioned, it attracted a few commercial fishermen, loggers, and trappers. Today its entire land area of 79,169 acres constitutes Northwest Angle State Forest. The state of Minnesota owns 14,399 acres, and the remainder is part of the Red Lake Indian Reservation. The total population, for the most part concentrated at Angle Inlet and at two other villages on Magnuson's and Oak islands, is less than 100. Until Alaska was admitted to the Union in 1959, the Angle was distinctive as the northernmost point in the United States.[43]

Britain's failure to negotiate the cession of the Northwest Angle also assured the rapid close of the joint boundary commission. In June, 1875, when the British astronomers left for their homeland, Cameron and Campbell estimated another year was needed to complete the maps and final reports, which would be exchanged in London. Cameron became increasingly anxious to return to England, but Derby ordered him to remain in Ottawa until the Americans had finished marking the boundary, in case new problems arose.[44]

Gregory, who was to supervise the remaining field work, went in August, 1875, from Washington to Detroit, where the American share of the iron monuments were manufactured, and sent them by rail to Moorhead. After organizing a small party in St. Paul and obtaining a military escort at Fort Pembina, he hired additional men, teams, and wagons. Within five weeks Gregory's crew set and painted 43 markers west of Pembina and 17 to the east, erecting them midway between each of those placed by the British. Many of the sites for the American monuments had already been accurately staked by the British.[45]

Gregory also completed a list of two series of monuments from Angle Inlet to the summit of the Rockies. The first series, numbered one through seven, marked the 16-mile meridian line south from Angle Inlet; the second, numbered one through 382, identified the 49th parallel boundary westward from Lake of the Woods. Of the 77 monuments between the inlet and the Red River astronomical station, 51 were iron and 26 were earth or timber mounds or stone cairns. Although the markers were recorded by number and location, no numbers were inscribed on them. Thus there was no way to distinguish one from another on the ground. After discharging most of his men on October 7, Gregory checked the placement of markers and some of the British calculations at Angle Inlet. This work was completed rapidly, and he returned to Washington on November 2, 1875.

Although the boundary was well marked with the completion of the commission's field work, Cameron feared many monuments would be obliterated or altered in time, either by natural phenomena or vandalism. He therefore suggested they be inspected and repaired every five years. The British and American governments, however, did not establish such a program of boundary upkeep.[46]

When their office work was completed in the spring of 1876, Campbell and Twining sailed for London. On May 29 they exchanged reports with Cameron, Anderson, and Ward. Since the commissioners had previously agreed on all issues, the final reports were identical in their conclusions, though they differed in format and length. The American document, written largely by Twining, emphasized astronomical calculations. That of the British, while appropriately technical in places, offered more observations on the borderland and its Indian and mixed-blood residents. It contained George Dawson's geological study as well as much information about Dufferin, including the specifications of its buildings. The United States report was published in 1878 with surplus boundary commission funds. Its highly technical data on the survey locations of each monument and all reference points were of much value to future boundary surveyors who had to re-mark the entire line 40 years later.[47]

CHAPTER 11

The Boundary Marked, 1890–1925

PROBLEMS ARISING from the unmarked status of the Minnesota-Ontario border remained largely ignored for nearly a generation after the survey of the 1870s. By the end of the century a rush of settlers to the boundary area, along with activities in logging, mining, and railroad construction, contributed to the instability of relations between Canadians and Americans. A number of disputed land claims added to the critical need for additional surveying and marking of Minnesota's border, as well as of the entire line between the United States and Canada. To meet the need, the United States and Great Britain signed three more treaties in 1903, 1906, and 1908. During the following decade, while boundary commissioners worked out resolutions of remaining issues, the Minnesota section was measured or remeasured and marked. In 1925 the commissioners' recommendations were incorporated in a treaty which at last eliminated the problems of the looped line at Angle Inlet and the curved lines along the 49th parallel and established a permanent International Boundary Commission.

Until the Red River uprising resulted in the addition of Manitoba to the Dominion, the remote, inhospitable region stretching from Lake Superior to Lake of the Woods had continued to be regarded as Webster, Ashburton, and most of their contemporaries had thought of it—an area of no particular value. It was the need to connect Manitoba and eastern Canada that awakened the borderland.

The building of the Dawson Road by the military men sent out under Colonel Wolseley to quell the Riel Rebellion in 1870 created the main thoroughfare for immigrants pouring into Manitoba during the following decade. As laid out by Simon Dawson many years earlier, the 530-mile route began at Port Arthur with a 34-mile stretch of rough wagon road that bridged the Kaministikwia River on its way to Shebandowan Lake. From there it followed the waterways and portages of the "Old Road" and the traditional voyageurs' route to a landing at Harrison Creek in the Northwest Angle of Lake of the Woods. One of the welcome overnight stops was made at the oasis in the wilderness called Fort Frances. The remainder of the journey from the Angle to Winnipeg was completed over a wagon road. To speed the passage of travelers using the Dawson route, the Dominion government spent nearly $1,300,000 on improvements, building and replacing bridges, clearing boulders and brush, and laying corduroy roadbeds where necessary. It also put steamboats and tugs on many lakes en route, so that the traffic between Lake Superior and the Red River became a relay of people and goods by canoe, boat, horse-drawn wagon, tugboat, steam launch, and stagecoach. Despite the hardships it offered, thousands of people reached the Manitoba prairies via the Dawson Road before it was abandoned about 1882.[1]

With the coming of settlers, the inexorable frontier process of pushing the Indians aside took its course. By a treaty in 1873 Canada obtained the Ojibway lands between Lake Superior and Lake of the Woods. Farmers soon moved to the Canadian side of the Rainy River. Only three years later a tract was surveyed on the north side of the Rainy, and parcels of land were given free to bona fide settlers. The influx of farmers to this part of Ontario, which preceded the farming frontier on the United States side of the line by a generation, gave added importance to the borderland.

The opening of central Canada's agricultural frontier coincided with the construction of the Canadian Pacific Railway. When British Columbia entered the Dominion in 1871, Canada was committed to the building of a transcontinental railroad. At Fort William, the Lake Superior terminus, construction did not begin until 1875, but the track was completed to Winnipeg in 1882; three years later it reached Vancouver on the Strait of Georgia. Since it was built through an area north of the great white and red pine forests, the millions of board feet of lumber needed for trestles, bridges, ties, stations, and other structures had to be obtained farther south. As the rails were extended to Rat Portage (present Kenora), Canadian lumbermen illegally cut white and Norway pine in northern Minnesota. They floated logs to mills at Fort Frances and other locations on the Rainy River and towed rafts of them to mills on Lake of the Woods and at Rat Portage. This activity in logs and lumber transformed Fort Frances from a remote trading station into a bustling commercial center whose business persisted as the Canadian Pacific was constructed westward across the plains.[2]

As the railroad influenced the development of Fort Frances and the Rainy River and Lake of the Woods areas, it also helped boom Fort William and neighboring Port Arthur into twin cities at the Canadian head of Lake Superior. The growth of Fort William, which had stagnated with the decline of the fur trade, had been reawakened in 1855 by the completion of the Sault Ste. Marie canal and had increased when the Dawson Road was in use in the 1870s. It was also boosted in 1868 by the discovery of silver on tiny Silver Islet, about a mile off Thunder Cape. For some 15 years, the mines near Fort William were reputed to be the world's richest. When additional silver, gold, and iron deposits were found on the mainland, many of the town's promoters believed its future lay in mining.

The island produced silver valued at over $3,000,000, while the yield of mainland mines approached $2,000,000. By the time depletion and rising production costs closed down the Silver Islet mine in 1884, however, Fort William had found its destiny as a grain port.[3]

The significance of the Canadian Pacific Railway to Fort William and Port Arthur became evident during the 1880s. Since the railroad was the only artery connecting the vast grainfields of the Canadian central plains with lake transportation, the wheat trade flowed through the twin ports. The demands of the trade, which ran to millions of bushels annually, led to the construction of storage and transshipment facilities, as well as harbor improvements, soon after the first grain began to arrive in 1881. By the end of the decade, the place of Fort William and Port Arthur in Canadian commerce was secure, and their status as the population center of western Ontario was assured.[4]

The promoters of Fort William and Port Arthur directed most of their efforts along the Canadian Pacific, but other tentacles of their influence extended southwestward toward the boundary. Encouraged by prospects of a railroad link with Duluth and hopes of silver and iron mines in the Gunflint Lake area, they led the way in building the Port Arthur, Duluth and Western Railway. Construction of this short line, which was subsidized by the government of Ontario, began a few years after the first mine opened on the Vermilion Iron Range in Minnesota—an event that touched off excited prospecting on both sides of the border. American interest in the area increased dramatically with the first shipment of iron ore from Tower to Two Harbors in 1884, and the founding three years later of Ely, where the productive Chandler Mine was located, touched off a frantic search for more deposits both north and south of the Vermilion Range. In 1889 a Minnesota company hauled mining equipment up what became the Gunflint Trail to the Paulson Mine, an ore discovery at Gunflint Lake. Three years later the railroad was completed for some 85 miles from Port Arthur. Instead of connecting with Duluth, however, it stopped at the border, where it met the tracks of the mining company's line running just over five miles to the Paulson Mine.[5]

Although the Gunflint area failed to produce marketable quantities of iron or silver ore, the Port Arthur, Duluth and Western Railway became an important logging line. In the wake of its construction, Canadian lumbermen claimed land near an unmarked, and in some areas unknown, boundary. During the 1890s the railroad helped open only a small section of the borderland. Later, however, it became part of the Canadian Northern Railway, which, when completed from Lake Superior to Fort Frances in 1901, provided ready access to many areas near the boundary.

Further American interest in the borderland was spurred by the Rainy Lake gold rush inspired by the discovery of the precious metal on Little American Island in July, 1893. Within a year the center of activity—Rainy Lake City—had mushroomed into a straggly collection of tents, covered wagons, tar-paper shacks, and log cabins housing nearly 400 people. To serve the burgeoning population, entrepreneurs quickly established a newspaper, three hotels, a barber shop, three general stores, two restaurants, a hardware store, a butcher shop, and five saloons. Many aspiring argonauts, along with mining and sawmilling machinery and even steamboats, made the hard journey to their northern destination by train to Tower (the Minnesota railhead closest to the border lakes), boat across Vermilion Lake, a crudely fashioned portage road to Crane Lake, and commercial steamboat to Rainy Lake. Other prospectors arrived by steamboat from Kenora. Although it ran its course in only a few years, the gold rush enticed hundreds of Americans to the unmarked boundary country. Joining the goldseekers were lumbermen, commercial fishermen, and land claimants, who scattered throughout the region.[6]

As the boom at Rainy Lake City died, the village of Koochiching, later renamed International Falls, began to develop on the American side of the Rainy River across from Fort Frances in an important section of the lumbering frontier. Much of Koochiching's commerce in lumber and supplies was directed down the Rainy River to Kenora. American boatmen joined Canadians in the river traffic, which as early as 1890 had numbered more than 20 small steamboats operating between Fort Frances and Lake of the Woods. Along with their business in transporting goods and lumber, the Americans engaged in commercial fishing and tourism. Their activities stimulated the border rivalry with Canadians, because the location of their commonly used routes in relation to the unmarked boundary in Lake of the Woods was not clear to either Canadian or United States customs officials.

Conflicting land claims were particularly bothersome in areas where there was no natural boundary. While it was not difficult to judge the route of the border along streams where both banks were visible, tracing it through larger lakes could not be done with precision even by surveyors in the Canadian Department of Crown Lands and the United States General Land Office. These men did not have copies of the boundary commission maps used by Webster and Ashburton, nor did they seem to be aware of the mid-water line principle. Many of them believed the boundary followed the deepest channel, regardless of its distance from either shore. As a result identifying the nationality of islands in such irregularly shaped bodies of water as Lac la Croix was a confused effort at best. During the 1880s and 1890s parts of many islands were hurriedly claimed by prospectors hoping to discover gold. Without an accurate survey to determine jurisdiction, conflicting patents were held by claimants from both the United States and Canada. Amid the tension only a spark was needed to ignite a boundary controversy in the 1890s.[7]

The catalyst was Frank Gardner, a resident of Rat Portage. In 1882 and 1883 Gardner had purchased lands in St. *Louis County*, Minnesota, including a portion of Coleman Island in Lac la Croix, which had been platted by the United States General Land Office. He accordingly paid property taxes to St. Louis County. About ten years later when he planned to cut some timber, he was informed that the government of Ontario would stop him because the Canadian survey of 1891 placed the island in Canada. On October 2, 1894, Gardner complained to the United States General Land Office. He was told by Edward A. Bowers, the acting commissioner, that after his office had issued the patent, it had no further jurisdiction. "As the question raised by you appears to be international in its character," Bowers advised, "it is suggested that you call the attention of the State Department to the matter."[8]

Gardner did so. He also complained to Congressman Charles A. Towne of Duluth, who represented northeastern Minnesota in the House of Representatives. Towne was sympathetic, not only because he wanted the boundary surveyed and marked, but because he was among those who thought Webster and Ashburton had erred in deciding on a line that was part land and part water. He chose to believe, as Porter had in the 1820s, that it should follow the most continuous water passage.

Like a number of other Minnesotans at that time, Towne harbored some hope of securing for the United States the area known as Hunter Island, even though the Webster-Ashburton Treaty firmly established the boundary south of it. Citing over a dozen 18th- and 19th-century French, British, and American maps, he wrote to Congressman Joel P. Heatwole, chairman of the House Subcommittee on Foreign Affairs, and easily proved that cartographers disagreed over the course of the waterways in the border region. "It will be seen that there is enough difference in these maps as to Hunters Island," he wrote, "to make good my contention that there is much reason to doubt the exact location of the boundary line between Minnesota and Canada from Lake Superior to the Lake of the Woods, and as to whether Hunters Island is rightfully regarded and held as Canadian territory."

In his search for supporting evidence, Towne was assisted by some of his constituents. Roscoe W. Gilkey, a former surveyor and timber cruiser from Duluth, informed him that Hunter Island was not an island at all, but a peninsula connected to Minnesota by a narrow isthmus. Although this fact did not alter the Webster-Ashburton

Treaty, it seemed to the congressman and his supporters to be an adequate reason for attempting a boundary adjustment.

Towne's contention was further supported, and perhaps partially formulated, by George R. Stuntz, a surveyor and pioneer in the opening of the Vermilion Iron Range who had four decades of experience in northern Minnesota. Along with some congressmen, Stuntz was angry because President Grover Cleveland's administration had taken a stand in the border controversy between British Guiana and Venezuela—in which the United States had no territorial interest whatsoever—while ignoring its own problems. In January, 1896, Stuntz suggested that "While adjusting the boundary for Venezuela, would it not be advisable to adjust the Alaskan boundary, and also come nearer home and adjust the boundary between our own Minnesota and Canada?" He deplored the crookedness of the Minnesota-Ontario border and wanted it straightened by drawing the line north of Hunter Island. This should be done, he said, because the boundary commissioners of the 1820s had diverged from the most continuous waterway "whenever there was a plausible show to get a strip of Uncle Samuel's territory."

Meanwhile the confusion over steamboat routes and the unmarked boundary in Lake of the Woods came to a head in a misunderstanding over Oak Island near the Northwest Angle. As they had for years, steamboat captains commonly used the channel passing south and west of the island. Some local residents, wrongly assuming the channel followed the boundary, therefore believed Oak Island belonged to Canada. In the fall of 1895 Richard Olney, United States secretary of state, received reports that the Canadian Department of Marine and Fisheries was "taking steps" to secure Oak Island. He promptly notified Sir Julian Pauncefote, British ambassador to the United States, that the island was referred to as "No. 1" in the Webster-Ashburton Treaty, which placed it in the United States. In reply Pauncefote forwarded a report from the Canadian Privy Council stating the rumor was "entirely without foundation." The government had merely investigated the claims of "certain parties" and "old settlers" who contended the boundary in Lake of the Woods followed the steamboat channel, the council explained. The report confirmed that Canadian officials, concerned only with the issuance of fishing licenses, were satisfied that Oak Island and island No. 1 were the same. Although the incident proved to be no issue, it strengthened Towne's argument for congressional action.[9]

As his lever to open a discussion of Hunter Island in Congress, Towne used Gardner's complaint. His principal supporter was Representative Stephen R. Harris of Ohio, who was concerned about alleged Canadian interference with American fishermen on Lake Erie. Together they persuaded the House Committee on Foreign Affairs to endorse their call for a boundary survey. Early in 1896 the House passed resolutions supporting both a survey and Towne's request for an adjustment of the line at Hunter Island. The State Department, however, preferred not to escalate these matters. After studying them at length, Assistant Secretary Alvey A. Adee stated the department's position. "The circumstance that continuous water communication may exist in fact north of the tract known as Hunters Island appears, however, to be immaterial in view of the precise mention" of the boundary line in the Webster-Ashburton Treaty. This conclusion, along with the department's concern with other issues and the perhaps not coincidental withdrawal of Ontario's claim to Gardner's Coleman Island holdings, temporarily quieted the discussion in Congress.[10]

Towne, however, was furious. The considerable publicity he received drew Canadian attention to the Hunter Island area. William F. King, the astronomer of Canada, sent A. J. "Jack" Brabazon, a dominion surveyor, to investigate the validity of American claims to Hunter Island. In June, 1896, Brabazon and two assistants rode the Port Arthur, Duluth and Western Railway from Fort William to Gunflint Lake. At the lake's western end they found two small trading posts—one American and one Canadian—on opposite ends of the railroad trestle. They also met a United States customs officer residing near the American post and observed the activities of American prospectors and Canadian lumbermen near the boundary.[11]

Brabazon, who carried copies of the maps signed by Webster and Ashburton, first led his men from Gunflint Lake eastward as far as the headwaters of the Pigeon River—there being no question about the boundary from Fowl Portage to Lake Superior. Then they returned to Gunflint Lake and took their reconnaissance westward to Kettle Falls at the outlet of Namakan Lake. As they surveyed the mid-water line and compared it to the boundary on the maps drawn by Porter's and Barclay's men, they discovered that a number of islands were not shown and others were mislocated. The problem of omitted and improperly placed islands was especially acute in the larger lakes, such as Saganaga, Lac la Croix, and Namakan. In his report Brabazon specifically identified by the officially assigned numbers the islands that were either misplaced or of different dimensions than those recorded in the 1820s. He also noted the location of any newly discovered islands with respect to the numbered ones on the official maps.

When Brabazon's survey ended on July 24 he had covered about 210 miles of the boundary. His first conclusion was that much of the surveying done in the 1820s was slipshod. "It is quite evident from the discrepancies heretofore mentioned," he noted, "that when an accurate survey of the lakes is made, the positions and extent of many of the islands, bays and channels will be found to differ considerably from those shown on the maps of 1842." Despite numerous minor errors, however, the boundary as laid down on the Article 7 maps could be easily followed. Brabazon's report, which was presented to King on February 1, 1897, left the way open for a future survey to make adjustments not in miles but in yards, and it relaxed Canadian anxiety over American pretensions to Hunter Island.

Apparently the report was not shown to the United States Department of State until six years later, but Brabazon's mission did not go unnoticed in Minnesota. Only three days after the Canadian finished his work, he was met near International Falls by Alexander N. Winchell, a youthful mineralogist and geologist studying the iron lands of the border region. As a result of their conversation, Winchell concluded that "The Canadian government has not waited for a joint survey to inform itself concerning the actual condition of the boundary; but it has quietly sent out a party of surveyors at its own expense to trace the line from Pigeon point to the Lake of the Woods." Brabazon, said Winchell, was "satisfied that the Treaty of Washington [*Webster-Ashburton Treaty*] is in agreement with the physical features."[12]

After Brabazon's reconnaissance there was little chance that Great Britain and Canada would consider relinquishing Hunter Island. The ill-founded Minnesota claim persisted for a time, however, largely because of the efforts of Winchell and his father, Newton H., archaeologist, author, and head of the state's geological survey. In an article entitled "Minnesota's Northern Boundary," written in 1895 and published in the *Minnesota Historical Society Collections* in 1898, Alexander Winchell reiterated the contention that the boundary should have followed the most continuous water passage. He found it "hard to understand why Mr. Webster, in the treaty of 1842, did not insist upon the line through the water courses which was clearly intended by the treaty of 1783."

Although there was virtually no hope of persuading the State Department to support a claim to Hunter Island, Newton Winchell continued to investigate the subject. In 1907, when it seemed the United States and Great Britain would soon agree to survey and mark the line as defined by the Webster-Ashburton Treaty, his conclusions were at last published in *Science* magazine. The United States, he said, had lost about 2,500 square miles of land along Minnesota's northern boundary because the line diverged from the most continuous water passage at the Kaministikwia River, Hunter Island, and the northernmost canoe route from Rainy Lake to Lake of the Woods. This contention, which unfortunately revealed inadequate historical investigation, was based on various old maps showing divergent waterways and on Winchell's undocumented conclusion that the treaty makers in 1783 had intended the boundary to follow consistently the most continuous water passage from Lake Superior to the northwest point of Lake of the Woods.[13]

Nevertheless Winchell recognized that Webster had signed away any hope of extending Minnesota farther northward. By naming specific boundary lakes, the infamous treaty had cut off "further uncertainty and controversy," denying the United States an opportunity to gain a line along the most continuous water route. He did not criticize Webster personally. Rather he faulted the boundary commissioners, whose advice Webster had followed, for being influenced by "the Canadian *voyageurs* . . . the only men acquainted with the region . . . who were then British subjects" looking for ways "to shift the flexible boundary line farther and farther toward the south." Winchell's effort was a futile exercise which raised no serious doubts about the validity of the boundary line fixed by Webster and Ashburton, for the United States had no historical or legal reasons for claiming Hunter Island. His writings serve, however, to epitomize the Minnesota school of thought that tried to promote the acquisition of the controversial area by the American government.

The congressional resolutions of 1896 demonstrated broad support for a survey east of Lake of the Woods, but the project was neglected in favor of other critical issues. Among Congress' concerns was the long-lived controversy over the boundary between the southern Alaskan Panhandle and British Columbia. The Canadian government's failure to reconcile its differences with the Americans prompted Great Britain to take matters into its own hands in 1897. The British Foreign Office and the United States Department of State established a joint high commission, which met in 1898–99 to discuss a wide range of problems—including the boundary from Lake Superior to Lake of the Woods. Four years later the Alaskan boundary dispute was settled by a joint tribunal, established under the Treaty of 1903, which delineated a border largely in support of the line that had been proposed by the United States.[14]

The decision of the Alaskan tribunal fostered a climate of improved diplomatic relations between Great Britain and the United States, during which they were able to settle other boundary questions. To survey and mark the Alaskan Panhandle border, Canada's astronomer William King and Otto H. Tittmann, director of the United States Coast and Geodetic Survey, were named to head a joint commission. Between 1903 and 1908 they also had the task of resurveying and re-marking the boundary from the Rockies west to the Gulf of Georgia. In 1906 they were given the added responsibility of measuring and marking the 141st meridian from the Alaskan Panhandle line to the Arctic Ocean.[15]

During this era of activity other neglected sections of the boundary were brought to public attention. The line through Passamaquoddy Bay had never been surveyed and marked, and there were complaints about inadequate marking along other portions of the northeast border. In 1903 these problems received publicity in an article written for *National Geographic Magazine* by John W. Foster, former secretary of state. In his historical summary Foster mentioned particularly the boundary west of Lake Superior. "It is charged by Canada," he wrote, "that the United States Land Office has surveyed, platted, and sold to Americans a considerable extent of land on the Minnesota-Wisconsin frontier which really belongs to Canada." Alluding to Brabazon's work, he implied that the United States was also a wronged party, because "The Government of the Dominion has sought on its own account to survey and mark the boundary in that region without the cooperation of the American authorities, but our Government has not accepted this survey."[16] Foster's reference to Wisconsin was in error, as was his statement that Brabazon had marked the boundary. Nevertheless his article again pointed to the need to survey and mark Minnesota's northern border so it would become identifiable upon the ground.

The Foreign Office and the State Department were determined that, for the first time in the history of the United States-Canada boundary, the entire line would be surveyed and marked in an atmosphere free of dispute. Seemingly it was at last possible to approach the project methodically without inflammatory pressures. The State Department employed as its principal consultant Chandler P. Anderson, a Wall Street lawyer who had been the United States secretary of the joint high tribunal in 1898–99 and the American associate counsel of the Alaskan boundary tribunal in 1903. A competent historical researcher as well as a legal expert, Anderson made specific recommendations concerning the authority of existing treaties and identified those problems which could be resolved only through a new agreement. He prepared a memorandum and a draft of a possible new treaty on the northern boundary. His memorandum reviewed each section of the line, identifying its origin in *existing treaties*, its previous surveys, and its current status, and suggesting that parts of it should be measured under the authority of old agreements and other unmarked sections under a new treaty.[17]

Officials in the State Department and the Foreign Office rejected Anderson's proposal. Instead they wanted one document that would provide for the necessary work along the entire border. The result was the Treaty of 1908, which authorized surveys in Passamaquoddy Bay, *along* the St. Croix River, and from the mouth of the Pigeon River to the northwest point of Lake of the Woods, and resurveys from the source of the St. Croix to the St.

Lawrence and from Lake of the Woods to the summit of the Rocky Mountains. The treaty endorsed the nearly completed resurvey of the line west of the Rockies and called for final mapping and marking of the short stretch between the 49th parallel and the Pacific. To accomplish this work Great Britain and the United States each agreed to appoint "an expert geographer or surveyor as commissioners."[18]

In addition the 1908 pact provided for the re-establishment of the boundary through the St. Lawrence River and the Great Lakes from St. Regis, New York, to the mouth of the Pigeon River. But this time the task was given to a joint Canadian-American body already in existence. Under Article 4 it was assigned to the International Waterways Commission, which had been created in 1905 by concurrent Canadian and United States statutes to co-ordinate such common problems as fishing and water flow in the St. Lawrence and the Great Lakes.

Soon after the treaty was ratified, Great Britain and the United States named King and Tittmann as the Canadian and American commissioners under the survey and resurvey articles. Both men were still actively fulfilling their earlier assignments. From 1908 to 1925 they and their successors worked under the authority of the award of the Alaskan tribunal of 1903, the Alaskan boundary Treaty of 1906, and the Treaty of 1908. In practice this meant the commissioners jointly planned surveys and resurveys, shifting their field parties as necessary along the line from the Atlantic to the Pacific and north to the Alaskan border.[19]

The full-time staffs of the United States and Canadian commissions normally numbered about 20 men each. The commissioners co-ordinated the field work, which was supervised by their two chief engineers, each of whom often led one of his country's surveying parties. A unit usually consisted of a head surveyor, one or two assistants, and a number of seasonal laborers hired in the locale of the assignment. The number of groups at work depended upon the scope of the season's project. In general progress was regulated by the weather or the condition of the ground; in one instance, however, the lack of funds near the end of the fiscal year delayed the American surveyors until well into July. To support the survey the United States government annually provided about $140,000 in the State Department appropriation. Tittmann was paid nothing extra for his service as commissioner, because he received a salary from the Coast and Geodetic Survey. In 1915, when Edward C. Barnard succeeded Tittmann, the survey budget was increased to include an annual salary of $5,000 for the commissioner. Canadian expenses were comparable to those of the United States.[20]

The efforts on the Minnesota-Canada border were carried out in two separate projects. From the northwest point of Lake of the Woods westward to the summit of the Rockies the line had to be resurveyed and remonumented; from the northwest point eastward to Lake Superior the boundary had never been surveyed and marked. By the end of the 1911 season the American and Canadian parties had nearly completed the resurvey across the plains to the Red River. One of their most aggravating problems was Cameron's legacy of curved lines between monuments, which were difficult to locate on the ground.[21]

The work from the Red River to the northwest point of Lake of the Woods was assigned to the United States. Using horse-drawn sleighs, the American crew distributed cast-iron monuments and other heavy materials along the marshy line in February and March, 1912. With the coming of the spring thaw the men set to work, completing the resurvey and remonumenting along the 49th parallel to the lake by September. Late in that month they established camp on Harrison Creek at Angle Inlet, then spent several weeks conducting a detailed topographic and hydrographic survey of the immediate area. Part of their purpose was to redetermine the location of the northwesternmost point of Lake of the Woods, which the commissions of the 1870s had failed to mark. Once again taking advantage of frozen ground in the winter of 1913, the Americans used teams and sleighs to drop materials along the 16-mile meridian, marking the boundary for mapmaking purposes on the ice-topped lake as well as on land. With this advance preparation, the setting of the monuments was accomplished soon after the ground thawed.[22]

The cast-iron monuments erected along the boundary in 1912 and 1913 were similar to those set in the 1870s. They had the same dimensions—eight feet high, eight inches square at the bottom, and four inches square at the top—with a pyramidal cap, the point of which was to be exactly on the line. Their corners were more rounded than those of the originals, however, and since their thicker iron shell was filled with concrete rather than wood, they weighed about 95 pounds more. The new monuments had a three-foot base set in concrete with a five-foot shaft above ground.

On the flange of each marker was a small brass plate inscribed with such details as the elevation. The monuments along the 49th parallel bore in raised letters the words "CANADA" on the north side, "UNITED STATES" on the south, "CONVENTION OF 1818" on the east, and "TREATY OF 1908" on the west. Along the meridian line the shafts were turned so "CANADA" faced west and "UNITED STATES" east. In addition to the markers set on the boundary, the Americans in 1913 placed two cast-iron monuments on opposite shores of Angle Inlet to serve as references for the southernmost intersection of the 1783 and 1818 lines. No others were erected north of that point. The two special monuments bore only the words "REFERENCE MARK" on the sides toward the inlet.

The Canadian and American parties, working independently, completed the task of erecting monuments in 1913. The final work of numbering the markers from the Red River westward was carried out as a special project after all had been set. The system used was the reverse of that employed in the 1870s, for the monuments were numbered consecutively eastward beginning with 0 at Point Roberts on the Gulf of Georgia and ending with 925 at the northwest point on the meridian line at Angle Inlet. A three-man American team sent to the Rockies in 1914 moved with dispatch to continue the numbering task until they encountered the infamous swamps east of the Red River early in November. There they delayed the work until the ground froze solid, then completed it on December 14.

The second part of the Minnesota effort—surveying and marking for the first time the boundary between the northwest point of Lake of the Woods and the mouth of the Pigeon River—proved to be the single most arduous project authorized by the Treaty of 1908. Some field work was done annually during the ten years from 1908 to 1918, but the final definition of the line required additional efforts in 1921, 1922, 1925, and 1926. Beginning with a meeting of King and Tittmann in December, 1908, the boundary commissioners over the years formulated several general rules to govern the survey and the marking of the border. They agreed the demarcation would consist of a series of straight lines, which should conform as closely as possible to the curved lines shown on the original maps prepared by Barclay's and Porter's men. In keeping with the dictates of the 1908 treaty, they concurred that the border "so far as practicable, shall be a water line and shall not intersect islands." Through the major stream, the Rainy River, the boundary was to be established midway between the banks, except where it passed islands, each of which had to be left in its entirety to either Canada or the United States. To avoid dividing four islands, the commissioners found it necessary to adjust the direct route of the 1820s from near Oak Island in Lake of the Woods to a point near the mouth of the Rainy River.[23]

Although these guidelines evolved over nearly two decades, Tittmann and King had agreed from the beginning on a thorough triangulation survey of the boundary starting at the mouth of the Pigeon River. A small American party, headed by W. B. Fairfield, an engineer employed by the United States Coast and Geodetic Survey, began the work modestly in 1908. By October, 1911, the surveyors reached Gneiss Lake, then known as Round Lake, having spent three seasons and part of a fourth conducting a triangulation survey involving continual traversing back and forth between Canada and the United States—a task inhibited by the steep, rocky terrain, especially along the Pigeon River. The crews did not set any permanent monuments, but they placed temporary markers identifying reference points and recorded all their calculations as well as the exact location of all triangulation stations. They also cleared a 20-foot vista strip over the long Watap Portage between Mountain and Watap lakes, one of only three places on the entire Lake of the Woods-Lake Superior boundary where there was no connecting waterway.

The pace of the triangulation survey increased in 1912 when a Canadian party, having finished its work west of the Red River, was assigned to the Lake of the Woods area. This group, headed by James J. McArthur, who later served as Canada's boundary commissioner, searched unsuccessfully for David Thompson's monument, conducted a survey from the northwest point east to Oak Island, and placed permanent reference markers on land flanking the boundary. Meanwhile Fairfield's men progressed along the line from Gneiss Lake to the west end of Knife Lake. As in previous years they traveled by canoes along the border. At the end of the season they relied upon logging companies in the region for storing equipment and for transportation by boats to nearby railroads in either Minnesota or Ontario.

The work was greatly accelerated in 1913 by four crews—three American and one Canadian. Fairfield's men continued westward; the two other United States parties, which were much larger, and McArthur's Canadian unit worked alternate sections of the boundary from Baudette, near the mouth of the Rainy River, eastward to Lac la Croix. As they progressed they identified turning points along the mid-water line and placed permanent monuments on both banks of the Rainy River and on the islands in the larger lakes. At the end of the 1914 season the Americans working from the east had reached Crooked Lake, and the surveyors coming from the west were at Lac la Croix.[24]

By July, 1914, King and Tittman could report encouraging progress, not only along the Minnesota-Ontario boundary but in other sections of the United States-Canada border as well. Tittman informed Secretary of State William Jennings Bryan that the line was completed in Alaska, west of the Rockies, and along the short 20-mile stretch in Passamaquoddy Bay. He also reported that most of the work had been done between Lake of the Woods and Lake Superior. The one major remaining project was to re-establish just over a third of the 658-mile northeast boundary from the source of the St. Croix to the St. Lawrence.[25]

While Tittmann was satisfied with the commission's accomplishments, he was disturbed by confirmed reports of disputed ownership of numerous islands in the Minnesota-Ontario border lakes. He informed the State Department "that some small islands belonging to the United

States have been surveyed by the Canadian Land Office and probably granted to private owners by Canada and vice versa islands belonging to Canada have been surveyed by the U.S. Land Office and granted by the United States." As the survey advanced, he predicted, additional small islands would be noted, "the nationality of which is not now known, but will become known as soon as the Commissioners have fixed the boundary." To minimize problems Tittman wanted the secretary of the interior to temporarily withdraw from entry any public lands on islands within two miles of the boundary. He also asked for the General Land Office plats of the entire area from Lake of the Woods to Lake Superior, so they could be compared with the boundary maps being prepared.[26]

The survey clarified the legal status of numerous islands, some of which were transferred from one country to the other. Such transfers apparently were not always communicated to local officials, however, as the case of so-called Warren Island in Lac la Croix illustrates. In 1884 George H. Warren of Minneapolis and a partner received a United States patent to the island. For over 50 years Warren and his heirs paid taxes to St. Louis County. When the United States government attempted to purchase the property from the Warren estate in the early 1930s, it was discovered that the island lay on the Canadian side of the new line surveyed under the 1908 treaty. Neither St. Louis County nor Ontario officials seem to have been aware of the error.[27]

The scope of the Minnesota-Ontario boundary project was greatly reduced in 1915, when most of the surveyors were sent to the Maine-Quebec highlands. Remaining in the area were a Canadian group of about two dozen men working on Lac la Croix and a United States party of about 20 on Crooked Lake. The following season the Americans set permanent monuments on a section of the line east of Crooked Lake, while the Canadians completed the basic survey to that point from the west. Eight years after the work had begun, the east and west surveys were joined, and the original surveying program was complete. In the meantime, however, the commissioners had decided to undertake more detailed mapping and monumenting than had been anticipated in 1908. Thus during 1917 and 1918 Americans and Canadians completed contour maps of the border waters and adjacent lands and rechecked turning points in narrow waterways. Only after this was done could permanent monuments be placed on the easternmost section of the line along the Pigeon River—the first area to be surveyed in 1908 and the last to be marked a decade later.[28]

The 426-mile border from the northwest point of Lake of the Woods to the mouth of the Pigeon River was defined with 1,373 reference markers placed on lake shores, islands, and stream banks and nine boundary monuments erected on the three portages—Swamp, Height of Land, and Watap. The former, comprised of several types, were numbered consecutively from west to east with the even numbers in the United States and the odd numbers in Canada. The most common were 1,279 short bronze posts two inches square. Two cast-iron reference markers were set at the most northwest point of Lake of the Woods. From there to the lower Rainy River near Baudette the line was referenced with 84 wrought-iron monuments measuring three feet long and two inches square. Seven bronze disks were placed along the lower Pigeon River to provide additional reference points after the bronze posts had been drilled into place. The nine monuments erected on the three portages were numbered on the boundary maps in a separate series from the reference markers, with numbers one through three on Swamp Portage between Swamp and Cypress lakes, four through six over Height of Land Portage connecting North and South lakes, and seven through nine on Watap Portage. Among the monuments were five-foot bronze obelisks and short, conical posts of bronze and of aluminum-bronze.[29]

After the major field work was completed in 1918, the boundary surveys under the Treaty of 1908 lingered on while all calculations were rechecked and recorded, complete sets of official maps were prepared, and final reports were written. The official report on the line from the northwesternmost point of Lake of the Woods to Lake Superior was published in 1931; that on the boundary from the Gulf of Georgia to Lake of the Woods appeared in 1937. Not until these documents were made public was the work authorized in 1908 finally completed.

While the last details of the 1908 surveys were being finished, the United States, Great Britain, and Canada worked to quiet once and for all the long-standing problems of Cameron's curved lines between monuments and the looped line in the northwest area of Angle Inlet. Both commissioners urged that a new treaty be negotiated to deal with these and other boundary questions, but their governments were slow to act. For a time the discussions were held in abeyance while the three nations dealt with World War I and its postwar settlements. Early in 1920 American commissioner Edward Barnard again reminded the State Department of the unresolved matters. After noting that only some monumenting in the St. Croix River area was required to complete the field work under the 1908 treaty, he reviewed various proposals made by the commissioners over the years. Included were a recommendation to define an additional course along the boundary in Passamaquoddy Bay, which had been set by a treaty in 1910, and a call for the creation of a permanent joint commission to maintain the 5,526-mile boundary between the United States and Canada. Although the State Department was unconvinced of the need for a permanent commission, it assured Barnard that the matter would be looked into "at the appropriate time."[30]

The appropriate time came slowly. Not until nearly five years after the State Department invited Barnard to draft a treaty was an agreement completed with Canada. Some of the delay was caused by the department's unwillingness to ask Congress to create another long-lived commission. In fact early treaty drafts provided that the joint body could be abolished by unilateral action of either country after six years. Among the first prominent supporters of a permanent commission was John W. Davis, United States ambassador to Great Britain, who publicized the United States-Canada line as "The Unguarded Boundary." He believed a new treaty would be an indication of "international friendship," buttressing what he thought should be the major foreign policy of the United States—"the sedulous cultivation of the self-governing dominions of the British Empire and encouragement of their disposition toward independent action."[31] In other words the ambassador supported Canada's quest to control its own foreign affairs, an aim stimulated by its participation in World War I.

The Dominion government assumed treaty-making powers shortly before a boundary convention was written and ratified in 1925. This agreement is the most recent boundary treaty affecting the Minnesota-Canada line and the first to be negotiated between the United States and Canada. Its provisions carried out the major recommendations of the boundary commissioners.[32]

Article 1 shifted the northwesternmost point of Lake of the Woods due south nearly a mile to the most southerly intersection of the 1783 and 1818 lines. This meant Minnesota lost to Canada the two and half acres of water area enclosed in the looped line. Article 2 provided for straight lines connecting monuments from Lake of the Woods to the summit of the Rocky Mountains. The treaty noted that the difference between curved and straight courses averaged only four inches and in no case exceeded one and eight-tenths feet.

The third article defined an additional course in Passamaquoddy Bay, and the fourth continued the positions of joint boundary commissioners created by the 1908 treaty. These officials were specifically and jointly "empowered and directed: to inspect the various sections of the boundary line between the United States and the Dominion of Canada and between Alaska and the Dominion of Canada at such times as they shall deem necessary; to repair all damaged monuments and buoys; to relocate and rebuild monuments which have been destroyed; to keep the boundary vistas open; to move boundary monuments to new sites and establish such additional monuments and buoys as they shall deem desirable; to maintain at all times an effective boundary line . . . and to determine the location of any point of the boundary line which may become necessary in the settlement of any question that may arise between the two governments."

Since 1925 the International Boundary Commission's principal task has been to maintain the boundary as numerous features along it have been changed by road construction, lumbering, altered water levels, erection of advertising signs, vandalism, and natural erosion and the growth of vegetation. Such changes constantly challenge the commission, which is responsible for maintaining a visible marking of the line on the ground, recording accurately all newly erected monuments and calculations necessary to redefine the boundary at any given point, and regulating certain activities, such as construction across the border or on the vista.

Officially the commission is a single body, with the American section headquartered in Washington, D.C., and the Canadian based in Ottawa. Each country provides its own commissioner, staff, and funding. The two commissioners usually meet several times a year in their headquarters cities or at boundary sites to plan and inspect field work and to take regulatory action. In some instances maintenance and regulation are shared with several other agencies. One of these is known as the International Joint Commission, which lately has become more involved with environmental aspects affecting the boundary waters. Among the proposals for construction considered by the commissioners are those dealing with power transmission lines, pipelines, billboards, authorized and unauthorized roads, buried telephone cables, and fences.[33]

The two sections are modestly staffed, normally with three or four engineers and an administrative assistant in addition to the commissioner. Their task of maintaining the 5,526 miles of boundary separating Canada and the contiguous United States and Alaska is an enormous one. During the first decade following ratification of the 1925 treaty, the commissioners planned to inspect the entire line at least once during each ten-year period. This plan was not continued. The commission sends personnel into the field each year, as it has since 1925, with the size of the crews determined by the type and amount of work to be done. In 1978 the commissioners developed a schedule of projects to be undertaken during the following 15 years.[34]

Because most of the boundary between Minnesota and Canada runs through water or swamp, its monuments are subject to natural deterioration and require regular maintenance. In the decade of the 1960s, for example, engineers and the commissioners worked on the Minnesota line during parts of six years. Late in 1977 and during January, 1978, a party of six men again checked the border between Minnesota and Manitoba, clearing the vista along the meridian line of the Northwest Angle and along the 49th parallel to the west during the winter. Like those who coped with the same section in the 1870s, the

LOGGERS in Minnesota's north woods about 1890 took a break for lunch from the swingdingle. Much of the timber cut during this era was illegally sold to Canadian mills at Fort Frances and Kenora. A congressional act passed in 1902 to stop the practice also resulted in opening Minnesota land along the Rainy River to homesteaders.

THE STEAMER "D. L. Mather" was one of many that towed log rafts through Lake of the Woods to sawmills in 1901, when this photograph was taken near Oak Point.

CONGRESSMAN Charles A. Towne of Duluth led the last fight by Minnesotans and others in 1896 to adjust the boundary between Lake Superior and Lake of the Woods in order to secure Hunter Island for the United States. Although the effort was futile, it brought to public attention the critical need to mark Minnesota's northern border on the ground.

LUMBER-SHIPPING activities on the bank of the Rainy River at Fort Frances, Ontario, indicate that the settlement had developed from a remote trading station to a bustling commercial center by 1901, when this photo was taken. The same year the railroad reached the town, adding to its importance.

GOLD enticed hundreds of prospectors and businessmen to Rainy Lake City by 1895, just two years after the precious metal was discovered on nearby Little American Island in Rainy Lake. Although the rush was short-lived, it attracted many permanent settlers to the northern border region.

INTERNATIONAL FALLS about 1902, when the village was still called Koochiching, was on the verge of a boom triggered by the construction in 1905–10 of a dam over Koochiching Falls in the Rainy River. Completion of the dam helped transform the town into one of Minnesota's paper-producing centers.

WORK CREWS, wagons, and supplies of the international boundary commission working under the Treaty of 1908 rode the flatcars of the Duluth, Rainy Lake and Winnipeg Railroad in 1913 to reach the border area. The logging line crossed the boundary between Ranier, Minnesota, and Fort Frances, Ontario. Courtesy National Archives, Washington, D.C.

MOSQUITOES, flies, and swamps constituted the most difficult challenges to surveyors and workmen measuring and marking Minnesota's northern boundary between 1908 and 1918. Both men and horses wore protective coverings against insect bites in 1912, but nothing could stop them or the wagons from sinking into the muddy morass. Courtesy National Archives.

WEARING HIP BOOTS, boundary workers in 1912 erected a monument in the swamps. The heavy cast-iron markers and materials used to set them were carried to this section of the border on the men's backs. Courtesy National Archives.

A 1972 PHOTOGRAPH of the author and the monument on the northernmost point of the meridian line at Northwest Angle illustrates how markers become tilted over time. Courtesy William E. Lass.

BRONZE-POST MONUMENTS were the most common among the 1,373 reference markers set along the 426-mile border from Lake of the Woods to Lake Superior. They measured two inches square, seven inches high, with a round, ten-inch shank. The split shank was driven over a wedge placed at the bottom of a drilled hole, holding the marker firmly in solid rock. From International Boundary Commission, *Joint Report . . . Lake of the Woods to Lake Superior* (1931).

THE BOUNDARY between the northwest point of Lake of the Woods and Baudette was referenced with 84 wrought-iron monuments set in a square concrete base with only the upper foot above ground. This marker was erected on Rose Island in Lake of the Woods about 1913. Photo by William E. Lass, 1972.

REFERENCE MARKER number 1112 was imbedded in rock near a lodge on Gunflint Lake. Photo by William E. Lass, 1973.

PORTAGING equipment used by the United States boundary commission in 1913 included this narrow-track railroad and handcar that transported men, materials, and canoes over Prairie Portage between Birch and Carp lakes. From International Boundary Commission, *Joint Report . . . of the Boundary . . . from the Northwestern Point of Lake of the Woods to Lake Superior* (1931).

A CAST-IRON MONUMENT, number 833, has marked the boundary at Emerson, Manitoba, since it was erected in 1913. Photo by William E. Lass, 1972.

THE INTERNATIONAL Boundary Commission placed a set of ornamental monuments at the border crossing of Highway 75 at Emerson, just east of marker number 833. These markers are made of concrete covered with a polished, quartz-aggregate surface and rise about five feet above the base.
Photo by William E. Lass, 1971.

A SHORT, conical, bronze post, photographed by the author with guide Louie Reid, marks the boundary at the lower end of Height of Land Portage connecting North and South lakes. This type of marker, set in a concrete base, is held erect by a circle of concrete formed by removing the bottom of a galvanized washtub, inverting it over the post, and filling it with cement. Three similar markers of aluminum-bronze were set on Watap Portage between Mountain and Watap lakes. The Swamp Portage line between Cypress and Swamp lakes was marked with one conical bronze post and two five-foot, bronze obelisks. Photo by William E. Lass, 1973.

THE INTERNATIONAL Boundary, established on the principle of a mid-water line, zigzags its way between turning points in Loon Lake and Lac la Croix. Because much of the terrain between Lake Superior and Lake of the Woods is similar to that in this photograph, it is difficult for most people to visualize the border in that section of Minnesota. Photo by Royal Canadian Air Force, from International Boundary Commission, *Joint Report . . . Lake of the Woods to Lake Superior* (1931).

AFTER HEAVY RAINS and flooding in the 1960s, erosion toppled reference markers on the banks of the Rainy River. In 1968 employees of the International Boundary Commission relocated this monument farther away from the river. Courtesy Canadian Section, International Boundary Commission.

AN ALL-TERRAIN vehicle, used in 1966 for field work by the International Boundary Commission, crossed a temporary bridge over Poplar Creek along the meridian line on the Northwest Angle. Such vehicles make the transporting of workers and supplies in the marshy sections of Minnesota's northern boundary area a far less formidable task than it was in the 1870s and early 1900s. Courtesy United States Section, International Boundary Commission, Washington, D.C.

men found the swamps a severe test. Unlike their predecessors, however, they were able to use an all-terrain vehicle for greater ease of transportation. Of the 31 monuments on the portion of the boundary inspected in 1977–78, about a dozen required new obelisks and some 20 needed new concrete bases set on pilings. As they deteriorate or are lost, these and other markers will be replaced with newly designed monuments. One of the two new types is a four-foot shaft of high-strength, corrosion-resistant, and light-weight stainless steel. The other is a 400-pound, three-foot obelisk cut from white granite quarried in Quebec.[35]

In addition to its original responsibilities, the International Boundary Commission was given authority by the Treaty of 1925 to add markers identifying the border where it is crossed by highways and bridges. Between 1925 and 1937 pairs of specially designed ornamental monuments were erected at 14 crossings between the Gulf of Georgia and Lake of the Woods. One set was still in place in 1980 at Emerson, Manitoba, on opposite sides of Highway 75. A single marker, set in 1945, stood on the west side of the highway between Warroad, Minnesota, and Middleboro, Manitoba.[36]

To keep the boundary visible and to facilitate resurveying, the International Boundary Commission periodically clears the vista strip to a width of 20 feet at skyline height. From Lake Superior to Lake of the Woods, vistas are maintained only over the three portages. The remainder of Minnesota's border to the Red River must be kept cleared. Traditionally trees and brush were removed with saws and axes. Since the early 1960s the commission has used herbicides sprayed from tracked vehicles, which are able to move rapidly through swampy terrain. In some sections of the boundary, including the northern end of the meridian line at Northwest Angle, the vista may span up to 60 or 70 feet where it has become a roadway for logging vehicles.[37]

The existence of the vista has led to erroneous beliefs about it. Some people think the 20-foot clearing constitutes the boundary, which in truth legally consists of nothing more than a line no broader than its width upon a map. Others believe it represents a no-man's land along the border. For this view there are historical reasons dating back to 1908. About that time the boundary commissioners asked their governments' help in facilitating surveys of the line. In response President Theodore Roosevelt in 1908 withdrew from sale or entry all the public lands of the United States within 60 feet of the border. His proclamation affected only areas which had not been privately claimed, but there seems to have been a misconception from the start that it concerned all borderland. Over the next several decades Canadian provinces invoked similar measures. Thus, where there is publicly held land on both sides of the demarcation, a strip 120 feet wide remains as a boundary reservation, where surveying and vista-clearing are easily accomplished. In 1960 the International Boundary Commission received authority to enter private lands on both sides of the border for the purpose of cutting the vista.[38]

Over a period of 142 years of Anglo-American relations, the Minnesota-Canada boundary evolved from an impossible description in a treaty to a definite, officially fixed line identifiable at any point on land or water. The diplomatic phase of its history, which occurred before Minnesota was established, defined the border in treaties between the United States and Great Britain. The second phase—the surveying and monumenting of the boundary—coincided with the closing of the frontiers on both sides of the line. The Treaty of 1925, which ushered in the third phase, marked an important transition. It symbolized the end of the frontier struggle, with its hostilities, disputes, and uncertainties, and the beginning of a new era characterized by the recognition that both countries had reached their territorial limits with respect to each other. The evolution of the Minnesota-Canada boundary culminated in the present co-operative work by Canada and the United States in maintaining the peaceful border between the two nations.

Reference Notes

CHAPTER 1.
THE REVOLUTIONARY WAR
BOUNDARY SETTLEMENT—*Pages 3–18.*

[1] For a review of French activities in the New World from 1615 to 1763, and on the Treaty of 1763, see Ray A. Billington, *Westward Expansion: A History of the American Frontier,* 103–131 (4th ed., New York, 1974).

[2] The role of the boundary question in Anglo-French relations is thoroughly discussed in Max Savelle, *The Diplomatic History of the Canadian Boundary, 1749–1763* (Reprint ed., New York, 1968). On the Royal Proclamation, here and below, see Alfred L. Burt, *The Old Province of Quebec,* 76–78 (Reprint ed., New York, 1970). Canada consisted of the old province of Quebec until 1791, when it was split into Upper and Lower Canada; the Dominion of Canada was not established until 1867, after which the provinces as they are now known were formed. The terms "Canada" and "Canadians," as used in this book, generally refer to British North America and its inhabitants.

[3] Burt, *Old Province of Quebec,* 77–79; Clarence M. Burton, "The Boundary Lines of the United States under the Treaty of 1782," in *Michigan Historical Collections,* 38:133 (Lansing, 1912).

[4] A[lfred] L. Burt, *The United States, Great Britain, and British North America from the Revolution to the Establishment of Peace after the War of 1812,* 20–23 (Reprint ed., New York, 1961); Burt, *Old Province of Quebec,* 180, 186.

[5] Henry recalled his trading career in *Travels and Adventures in Canada and the Indian Territories,* edited by James Bain (Boston, 1901). On Grand Portage, here and below, see June D. Holmquist and Jean A. Brookins, *Minnesota's Major Historic Sites: A Guide,* 152–156 (Revised ed., St. Paul, 1972); John Parker, ed., *The Journals of Jonathan Carver and Related Documents, 1766–1770,* 130 (St. Paul, 1976).

[6] Nancy L. Woolworth, "Grand Portage in the Revolutionary War," in *Minnesota History,* 44:200 (Summer, 1975); Solon J. Buck, "The Story of the Grand Portage," in *Minnesota History Bulletin,* 5:18 (February, 1923); "Petition from the North-West Traders," May 11, 1780, published with "Note E. The North West Trade," in *Report on Canadian Archives, 1888,* 62 (Ottawa, 1889).

[7] Billington, *Westward Expansion,* 180–183; Samuel F. Bemis, *The Diplomacy of the American Revolution,* 57, 61–65, 67, 84–87 (Revised ed., Bloomington, Ind., 1957).

[8] Here and below, see Richard B. Morris, *The Peacemakers: The Great Powers and American Independence,* 17, 18 (New York, 1965); Paul C. Phillips, *The West in the Diplomacy of the American Revolution,* 114, 116, 119 (Reprint ed., New York, 1967).

[9] *Secret Journals of the Acts and Proceedings of Congress,* 2:138 (Boston, 1820). The 45th parallel runs through the northern edge of the Twin Cities; it is marked by a plaque on a boulder placed on the east side of Cleveland Ave. at Roselawn Ave. just north of St. Paul.

[10] *Secret Journals,* 2:224–228; Francis Wharton, ed., *The Revolutionary Diplomatic Correspondence of the United States,* 3:300–302 (Washington, 1889); Bemis, *Diplomacy of the American Revolution,* 174.

[11] Bemis, *Diplomacy of the American Revolution,* 101, 176; Phillips, *West in the Diplomacy of the American Revolution,* 128. Adams remained in Paris until July 27, 1780, when he went to Amsterdam to pursue diplomatic support. See Benjamin Franklin to the President of Congress, August 9, 1780, John Adams to the President of Congress, August 14, 1780, both in Wharton, ed., *Revolutionary Diplomatic Correspondence,* 4:21–23, 29.

[12] Morris, *Peacemakers,* 215; Bemis, *Diplomacy of the American Revolution,* 189; Wharton, ed., *Revolutionary Diplomatic Correspondence,* 4:505. All the appointed commissioners except Jefferson took part in the negotiations.

[13] Bemis, *Diplomacy of the American Revolution,* 190.

[14] ·[Edmond George Petty-Fitzmaurice] Fitzmaurice, *Life of William, Earl of Shelburne,* 2:118 (2nd ed., London, 1912).

[15] On Oswald, here and in the following three paragraphs, see *Dictionary of National Biography,* 14:1223 (New York, 1888); Fitzmaurice, *Shelburne,* 2:119; Bemis, *Diplomacy of the American Revolution,* 194, 195.

[16] "Notes for Conversation" of April 19, 1782, Franklin to John Adams, April 20, 1782, both in Albert H. Smyth, ed., *The Writings of Benjamin Franklin,* 8:472, 474 (Reprint ed., New York, 1970), hereafter cited as Franklin, *Writings.*

[17] Franklin, *Writings,* 8:527.

[18] Wharton, ed., *Revolutionary Diplomatic Correspondence,* 3:302, 5:87–94.

[19] Morris, *Peacemakers,* 287.

[20] Fitzmaurice, *Shelburne,* 2:124; Bemis, *Diplomacy of the American Revolution,* 203.

[21] Samuel F. Bemis, "Canada and the Peace Settlement of 1782–3," in *Canadian Historical Review,* 14:268 (September, 1933).

[22] Bemis, *Diplomacy of the American Revolution,* 205; Fitzmaurice, *Shelburne,* 2:165.

[23] Morris, *Peacemakers,* 306; Burt, *United States, Great Britain, and British North America,* 28; Wharton, ed., *Revolutionary Diplomatic Correspondence,* 6:23, 25–27. For more on the Mitchell map, see pp. 12–17, below.

[24] Morris, *Peacemakers,* 317; Bemis, in *Canadian Historical Review,* 14:276.

[25] Fitzmaurice, *Shelburne,* 2:175–182; Morris, *Peacemakers,* 330.

[26] Burt, *United States, Great Britain, and British North America,* 30; Morris, *Peacemakers,* 333, 338; Bemis, in *Canadian Historical Review,* 14:275.

[27] Wharton, ed., *Revolutionary Diplomatic Correspondence,* 5:805–807; Bemis, in *Canadian Historical Review,* 14:278.

[28] Morris, *Peacemakers,* 350, 354; Edgar W. McInnes, *The Unguarded Frontier: A History of American-Canadian Relations,* 72 (New York, 1942); Bemis, *Diplomacy of the American Revolution,* 230, 231; Fitzmaurice, *Shelburne,* 2:192. The term Northwest refers to the region north of the Ohio River later known as the Northwest Territory, established by the Ordinance of 1787, which embraced the present states of Ohio, Indiana, Illinois, Michigan, and Wisconsin and that part of Minnesota east of the Mississippi River. See R. Carlyle Buley, *The Old Northwest: Pioneer Period 1815–1840,* 1:vii, 111 (Bloomington, Ind., 1950); Charles O. Paullin, *Atlas of the Historical Geography of the United States,* plate 61 (Washington, D.C., 1932).

[29] Morris, *Peacemakers,* 350; Edward E. Hale and Edward E. Hale, Jr., *Franklin in France,* 2:162 (Reprint ed., New York, 1969).

[30] Frank Monaghan, ed., *The Diary of John Jay during the Peace Negotiations of 1782,* 13 (New Haven, 1934); Wharton, ed., *Revolutionary Diplomatic Correspondence,* 5:838, 839. Adams arrived in Paris on October 26, 1782, from the Netherlands, where he had completed a successful diplomatic mission.

[31] Wharton, ed., *Revolutionary Diplomatic Correspondence,* 6:113.

[32] Wharton, ed., *Revolutionary Diplomatic Correspondence,* 5:851.

[33] Wharton, ed., *Revolutionary Diplomatic Correspondence,* 5:856; Burt, *United States, Great Britain, and British North America,* 31.

[34] George W. Brown, "The St. Lawrence in the Boundary Settlement of 1783," in *Canadian Historical Review*, 9:230 (September, 1928); Charles F. Adams, ed., *The Works of John Adams*, 8:20 (Boston, 1853); Wharton, ed., *Revolutionary Diplomatic Correspondence*, 5:853.

As ultimately worded in Article 8 of the final treaty, this provision read: "The Navigation of the River Mississippi from its Source to the Ocean, shall for ever remain free and open to the Subjects of Great Britain and the Citizens of the United States." Hunter Miller, ed., *Treaties and Other International Acts of the United States of America*, 2:100 (Washington, D.C., 1931).

[35] Wharton, ed., *Revolutionary Diplomatic Correspondence*, 5:851; Fitzmaurice, *Shelburne*, 2:201; Morris, *Peacemakers*, 362, 367; Clarence W. Alvord, "When Minnesota Was a Pawn of International Politics," in *Minnesota History Bulletin*, 4:314, 317 (August–November, 1922).

[36] Wharton, ed., *Revolutionary Diplomatic Correspondence*, 6:132; Jay to Lord Grenville, September 4, 1794, in *American State Papers, Foreign Relations*, 1:491 (Washington, D.C., 1832), hereafter cited as *ASP, FR*.

[37] Hale and Hale, *Franklin in France*, 2:180, 184, 189; Miller, ed., *Treaties*, 2:96–100.

[38] Miller, ed., *Treaties*, 2:96; Bemis, *Diplomacy of the American Revolution*, 234n.

[39] Miller, ed., *Treaties*, 2:97.

[40] Wharton, ed., *Revolutionary Diplomatic Correspondence*, 6:107; McInnes, *Unguarded Frontier*, 71.

[41] Burt, *United States, Great Britain, and British North America*, 34; Annah May Soule, "The International Boundary Line of Michigan," in *Michigan Historical Collections*, 26:608 (Lansing, 1896).

[42] Burt, *United States, Great Britain, and British North America*, 34.

[43] Burt, *United States, Great Britain, and British North America*, 34; the quote appears in Alvord, in *Minnesota History Bulletin*, 4:318.

[44] Great Britain's interest in the commercial development of the interior is well described by Brown, in *Canadian Historical Review*, 9:223–238.

[45] Miller, ed., *Treaties*, 3:349. On Mitchell, here and below, see Edmund Berkeley and Dorothy Smith Berkeley, *Dr. John Mitchell: The Man Who Made the Map of North America* (Chapel Hill, N.C., 1974), which emphasizes Mitchell's scientific and medical attainments. See also *Dictionary of American Biography*, 13:50 (New York, 1934); *Dictionary of National Biography*, 38:70 (1894); "John Mitchell's Map of the British and French Dominions in North America," compiled and edited by Walter W. Ristow from various published works of Lawrence Martin, in *A La Carte: Selected Papers on Maps and Atlases*, 102–113 (Washington, D.C., 1972); Gordon W. Jones, "The Library of Doctor John Mitchell of Urbanna," and John F. Dorman and James F. Lewis, "Doctor John Mitchell, F.R.S., Native Virginian," both in *Virginia Magazine of History and Biography*, 76:441–443, 437–440 (October, 1968).

[46] Miller, ed., *Treaties*, 3:330, 333.

[47] The various editions of the map are extensively described by Miller, ed., *Treaties*, 3:328–356, who based his study on a manuscript entitled "Mitchell's Map, An Account of the Origin and Uses of the Most Important Map in American History," by Lawrence Martin, chief of the Division of Maps in the Library of Congress from 1925 to 1933. The library's efforts to locate Martin's manuscript since his death in 1955 have been unsuccessful. Richard W. Stephenson, Geography and Map Division, Library of Congress, to the author, November 19, 1971.

[48] Charles C. Hyde, "Maps as Evidence in International Boundary Disputes," in *American Journal of International Law*, 27:311 (April, 1933).

[49] James White, "Boundary Disputes and Treaties," in Adam Shortt and Arthur G. Doughty, eds., *Canada and Its Provinces*, 8:837 (Toronto, 1914). Renville Wheat, comp., *Maps of Michigan and the Great Lakes, 1545-1845*, 21 (Detroit, 1967) and Robert W. Karrow, Jr., *Mapping the Great Lakes Region: Motive and Method*, [8] (Chicago, 1977), both attributed the origin of Isle Philippeaux to Jacques Nicolas Bellin, whose map of 1744 introduced it as one of six nonexistent islands in Lake Superior that were created and named to flatter influential government officials, especially Jean-Frederic Philippeaux de Ponchartrain, Comte de Maurepas.

[50] On the Indian's sketch map, see Lawrence J. Burpee, ed., *Journals and Letters of Pierre Galtier de Varennes de la Vérendrye and His Sons*, 53 (Toronto, 1927); N[ewton] H. Winchell and Warren Upham, *The Geology of Minnesota*, 1:18 (Minnesota Geological and Natural History Survey, *Final Report*—Minneapolis, 1884). See also *A New Map of Part of North America, from the Latitude of 40 to 68 Degrees* (originally published to illustrate Arthur Dobbs's *Remarks upon Captain Middleton's Defence*, London, 1744); Guillaume Delisle, *L'Amerique Septentrionale* (1722), taken from I. Covens and C. Mortimer, *Nieuve Atlas* (1730–39); Henry Popple, *A Map of the British Empire in America with the French and Spanish Settlements Adjacent Thereto* (London, 1733), all in Geography and Map Division, Library of Congress.

[51] Miller, ed., *Treaties*, 3:348; Lawrence Martin and Samuel F. Bemis, "Franklin's Red-Line Map Was a Mitchell," in *New England Quarterly*, 10:106, 109 (March, 1937).

[52] Adams, *Works*, 8:20, 210, 392, 398, 519; Miller, ed., *Treaties*, 3:329; Franklin, *Writings*, 10:93 (London, 1907).

[53] Miller, ed., *Treaties*, 3:330, 4:404n (1934); Franklin, *Writings*, 8:637. See also Chapter 7, below.

[54] The Jay copy refers to a first impression of the third edition of Mitchell's map that was held by the family of John Jay until 1843 and later added to the collections of the New York Historical Society. Martin believed it was used during the opening phases of the Paris negotiations in 1782. The King George copy, so called because it was in the library of George III before its transfer to the British Museum, was a fourth edition of the map. Martin concluded that it was used during the period of the peace negotiations. Miller, ed., *Treaties*, 3:341–349.

[55] For descriptions of the advantages of Mitchell's errors to the United States, see Alfred J. Hill, "How the Mississippi River and the Lake of the Woods Became Instrumental in the Establishment of the Northwestern Boundary of the United States," in J[acob] V. Brower, *The Mississippi River and Its Source*, 305–352 (*Minnesota Historical Collections*, vol. 7, 1893); Alexander N. Winchell, "Minnesota's Northern Boundary," in *Minnesota Historical Collections*, 8:185–212 (St. Paul, 1898).

[56] S[imon] J. Dawson, "Memorandum on Early Maps of the Disputed Territory," 275, in *Statutes, Documents and Papers Bearing on the Discussion Respecting the Northern and Western Boundaries of the Province of Ontario* (Toronto, 1878).

[57] Here and the following two paragraphs, see Brown, in *Canadian Historical Review*, 9:231, 233, 236.

[58] Frobisher to Adam Mabane, April 19, 1784, in *Report on Canadian Archives, 1888*, 63. On the founding of the North West Company, see Gordon C. Davidson, *The North West Company*, 1–31 (Reprint ed., New York, 1967).

[59] Benjamin and Joseph Frobisher to Governor Frederick Haldimand, October 4, 1784, in *Report on Canadian Archives, 1890*, 48–51 (Ottawa, 1891); Davidson, *North West Company*, 47, 105. For Umfreville's account of the exploration, see Robert Douglas, ed., *Nipigon to Winnipeg* (Ottawa, 1929).

[60] Samuel F. Bemis, *Jay's Treaty: A Study in Commerce and Diplomacy*, 10 (New York, 1923); Davidson, *North West Company*, 22.

CHAPTER 2.

THE NORTHWEST BOUNDARY GAP—
Pages 19 to 27.

[1] Samuel F. Bemis, "Jay's Treaty and the Northwest Boundary Gap," in *American Historical Review*, 27:468–470 (April, 1922); Bernard Mayo, ed., *Instructions to the British Ministers to the United States, 1791-1812*, 29n (*American Historical Association Report for 1936*, vol. 3, Washington, D.C., 1941).

[2] Billington, *Westward Expansion*, 207–209, 216, 218.

³ Billington, *Westward Expansion*, 223; Davidson, *North West Company*, 272.

⁴ Bemis, in *American Historical Review*, 27:468–470; Mayo, ed., *Instructions to British Ministers*, 29n.

⁵ Mayo, ed., *Instructions to British Ministers*, 25. For a full discussion of the Indian buffer state see Bemis, *Jay's Treaty*, 109–133.

⁶ Mayo, ed., *Instructions to British Ministers*, 28.

⁷ Here and below, see Thomas Jefferson, "Notes of a Conversation with Mr. Hammond," June 3, 1792, in Paul L. Ford, ed., *The Writings of Thomas Jefferson*, 1:195 (New York, 1892); Bemis, in *American Historical Review*, 27:471; Alvord, in *Minnesota History Bulletin*, 4:321; Bemis, *Jay's Treaty*, 104, 107, 122, 132.

⁸ Burt, *United States, Great Britain, and British North America*, 110–120, 130–140.

⁹ *ASP, FR*, 1:472–474.

¹⁰ Bemis, *Jay's Treaty*, 221; *ASP, FR*, 1:488. Grenville also asked for free commerce on the American side of any common boundaries, for the British government had been well informed about Grand Portage and the Great Lakes fur trade by traders Isaac Todd and Simon McTavish before the negotiation of Jay's Treaty. They had reported that the value of Canadian fur exports in 1789–94 averaged £250,000. Of this amount £100,000 worth was said to have come through Detroit, Michilimackinac, and Niagara, and nearly an equal amount came from the area west of Lake Superior. They complained that the boundary stipulations of the peace treaty could deprive them of the most useful grounds on the St. Marys River, the outlet of Lake Superior, and of Grand Portage, which they stated "is situated on the American side of the line about 6 Miles from the Water Communication, which is inaccessible for a considerable distance, on account of Falls, & Rapids; nor is it possible to make a carrying place on our Side of the Line, the Mountains are so Steep." Todd and McTavish concluded with the warning that the valuable trade of the northwest could be preserved only through the retention of Grand Portage and the St. Marys posts. "Memoir in Regard to the Fur Trade, circa 1794," in Davidson, *North West Company*, 277–279.

¹¹ Here and three paragraphs below, see Jay to Grenville, September 1, 4, 5, 1794, in *ASP, FR*, 1:490, 491, 492; Bemis, *Jay's Treaty*, 289. Grenville was relying on William Faden's map, which correctly showed the Mississippi rising south of Lake of the Woods. As Jay pointed out, however, the map did not accurately locate the northernmost source of the Mississippi, and, in fact, conjectured as to the upper Mississippi's true course. William Faden, *Map of the United States of North America with the British Territories and Those of Spain according to the Treaty of 1784*, ([1793]), in Geography and Map Division, Library of Congress.

¹² Bemis, *Jay's Treaty*, 178, 246, 250, 263.

¹³ Here and below, see Miller, ed., *Treaties*, 2:246, 248.

¹⁴ For a full discussion of the treaty, see Burt, *United States, Great Britain, and British North America*, 141–165.

¹⁵ Buck, in *Minnesota History Bulletin*, 5:23.

¹⁶ Roderic[k] McKenzie, "Reminiscences," in L. R. Masson, ed., *Les Bourgeois de la Compagnie du Nord-Ouest*, 1:46 (Reprint ed., New York, 1960); Alexander Mackenzie, *Voyages from Montreal, on the St. Laurence, Through the Continent of North America, to the Frozen and Pacific Oceans; In the Years 1789 and 1793*, map following preface (London, 1801).

¹⁷ Eric W. Morse, *Canoe Routes of the Voyageurs: The Geography and Logistics of the Canadian Fur Trade*, 23 (Toronto, 1962). The boundary surveyors who worked under Article 7 of the Treaty of Ghent in the 1820s determined that the distance from Lake Superior to Rainy Lake by the Pigeon River route was 207.86 miles, whereas the distance via the Kaministikwia was 263.34 miles; Henry Y. Hind, *North-West Territory: Reports of Progress*, 190 (Toronto, 1859).

¹⁸ L[awrence] J. Burpee, ed., "Some Letters of David Thompson," in *Canadian Historical Review*, 4:123 (June, 1923); "Boundary Between the United States and Great Britain," in 25 Congress, 2 session, *House Executive Documents*, no. 451, pp. 123, 126, 128 (serial 331).

¹⁹ Christopher Gore to Lord Hawkesbury, September 22, 1802, in *ASP, FR*, 2:588 (1832).

²⁰ 25 Congress, 2 session, *House Executive Documents*, no. 451, p. 126.

²¹ Davidson, *North West Company*, 105; Buck, in *Minnesota History Bulletin*, 5:23. On the building and naming of Fort William, see Susan Campbell, *Fort William: Living and Working at the Post*, 12–14 (*Fort William Archaeological Project Series*—1976). The post has been reconstructed about ten miles up the Kaministikwia from its original site on Thunder Bay.

²² Mackenzie, *Voyages*, lviii, wrote that Thompson was sent out "expressly" to determine the locations of Lake of the Woods and the Mississippi. In his *Narrative*, written decades after the exploration, Thompson recalled that he had been asked to determine the positions of the North West Company's posts relative to each other and to the 49th parallel, which he erroneously stated had been fixed in 1792 as the international boundary from Lake of the Woods to the Rocky Mountains. Since that boundary was not agreed upon until the Convention of 1818, he could not have been told it was the demarcation in 1797. J. B. Tyrrell, ed., *David Thompson's Narrative of His Explorations in Western America, 1784–1812*, 170 (Reprint ed., New York, 1968).

²³ David Thompson Journal, August 25, 1797, photocopy in David Thompson Papers, Minnesota Historical Society (MHS) Division of Archives and Manuscripts, original in Ontario Department of Public Records and Archives, Toronto. Thompson's assumption that Rat Portage was the northwesternmost point of Lake of the Woods handicapped him a quarter century later when he was instructed to determine that point as part of an official boundary survey. See p. 45, below. See also Richard Glover, ed., *David Thompson's Narrative, 1784–1812*, lxxviii–lxxxii (Toronto, 1962). On p. 186, Thompson again presented erroneous information about the international boundary near Pembina on the Red River. He described how, during March 14–20, 1798, he determined that the fur post there was at latitude 48° 58′ 24″ N. Then, he recalled, he pointed out the 49th parallel in order that the inhabitants could remove themselves to British territory.

²⁴ Here and below, see Thompson Journal and "Record of Distances and Observations, 1798," entries for April 26 and 27, both in Thompson Papers. On Henry Rowe Schoolcraft's 1832 discovery, see his *Narrative of an Expedition through the Upper Mississippi to Lake Itasca, the Actual Source of This River* (New York, 1834).

With the exception of only one spot—the outflow of Turtle Brook from Fox Lake—it is impossible to determine the precise locations from which Thompson's observations were taken. At that point Thompson's measurement of 47° 37′ 19″ N and 95° 8′ 35″ W compares with the present one of 47° 36′ 8″ N and 94° 50′ W. The other points Thompson measured on Turtle Lake proper must have been at about the present 94° 51′ W, so he placed the lake roughly 19 minutes too far west. At the latitude of Turtle Lake a degree of longitude is nearly 47 miles. Erwin Raisz, *Principles of Cartography*, 149 (New York, 1962).

²⁵ Mackenzie, *Voyages*, map following preface, lviii. According to David Thompson, Mackenzie's fur trade history was actually written by Roderick McKenzie; see John J. Bigsby, *The Shoe and Canoe*, 1:115 (Reprint ed., New York, 1969).

In accounting for the slight difference in Turtle Lake's longitude as reported by Mackenzie and as entered by Thompson in his "Record of Distances and Observations," Thompson Papers, the distinct possibility of a transcribing or printing error during the book's production cannot be ruled out.

²⁶ Mackenzie, *Voyages*, lviii, 399. On the St. Louis River–Savanna Portage route, see Holmquist and Brookins, *Minnesota's Major Historic Sites*, 158–163.

²⁷ John W. Davis, "The Unguarded Frontier," in *Geographical Review*, 12:590 (October, 1922); H. George Classen, *Thrust and Counterthrust: The Genesis of the Canada-United States Boundary*, 9–11 (Chicago, 1967).

²⁸ Davis, in *Geographical Review*, 12:590; Burt, *United States, Great Britain, and British North America*, 185. On the St. Croix River survey, see John B. Moore, *History and Digest of the International Arbitrations to which the United States has been a Party*, 1:1–43 (Washington, D.C., 1898), also printed in 53 Congress, 2 session, *House Miscellaneous Documents*, no. 212 (serial 3267).

²⁹ *ASP, FR,* 2:585, 587 (1832); Madison to King, June 8, 1802, in William R. Manning, ed., *Diplomatic Correspondence of the United States: Canadian Relations 1784–1860,* 1:157 (Washington, D.C., 1940).

³⁰ Manning, ed., *Diplomatic Correspondence,* 1:158.

³¹ Manning, ed., *Diplomatic Correspondence,* 1:539; *ASP, FR,* 2:588, 589.

³² Gore to Madison, October 6, 1802, Hawkesbury to Gore, October 4, 1802, both in *ASP, FR,* 2:587, 589.

³³ Manning, ed., *Diplomatic Correspondence,* 1:161. Madison did not mean that his proposed line from Lake of the Woods to the nearest source of the Mississippi (which he believed was Turtle Lake) would necessarily give Great Britain access to a navigable portion of the stream. Rather, he reasoned that there might be unknown navigable branches even closer to Lake of the Woods.

³⁴ King to Madison, February 28, December 9, 1803, in *ASP, FR,* 2:590, 591; to Hawkesbury, April 10, 1803, in Charles R. King, ed., *The Life and Correspondence of Rufus King,* 4:245 (New York, 1897); to Madison, May 13, 1803, in Manning, ed., *Diplomatic Correspondence,* 1:556. In his letter to Madison, December 9, 1803, King noted that he had sent the draft to Hawkesbury on April 11.

³⁵ Manning, ed., *Diplomatic Correspondence,* 1:557; King to Madison, May 13, 1803, in *ASP, FR,* 2:590.

³⁶ King to Hawkesbury, May 14, 1803, in Manning, ed., *Diplomatic Correspondence,* 1:558. The same letter under the date May 15, 1803, appears in King, ed., *Life and Correspondence,* 4:262.

³⁷ Miller, ed., *Treaties,* 2:499; Livingston to Madison, June 8, 1802, in *ASP, FR,* 2:519.

³⁸ Talleyrand to Duc Denis Decrés, October 2, 1802, in James A. Robertson, *Louisiana under the Rule of Spain, France, and the United States 1785–1807,* 2:141n (Cleveland, 1911). For a full discussion, see Richard R. Stenberg, "The Boundaries of the Louisiana Purchase," in *Hispanic American Historical Review,* 14:32–64 (February, 1934).

³⁹ Miller, ed., *Treaties,* 2:500.

⁴⁰ Livingston to Madison, May 20, 1803, in *ASP, FR,* 2:561.

⁴¹ Jefferson, "The Limits and Bounds of Louisiana," in *Documents Relating to the Purchase and Exploration of Louisiana,* 27, 28–32, 37 (Boston, 1904), hereafter cited as "Limits and Bounds."

⁴² Miller, ed., *Treaties,* 2:498.

⁴³ *ASP, FR,* 2:584. The other two committeemen were Senators Wilson C. Nicholas of Virginia and Robert Wright of Maryland. Charles F. Adams, ed., *Memoirs of John Quincy Adams,* 1:269, 271, 273 (Reprint ed., Freeport, N.Y., 1969); Adams to Madison, December 16, 1803, King to Madison, December 9, 1803, both in *ASP, FR,* 2:590, 591.

⁴⁴ Here and below, see Jefferson, "Limits and Bounds," 40–45. On the Treaty of Utrecht at the end of the War of Spanish Succession, see Frances G. Davenport, ed., *European Treaties Bearing on the History of the United States and Its Dependencies,* 3:193–214 (Washington, D.C., 1937); see also Thomas Hutchins, *An Historical Narrative and Topographical Description of Louisiana, and West Florida,* 7 (Reprint ed., Gainesville, Fla., 1968).

⁴⁵ *ASP, FR,* 2:574.

⁴⁶ Adams, *Memoirs,* 1:294. Samuel F. Bemis, *John Quincy Adams and the Foundations of American Foreign Policy,* 125 (New York, 1949), overstated Adams' role in causing the convention to be modified and ignored Jefferson's influence. Jefferson's part in the deletion of Article 5 was both recognized and resented by some opposition Federalists who deplored his territorial ambitions. See, for example, Timothy Pickering to King, March 3, 1804, in King, ed., *Life and Correspondence,* 4:363.

⁴⁷ Manning, ed., *Diplomatic Correspondence,* 1:167, 168; James F. Zimmerman, *Impressment of American Seamen,* 93 (New York, 1925).

⁴⁸ Madison to Monroe, March 5, 1804, in *ASP, FR,* 3:90 (1832); Zimmerman, *Impressment of American Seamen,* 91–115.

⁴⁹ For a summary of Monroe's unsuccessful efforts to resolve questions of neutral rights and a commercial agreement with Hawkesbury, here and below, see Monroe to Madison, April 15, June 3, 1804, in *ASP, FR,* 3:91, 93.

⁵⁰ *ASP, FR,* 3:97; Monroe to Charles James Fox, British secretary of state for foreign affairs, February 25, 1806, in Manning, ed., *Diplomatic Correspondence,* 1:580.

⁵¹ Burt, *United States, Great Britain, and British North America,* 197.

CHAPTER 3.
THE NORTHERN BOUNDARY
OF LOUISIANA TERRITORY—*Pages 28 to 34.*

¹ Manning, ed., *Diplomatic Correspondence,* 1:567. A copy of Huske's map, entitled *A New and Accurate Map of North America: Wherein the Errors of All Preceeding [sic] British, French and Dutch Maps, respecting the Rights of Great Britain, France, & Spain, & the Limits of each of his Majesty's provinces, are corrected,* is in North America file, Geography and Map Division, Library of Congress.

² Max Savelle, "The Forty-Ninth Degree of North Latitude as an International Boundary, 1719: The Origin of an Idea," in *Canadian Historical Review,* 38:183–190 (September, 1957); Davenport, ed., *European Treaties,* 3:193–214.

³ Savelle, in *Canadian Historical Review,* 38:192; *Statutes, Documents and Papers on Boundaries of Ontario,* 359–370, 376.

⁴ See, for example, Thomas Salmon, *Modern History; or, the Present State of All Nations,* 3:602 (3rd ed., London, 1745); William Douglass, *A Summary, Historical and Political, of the First Planting, Progressive Movements, and Present State of the British Settlements in North-America,* 1:8 (Boston, 1747); *Statutes, Documents and Papers on Boundaries of Ontario,* 136cc–ee, p–r. For more on maps which erroneously showed the 49th parallel boundary, see Charles O. Paullin, "The Early Choice of the Forty-ninth Parallel as a Boundary Line," in *Canadian Historical Review,* 4:129 (June, 1923).

⁵ Beckles Willson, *America's Ambassadors to England (1785–1929): A Narrative of Anglo-American Diplomatic Relations,* 77–89 (New York, 1929); on Pinkney, see *Dictionary of American Biography,* 14:626–629 (New York, 1934).

⁶ Madison to Monroe, May 15, 1806, to Monroe and Pinkney, May 17, 1806, Monroe and Pinkney to Madison, November 11, 1806, January 3, 1807—all in *ASP, FR,* 3:119–124, 137–140, 142–147; Irving Brant, *James Madison: Secretary of State 1800–1809,* [4]:372 (Indianapolis, 1953).

⁷ Monroe and Pinkney to Madison, April 22, 1807, in *ASP, FR,* 3:160. As examples of the slow mail service, the letter written by the negotiators to Madison on November 11, 1806, reached him on February 1, 1807, and his response of February 3 arrived in London on April 6.

⁸ On the negotiations and proposed articles of the new treaty, see Monroe and Pinkney to Madison, April 25, 1807, and enclosure, in *ASP, FR,* 3:162–165.

⁹ Here and below, see *ASP, FR,* 3:162, 164, 165; John M. Gray, *Lord Selkirk of Red River,* 16–26, 46 (Reprint ed., Toronto, 1964); Manning, ed., *Diplomatic Correspondence,* 1:589n, 591n.

¹⁰ Manning, ed., *Diplomatic Correspondence,* 1:179, 180.

¹¹ Brant, *Madison,* [4]:372; *ASP, FR,* 3:154. On the Berlin Decree and the Order of Council, see Frank A. Updyke, *The Diplomacy of the War of 1812,* 84 (Reprint ed., Gloucester, Mass., 1965).

¹² Manning, ed., *Diplomatic Correspondence,* 1:176. On the "Chesapeake" affair, see Henry Adams, *History of the United States of America,* 4:1–26 (New York, 1921); Bradford Perkins, *Prologue to War: England and the United States, 1805–1812,* 140–146 (Berkeley, 1970). See also Monroe to Theodore Lyman, Jr., April [?], 1817, in Stanislaus M. Hamilton, ed., *The Writings of James Monroe,* 6:20 (New York, 1902).

¹³ William Mainwaring, Hudson's Bay Company, to Holland and Auckland, March 24, 1807, in Great Britain, Foreign Office Records, series 5 (hereafter cited as FO/5), vol. 54, p. 25, microfilm copy in Public Archives of Canada, Ottawa; original in the Public Record Office, London. British acceptance of the 49th parallel is further substantiated by that government's conduct after 1807, when

it failed to seek out and publicize proof that the commissioners under the Treaty of Ghent had not fixed the line, and during negotiations in both 1818 and 1826, when it did not challenge the Americans' claim to a boundary based on the Treaty of Utrecht. See pp. 33, 53, below; Raymond Walters, Jr., *Albert Gallatin: Jeffersonian Financier and Diplomat*, 335–339 (New York, 1957); Henry Adams, ed., *The Writings of Albert Gallatin*, 3:511–513 (Philadelphia, 1879), hereafter cited as Gallatin, *Writings*. Whether full knowledge of the actual boundary history following the Treaty of Utrecht would have altered the agreement on the 49th parallel is questionable. The Hudson's Bay Company's requests for the 49th in 1714 and later would have served as a certain precedent in drawing the boundary in the 19th century. See Paullin, in *Canadian Historical Review*, 4:127–131.

The myth that Anglo-French commissioners had agreed upon the 49th parallel was ultimately exposed by Robert Greenhow, a U.S. State Dept. interpreter and publicist of American expansion. For his attempt to discredit the alleged legal basis for the 49th parallel boundary and to justify U.S. claims in Oregon north of that line, see "Summary of Facts Respecting the Northwest Coast of America," published in the *Washington Globe*, January 15, 1840, p. 3. His condemnation of the Utrecht boundary claim was based on negative evidence from secondary sources, specifically Adam Anderson, *An Historical and Chronological Deduction of the Origin of Commerce* (published in five editions in London between 1764 and 1801) and David Macpherson, *Annals of Commerce* (London, 1805). His arguments were elaborated and expanded in *Memoir, Historical and Political, on the Northwest Coast of North America, and the Adjacent Territories* (New York and London, 1840) and *The History of Oregon and California and the Other Territories on the North-West Coast of North America* (Boston, 1844). Although Greenhow's conclusions were generally accepted at the time, the Oregon boundary was finally based on the well-entrenched myth and set along the 49th parallel in 1846. See Chapter 7, below.

14 Here and below, see Julius W. Pratt, "Fur Trade Strategy and the American Left Flank in the War of 1812," in *American Historical Review*, 40:248 (January, 1935); Louis A. Tohill, *Robert Dickson, British Fur Trader on the Upper Mississippi: A Story of Trade, War, and Diplomacy*, 19, 27–29, 43 (Ann Arbor, 1927); Louise P. Kellogg, *The British Régime in Wisconsin and the Northwest*, 283–285, 314–321 (Madison, 1935).

15 James A. Jackson, *The Centennial History of Manitoba*, 36–39 (Toronto, 1970); Gray, *Selkirk*, 98; Evan Jones, *Citadel in the Wilderness: The Story of Fort Snelling and the Old Northwest Frontier*, 34, 38 (New York, 1966).

16 "Memorial of the Fur Traders in Regard to the American Boundary, 1814," in Davidson, *North West Company*, 296–301; Charles M. Gates, "The West in American Diplomacy, 1812–1815," in *Mississippi Valley Historical Review*, 26:501 (March, 1940).

17 Here and below, see *ASP, FR*, 3:700, 701, 704. See also Burt, *United States, Great Britain, and British North America*, 340, 345, 348.

18 Monroe to U.S. Peace Commissioners, August 11, 1814, U.S. Peace Commissioners to Monroe, August 12, 19, 1814—all in *ASP, FR*, 3:705, 706, 709. On the Treaty of Greenville, see Charles J. Kappler, comp. and ed., *Indian Affairs. Laws and Treaties*, 2:39–45 (Washington, D.C., 1904).

19 Walters, *Gallatin*, 279–282; British to U.S. Peace Commissioners, September 4, October 21, 31, 1814, in *ASP, FR*, 3:714, 725, 726; Fred L. Engelman, *The Peace of Christmas Eve*, 165–175, 219–229 (New York, 1962); Updyke, *Diplomacy of the War of 1812*, 286–294.

20 *ASP, FR*, 3:734, 735–738. See especially Articles 3–8; see also Engelman, *Peace of Christmas Eve*, 242, 284; Updyke, *Diplomacy of the War of 1812*, 243, 300, 320.

21 *ASP, FR*, 3:735–740; U.S. Peace Commissioners to Monroe, December 25, 1814, in *ASP, FR*, 3:733; Adams, *Memoirs*, 3:84–86.

22 Miller, ed., *Treaties*, 2:574, 576–580.

23 For the terms of the commercial convention of 1815 and the Rush-Bagot Agreement of 1817, see Miller, ed., *Treaties*, 2:595–600, 645–654.

24 Here and below, see United States, *Statutes at Large*, 3:332; Tohill, *Dickson*, 89–91; Lucile M. Kane, June D. Holmquist, and Carolyn Gilman, eds., *The Northern Expeditions of Stephen H. Long: The Journals of 1817 and 1823 and Related Documents*, 8 (St. Paul, 1978); Bemis, *Adams and the Foundations of American Foreign Policy*, 281–286; Dorothy O. Johansen and Charles M. Gates, *Empire of the Columbia: A History of the Pacific Northwest*, 110 (2nd ed., New York, 1967).

25 Here and below, see Adams to Rush, November 6, 1817, in *ASP, FR*, 4:370 (1834); Rush, *Memoranda of a Residence at the Court of London*, 93, 97 (Philadelphia, 1833); Rush to Adams, February 14, 1818, in Manning, ed., *Diplomatic Correspondence*, 1:834–837. For a biography of Rush, see J[ohn] H. Powell, *Richard Rush, Republican Diplomat 1780–1859* (Philadelphia, 1942).

26 Adams to Rush, May 21, 1818, to Gallatin, May 22, 1818, both in *ASP, FR*, 4:370, 371; Walters, *Gallatin*, 309.

27 *ASP, FR*, 4:375, 377, 378; Adams to Rush, July 30, 1818, in Manning, ed., *Diplomatic Correspondence*, 1:282.

28 Powell, *Rush*, 116–118; Rush, *Memoranda of a Residence*, 307; Rush to Adams, July 25, August 15, 28, 1818, in *ASP, FR*, 4:375, 379.

29 Walters, *Gallatin*, 310, 312.

30 Rush, *Memoranda of a Residence*, 371; Gallatin and Rush to Adams, October 20, 1818, and "Protocol of the fifth conference," held October 6, 1818, both in *ASP, FR*, 4:380, 391.

31 Miller, ed., *Treaties*, 2:659.

32 *ASP, FR*, 4:381, 391; Miller, ed., *Treaties*, 2:660.

33 Rush, *Memoranda of a Residence*, 381–414. Burt, *United States, Great Britain, and British North America*, 399–426, fully elaborated the importance of the convention.

CHAPTER 4.

ORGANIZING THE WILDERNESS SURVEY IN 1822—*Pages 35 to 39.*

1 Monroe to Bagot, April 12, August 15, 1816, in Manning, ed., *Diplomatic Correspondence*, 1:242, 252. The U.S. commissioners for Articles 4 and 5, respectively, were John Holmes of Massachusetts and Cornelius P. Van Ness of Vermont. On Barclay, below, see George L. Rives, ed., *Selections from the Correspondence of Thomas Barclay*, 1–46, 95, 312–318 (New York, 1894).

2 Rives, ed., *Correspondence of Thomas Barclay*, 357–365, 405–409; Castlereagh to Rush, February 28, 1818, in Manning, ed., *Diplomatic Correspondence*, 1:838; Robert McElroy and Thomas Riggs, eds., *The Unfortified Boundary: A Diary of the First Survey of the Canadian Boundary Line from St. Regis to the Lake of the Woods by Major Joseph Delafield*, 30–34 (New York, 1943), hereafter cited as Delafield, *Unfortified Boundary*. On the arbitration of the northeast boundary, see Chapter 7, below.

3 Monroe to Bagot, April 12, 1816, Bagot to Monroe, February 3, 1817, both in Manning, ed., *Diplomatic Correspondence*, 1:242, 820.

4 On Ogilvy, see W. Stewart Wallace, *The Dictionary of Canadian Biography*, 2:496 (Revised ed., Toronto, 1945); on Porter, below, see *Guide to the Microfilm Edition of the Peter B. Porter Papers in the Buffalo and Erie County Historical Society*, 1 (Buffalo, N.Y., 1968); Delafield, *Unfortified Boundary*, 36.

5 For the provisions under which the commissions were appointed, see Article 4 of the Ghent Treaty in Miller, ed., *Treaties*, 2:576.

6 Bagot to Adams, September 24, 1817, in Manning, ed., *Diplomatic Correspondence*, 1:831. On Hale, see Joseph Desjardins, *Guide to Parlementaire Historique de la Province de Quebec 1792–1902*, 30, 57 (Quebec, 1902); "La Famille Hale," in *Bulletin des Recherches Historiques*, 38:750 (October, 1932); W. Stewart Wallace, *The Macmillan Dictionary of Canadian Biography*, 292 (3rd ed., London and Toronto, 1963).

7 Delafield, *Unfortified Boundary*, 35, 36, 38–43; Herman L. Fairchild, *A History of the New York Academy of Sciences*, 64 (New York, 1887).

8 Miller, ed., *Treaties*, 2:580. For names of members of the British and American commissions in 1817, see Delafield, *Unfortified Boundary*, 36.

9 Delafield, *Unfortified Boundary*, 36; Anthony Barclay to Joseph Planta, April 7, 1825, in FO/5, vol. 200, p. 72. On Fraser, see Francis B. Heitman, *Historical Register and Dictionary of the United States Army*, 1:434 (Washington, D.C., 1903); Arthur Detmers, Buffalo and Erie County Historical Society, Buffalo, N.Y., to the author, June 20, 1975. On Bigsby, see *Dictionary of National Biography*, 2:489 (Reprint ed., 1949–50).

10 Tyrrell, *Thompson's Narrative*, xliv–lv.

11 Here and below, see Rives, ed., *Correspondence of Thomas Barclay*, 96, 206, 258, 356n, 416; Classen, *Thrust and Counterthrust*, 100; Anthony Barclay to the Earl of Aberdeen, July 19, 1828, in FO/5, vol. 240, pp. 324-327; Delafield, *Unfortified Boundary*, 266n. A manuscript copy of Barclay's elaborately worded commission is in "Boundary Claims, Arguments, and Miscellaneous Documents, 1818–26," Northern Boundary, Records Relating to International Boundaries, Record Group 76, National Archives, Washington, D.C., hereafter cited as NB/NARG 76. The commission was published with Gibbs Crawford Antrobus to John Quincy Adams, March 31, 1820, in Manning, ed., *Diplomatic Correspondence*, 1:923.

12 The St. Clair River and Lake Huron surveys are described in Delafield, *Unfortified Boundary*, 44–48; William A. Bird, *The Boundary Line Between the British Provinces and the United States*, 4 (Buffalo, N.Y., 1864).

13 Adams to Richard Rush, July 30, 1818, in Manning, ed., *Diplomatic Correspondence*, 1:282. While the act of March 3, 1821, and Secretary of State John Quincy Adams stated that the old rate was $4,444 per annum, Treasury Department officials authorized the actual payment of $4,444.44. See United States, *Statutes at Large*, 3:640; Adams to Rush, March 22, 1821, in Manning, ed., *Diplomatic Correspondence*, 2:4; Delafield, *Unfortified Boundary*, 45; Porter to Adams, February 9, 1822, in Letters Received from the U.S. Commissioner, NB/NARG 76; undated memo concerning Porter's salary, in Peter B. Porter Papers, roll 7B, frame 0099, hereafter abbreviated as 7B-0099, originals and microfilm owned by the Buffalo and Erie County Historical Society.

14 Here and below, see Porter to Adams, February 12, 1822, in Letters Received from the U.S. Commissioner, NB/NARG 76; Delafield, *Unfortified Boundary*, 64.

15 Barclay to Planta, January 21, 1822, in FO/5, vol. 170, p. 180.

16 Delafield, *Unfortified Boundary*, 63.

17 Porter to Adams, February 12, 1822, in Letters Received from the U.S. Commissioner, NB/NARG 76.

18 Porter to Adams, February 12, 1822, in Letters Received from the U.S. Commissioner, NB/NARG 76; Bird, *Boundary Line*, 8; Delafield to Porter, April 20, 1822, in Porter Papers, 7A-0391. On Ferguson, see *Appletons' Cyclopaedia of American Biography*, 2:433 (New York, 1887); on Whistler, see *Dictionary of American Biography*, 20:72 (1936).

19 Delafield to Porter, April 20, 1822, in Porter Papers, 7A-0391-0393. On Crooks's career, see David Lavender, *The Fist in the Wilderness* (New York, 1964).

20 Delafield, *Unfortified Boundary*, 368, 369; Delafield to Stuart, to Ferguson, and to Porter, each dated June 6, 1822, in Porter Papers, 7A-0419, 0422, 0425; to Adams, July 24, 1822, in Letters Received from the U.S. Agent, NB/NARG 76.

21 Delafield to Adams, July 24, 1822, in Letters Received from the U.S. Agent, NB/NARG 76; to Porter, April 20, 1822, in Porter Papers, 7A-0391-0393. Schoolcraft, later famed for his discovery of the source of the Mississippi River, was the mineralogist on the Cass expedition. On p. 264 of his *Narrative Journal of Travels through the Northwestern Regions of the United States . . . in the Year 1820* (Albany, N.Y., 1821), he mentioned the uncertain boundary west of Lake Superior and described two "grand routes"—one by way of Grand Portage and the other by way of the St. Louis River. Members of the American Article 7 commission were disturbed by Schoolcraft's remarks, because they appeared to make the St. Louis River route a viable boundary possibility, and because he described

the area between the St. Louis and Pigeon rivers as being "in dispute." They considered his choice of words both ill advised and untrue.

22 Barclay to Porter, May 25, 1822, Ferguson to Porter, July 9, 13, 1822—all in Porter Papers, 7A-0413, 0445, 0447; Porter to Adams, February 12, 1822, in Letters Received from the U.S. Commissioner, NB/NARG 76.

23 Ferguson to Porter, July 2, 1822, in Porter Papers, 7A-0439-0443.

24 Porter to Adams, June 21, 1822, in Letters Received from the U.S. Commissioner, NB/NARG 76; Porter to Ferguson, June 29, 1822, in Porter Papers, 7A-0433. After several months of "amicable negotiations" over the ownership of Grand Island in the Thousand Islands of the St. Lawrence River, Barnhart Island farther downstream, and Sugar, Fox, Stony, and Bois Blanc islands in the Detroit River, the agreement concerning Article 6 was signed on June 18, 1822. Delafield, *Unfortified Boundary*, 49-58; Classen, *Thrust and Counterthrust*, 93–102. See also Chapter 6, below. For detailed information on the work and conclusions of the Article 6 commission, see Journal of Proceedings for the period November 18, 1816–June 22, 1822, NB/NARG 76.

25 Ferguson to Porter, July 2, 1822, in Porter Papers, 7A-0439-0443.

26 Here and below, see Ferguson to Porter, August 1, 1822, in Porter Papers, 7A-0450-0452.

CHAPTER 5.
THE UNCERTAIN BOUNDARY, 1822–25—
Pages 40 to 49.

1 Hudson's Bay Company bill for supplies furnished the boundary commission, submitted to the Foreign Office, January 10, 1827, in FO/5, vol. 240, p. 216; Ferguson to Porter, August 20, 1822, in Porter Papers, 7A-0459; Thompson to Sayer, August 17, 1822, photocopy in Thompson Papers, MHS, original in Public Archives of Canada, Ottawa. Sayer was formerly a clerk for the North West Company in charge of a trading post "in the Countries between the Rainy Lake and the N W Coast of Lake Superior," according to a note Thompson appended to his copy of the letter.

2 Ferguson to Porter, August 1, 1822, in Porter Papers, 7A-0450.

3 Ferguson to Porter, August 20, 1822, in Porter Papers, 7A-0459. On Pigeon Falls, about 70 feet high, see Upham, *Minnesota Geographic Names*, 138.

4 Ferguson's report of October 27, 1826, in Boundary Claims, Arguments, and Miscellaneous Documents, NB/NARG 76.

5 Ferguson to Porter, September 23, 1822, in Porter Papers, 7A-0471.

6 Ferguson to Porter, August 20, 1822, in Porter Papers, 7A-0459.

7 Ferguson to Porter, September 23, October 14, 1822, January 20, 1823, in Porter Papers, 7A-0471-0473, 0500.

8 Ferguson to Porter, January 20, 1823, in Porter Papers, 7A-0500; to Bird, January 20, 1823, in Bird, *Boundary Line*, 4. A varying version of the latter is in Bird, "Reminiscences of the Boundary Survey between the United States and British Provinces," in Buffalo Historical Society, *Publications*, 4:6 (Buffalo, N.Y., 1896).

9 Ferguson to Porter, September 23, 1822, January 20, 1823, in Porter Papers, 7A-0471, 0500. On Schoolcraft, see Chapter 4, note 21, above.

10 Delafield to Porter, August 2, 1822, in Porter Papers, 7A-0453; Porter to Adams, August 20, 1822, in Letters Received from the U.S. Commissioner, NB/NARG 76; Adams to Porter, October 8, 1822, in Domestic Letters, vol. 20, p. 19, General Records of the Dept. of State, NARG 59; Delafield to Adams, September 24, 1822, in Letters Received from the U.S. Agent, NB/NARG 76.

11 Barclay to Canning, May 9, 1823; Francis Conynham, Foreign Office, to Barclay, July 11, 1823; Barclay to Conynham, September 15, 1823—all in FO/5, vol. 187, pp. 59, 87, 129.

12 Porter to Adams, December 20, 1822, in Letters Received from the U.S. Commissioner, NB/NARG 76; Barclay to Canning, May 10, 1823, in FO/5, vol. 187, p. 89.

13 Barclay to Canning, May 10, 1823, to Joseph Planta, July 5, 1823, both in FO/5, vol. 187, p. 89.

14 The trip and the fort are described in Bigsby, *Shoe and Canoe*, 2:232, 241, 242, 244–272, 273, 288. Fort La Pluie, renamed Fort Frances in 1830, was built in 1818 on a site within present-day Fort Frances, Ont. Grace Lee Nute, "Hudson's Bay Company Posts in the Minnesota Country," in *Minnesota History*, 22:271 (September, 1941). See also Hudson's Bay Company bill for supplies furnished the boundary commission, submitted to the Foreign Office, January 10, 1827, in FO/5, vol. 240, p. 217. McLoughlin and McGillivray had been a partner and chief director, respectively, of the North West Company before its merger with the Hudson's Bay Company in 1821. For biographical sketches, see W. Stewart Wallace, *Documents Relating to the North West Company*, 471, 482 (Toronto, 1934).

15 Bigsby, *Shoe and Canoe*, 2:292; field maps, 1823, photocopies in Thompson Papers, MHS, originals in Ontario Dept. of Public Records and Archives, Toronto. There are several dozen maps sketched on graph paper with each square representing one square mile. Most are dated and show Thompson's itinerary from present South Fowl Lake to Lake of the Woods. A dotted line on each map marks the projected boundary line as a middle course through lakes and streams.

16 Field maps, 1823, in Thompson Papers; Bigsby, *Shoe and Canoe*, 2:318; Thompson's report of February 20, 1824, in Boundary Claims, Arguments, and Miscellaneous Documents, 1818–26, NB/NARG 76.

17 International Boundary Commission, *Joint Report upon the Survey and Demarcation of the Boundary between the United States and Canada from the Northwesternmost Point of Lake of the Woods to Lake Superior*, 216 (Washington, D.C., 1931), hereafter cited as IBC, *Report of Boundary from Northwesternmost Point of Lake of the Woods to Lake Superior*.

18 Porter to Adams, December 20, 1822, in Letters Received from the U.S. Commissioner, NB/NARG 76.

19 For his journey, here and three paragraphs below, see Delafield, *Unfortified Boundary*, 375–381, 388–401, 406–418, 422, 425–430.

20 On the return trip, see Delafield, *Unfortified Boundary*, 431–499. It is of interest that the United States sent a second official party into the border area in 1823 led by Major Stephen H. Long. Also equipped with surveying instruments, Long reconnoitered the Kaministikwia route from September 5 to 15, about a month after Delafield. See Kane, *et al.*, eds., *Long Expeditions*, 218–228, and Chapter 6, below.

21 Porter to Adams, October 26, 1823, in Letters Received from the U.S. Commissioner, Delafield to Adams, October 9, November 28, 1823, in Letters Received from the U.S. Agent—all in NB/NARG 76.

22 Ferguson's report of February 20, 1824, and Thompson's report of the same date, in Boundary Claims, Arguments, and Miscellaneous Documents, NB/NARG 76.

23 Barclay to Porter, November 1, 1823, in Porter Papers, 7A–0511.

24 All officers of the joint boundary commission, including the commissioners, agents, secretary, assistant secretary, and surveyors, were required to sign formal oaths to carry out the purpose of the commission in a professional manner. Such oaths were signed at the commencement of the individual's employment but were not recorded with the joint commission until its next meeting.

Initially it was the intention of Great Britain and the United States to include the commissioners' salaries in the joint account. No specific salary was mentioned in the articles ratifying the Treaty of Ghent, but it was the understanding of both countries that the commissioners were to be paid at the same rate as those serving under the Treaty of 1794 (Jay's Treaty), namely, £1,000 annually. Great Britain paid its boundary commissioners more than that, however, and after passage of the 1821 law, the United States paid its commissioners much less. Therefore the two countries agreed in 1821, as a result of negotiations between Richard Rush, U.S. minister to Great Britain, and the Marquis of Londonderry (the former Lord Castlereagh), British secretary of state for foreign affairs, that each would pay its commissioner at its own rate and that these salaries would not be included in the joint expense account. Excerpt from Adams to Rush, March 22, 1821, Rush to Londonderry, May 7, 1821, to Adams, June 15, 1821, with Londonderry's note of June 13 attached—all in Porter Papers, 7A–0498–0501, 0503–0511.

25 The expenses approved at Albany were as follows: U.S. contingencies, April, 1822, to January, 1824, $3,132.51; U.S. salaries and wages, March, 1822, to March, 1824, $11,021.24; total, $14,153.75. British contingencies, June, 1822, to January, 1824, £1,207.11.6; British salaries and wages, January, 1822, to January, 1824, £2,273.4.1; total £3,480.7.7 or $13,923.52.

For purposes of computation the salaries and wages of the permanent commission members were placed in one category, and the contingency expenses for supplies, provisions, miscellaneous transportation, and wages of common laborers were put in another. Delafield's expense account attached to Delafield to Adams, March 13, 1824, in Letters Received from the U.S. Agent, and Journal of Proceedings for period February 16, 1824–October 17, 1826, pp. 101–107, both in NB/NARG 76.

On Porter's attitude toward Barclay's expenses, see Porter to Adams, August 20, 1822, in Porter Papers, 7A–0462–0466; Adams to Porter, October 8, 1822, in Domestic Letters, vol. 20, pp. 19–21, NARG 59; Porter to Adams, February 26, 1824, to Clay, October 18, November 8, 1826—all in Letters Received from the U.S. Commissioner, NB/NARG 76.

26 Thompson's report of February 20, 1824, in Boundary Claims, Arguments, and Miscellaneous Documents, NB/NARG 76.

27 Here and below, see Delafield's and Hale's reports presented at the Albany meeting of the board of commissioners, February 16–24, 1824, attached to Delafield to Adams, March 13, 1824, in Letters Received from the U.S. Agent, NB/NARG 76.

28 Barclay to Canning, March 10, 1824, in FO/5, vol. 187, pp. 229-233.

29 Thompson memorandum, February 23, 1824, Thompson to the board of commissioners, February 23, 1824, both in Boundary Claims, Arguments, and Miscellaneous Documents, NB/NARG 76.

30 Résumé of Albany meeting attached to Delafield to Adams, March 13, 1824, in Letters Received from the U.S. Agent, Porter to Adams, February 26, 1824, in Letters Received from the U.S. Commissioner, both in NB/NARG 76. The latter is quoted in Delafield, *Unfortified Boundary*, 82. Fond du Lac referred to the southwestern extremity of Lake Superior, where the St. Louis River empties into the lake.

31 See, for example, Porter to Adams, February 26, 1824, in Letters Received from the U.S. Commissioner, NB/NARG 76.

32 Journal of Proceedings for period February 16, 1824–October 17, 1826, p. 101, NB/NARG 76; Daniel Brent to Delafield, March 24, 1824, in Domestic Letters, vol. 20, p. 328, NARG 59; Thompson's undated report (October 25, 1824?) and Ferguson's report of October 26, 1824, both attached to Delafield to Adams, November 17, 1824, in Letters Received from the U.S. Agent, NB/NARG 76.

33 Barclay to Canning, March 10, 1824, in FO/5, vol. 187, pp. 229–233. Barclay seems to have been unaware that a similar opinion had been voiced in 1807 by British treaty negotiators Holland and Auckland. See p. 29, above.

34 Barclay to Canning, March 10, 1824, R. Wilmot Horton, undersecretary for colonial affairs, to Joseph Planta, November 10, 1824, Garry to Bathurst, October 30, 1824—all in FO/5, vol. 187, pp. 229–233, 305, 307–311.

Garry's endorsement of Barclay's proposal was apparently stimulated by his belief that Rat Portage would be lost to Great Britain if the boundary through Lake of the Woods was drawn according to terms of the Treaty of 1783. He had crossed Rat Portage in 1821 on his way from Fort William to the Red River settlements when he was negotiating the merger of the Hudson's Bay and North West companies. At that time he accepted David Thompson's conclusion that Rat Portage was the northwest point of Lake of the Woods. "Diary of Nicholas Garry," in Royal Society of Canada, *Proceedings and Transactions*, 2nd series, vol. 6, sec. 2, p. 128 (Ottawa, Toronto, and London, 1900).

35 Planta to His Majesty's Advocate General, December 8, 1824, Robinson to Canning, December 9, 1824, both in FO/5, vol. 187, pp. 328–331.

36 Foreign Office memorandum to Colonial Office, December 14, 1824, in FO/5, vol. 187, pp. 336–338; Planta to Barclay, February 12, 1825, in FO/5, vol. 200, p. 33.

37 Thompson's undated report attached to Delafield to Adams, November 17, 1824, in Letters Received from the U.S. Agent, NB/NARG 76.

38 Thompson Diary, August 10–September 7, 1824, in Thompson Papers; Ferguson's report of October 27, 1826, in Boundary Claims, Arguments, and Miscellaneous Documents, NB/NARG 76.

39 Daniel Brent, Dept. of State, to Delafield, March 24, 1824, in Domestic Letters, vol. 20, p. 328, NARG 59.

40 Delafield's statement to the boundary commissioners, October 25, 1824, Hale's statement of October 20, 1824, a copy of McGillivray to Hale, September 4, 1824—all attached to Delafield to Adams, November 17, 1824, in Letters Received from the U.S. Agent, NB/NARG 76. McGillivray's letter is published in 25 Congress, 2 session, *House Executive Documents*, no. 451, pp. 121–123.

41 Barclay to Canning, October 28, 1824, in FO/5, vol. 187, pp. 300–302; Journal of Proceedings for period February 16, 1824–October 17, 1826, p. 112, NB/NARG 76; Delafield, *Unfortified Boundary*, 82.

42 Journal of Proceedings for period February 16, 1824–October 17, 1826, pp. 109–112, NB/NARG 76. For more information on the maps, see Chapter 6, notes 8, 34.

43 Porter to Adams, November 10, 1824, in Letters Received from the U.S. Commissioner, and Delafield to John Quincy Adams, November 17, 1824, in Letters Received from the U.S. Agent, both in NB/NARG 76; the latter is quoted in Delafield, *Unfortified Boundary*, 86, 91.

44 Delafield to Adams, November 17, 1824, in Letters Received from the U.S. Agent, NB/NARG 76; Delafield, *Unfortified Boundary*, 87.

45 Canning to Barclay, December 13, 1824, in FO/5, vol. 187, pp. 181–184.

46 Sketch of Tiarks in *Allgemeine Deutsche Biographie*, 39:92–94 (Leipzig, 1895); Barclay to Ogilvy, October 22, 1817, in Rives, ed., *Correspondence of Thomas Barclay*, 387.

47 Thomas Barclay to Planta, May 21, 1822, Anthony Barclay to Planta, January 21, 1822, in FO/5, vol. 170, pp. 49, 128; Canning to Barclay, December 13, 1824, in FO/5, vol. 187, pp. 181–184; *Allgemeine Deutsche Biographie*, 39:92–94.

48 Here and below, see Canning to Barclay, December 13, 1824, and memorandum of Tiarks' opinion attached, in FO/5, vol. 187, pp. 181–184, 187.

49 Barclay to Planta, February 14, 23, 1825, in FO/5, vol. 200, pp. 62–65, 68.

50 Barclay to Planta, May 16, 1825, in FO/5, vol. 200, p. 76; Barclay to Fraser, April 9, 1825, in Porter Papers, 7A–0523; IBC, *Report of Boundary from Northwesternmost Point of Lake of the Woods to Lake Superior*, 218. On Hassler and his important work with the Coast Survey, later the U.S. Coast and Geodetic Survey, see A. Joseph Wraight and Elliott B. Roberts, *The Coast and Geodetic Survey 1807–1957: 150 Years of History*, 5–14 (Washington, D.C., 1957). His role in the expedition is not clear; he was not officially assigned to either commission. Perhaps he was invited by Tiarks, with whom he had become well acquainted during their work on the northeast boundary survey.

51 J[ohann] L. Tiarks, "N.W. Point of the Lake of the Woods," in *American Journal of Science and the Arts (Silliman's Journal)*, 15:43 (1829); the two pocket chronometers used by Tiarks were an Arnold, model number 2111, and a Morice, model number 201. His work on Lake of the Woods is also described in Barclay to Sir Edward Thornton, October 16, 1872, in FO/5, vol. 1456, p. 312.

52 Tiarks, in *American Journal of Science and the Arts*, 15:51, including numerous tables of his readings taken at Angle Inlet and Rat Portage. See also Tiarks' statement attached to Barclay to Planta, November 7, 1825, Barclay to Planta, October 5, 1825, both in FO/5, vol. 200, pp. 84, 90.

53 Hudson's Bay Company statement of supplies received by Anthony Barclay at Fort William on August 22, 1825, in FO/5, vol. 240, p. 296; IBC, *Report of Boundary from Northwesternmost Point of Lake of the Woods to Lake Superior*, 218; statement of expenses of Article 7 commission for the year ending January 5, 1826, by Richard Williams, in FO/5, vol. 240, p. 75; manuscript copy of Tiarks' report in Porter Papers, 7A–0532–0544; Barclay to Planta, October 5, November 7, 1825, in FO/5, vol. 200, pp. 90, 92. Tiarks' report was published four years later; see note 51, above.

54 Tiarks, "Remarks on the Seventh Article of the Treaty of Ghent," in FO/5, vol. 215, pp. 371–376.

55 Journal of Proceedings for period February 16, 1824–October 17, 1826, pp. 113–120, and Porter to Henry Clay, November 16, 1825, in Letters Received from the U.S. Commissioner, both in NB/NARG 76.

CHAPTER 6.

DISAGREEMENTS UNRESOLVED, 1826–27 — *Pages 50 to 62.*

1 Planta to Barclay, March 8, 1826, in FO/5, vol. 215, pp. 43–45; Barclay to Porter, April 25, 1826, in Letters Received from the U.S. Commissioner, NB/NARG 76.

2 Porter to Clay, May 15, 1826, in Letters Received from the U.S. Commissioner, NB/NARG 76; Clay to Porter, September 25, 1826, in Domestic Letters, vol. 21, p. 390, NARG 59.

3 Vaughan to Barclay, August 10, September 15, 26, 1826, Barclay to Planta, August 11, 1826—all in FO/5, vol. 215, pp. 166–172, 196–198, 201; Porter to Clay, August 28, 1826, Barclay to Porter, August 2, 1826, both in Letters Received from the U.S. Commissioner, NB/NARG 76; Clay to Porter, September 25, 1826, in Domestic Letters, vol. 21, p. 390, NARG 59.

4 Barclay to Canning, February 27, 1826, in FO/5, vol. 215, pp. 127–131; Ferguson to Porter, March 30, 1826, Delafield to Porter, April 16, 1826, both in Porter Papers, 7A–0556, 0561. Known by both names in the 1800s, St. George Island is now officially Sugar Island, so called because of its stands of sugar maple trees.

5 Journal of Proceedings for October 23, 1826, attached to Delafield to Clay, November 15, 1826, in Letters Received from the U.S. Agent, NB/NARG 76; Delafield, *Unfortified Boundary*, 48–61; Classen, *Thrust and Counterthrust*, 101; Joseph E. and Estelle L. Bayliss and Milo M. Quaife, *River of Destiny: The Saint Marys*, 70–72, 77–80 (Detroit, 1955). The journals for meetings of October 23, November 10, 1826, October 22–27, 1827, are published in *British and Foreign State Papers*, 57:803–823. Wolfe Island is at the head of the St. Lawrence River; Barnhart Island is near the site of St. Regis, N.Y. (see end sheet map).

6 Here and two paragraphs below, see Journal of Proceedings for period February 16, 1824–October 17, 1826, pp. 121–131, and for October 23, 1826, attached to Delafield to Clay, November 15, 1826; Hale's claim and argument, October 5, 1826, and Delafield's claim and argument, October 5, 1826—all in Letters Received from the U.S. Agent, NB/NARG 76. On Delafield's report, see also p. 62, below.

7 Here and below, see the further arguments and claims by Hale, October 6, 9, 1826, and Delafield's objections to them, October 7, 1826, both in Letters Received from the U.S. Agent; Journal of the New York meeting of the board of commissioners, October 4–17, 1826—all in NB/NARG 76.

8 Journal of Proceedings for October 17, 23, 1826, attached to Delafield to Clay, November 15, 1826, in Letters Received from the U.S. Agent, NB/NARG 76. For copies of the maps drawn by Article 7 surveyors and draftsmen, see Moore, *International Arbitrations*, vol. 6, maps 26–61; on these reproductions only those sections of the boundary line agreed upon by Porter and Barclay are indicated.

9 Here and the following two paragraphs, see Porter to Clay, October 31, 1826, in Letters Received from the U.S. Commissioner; David Thompson's sworn affadavit, June 3, 1827, in Report of the British Commissioner on Article 7, October 25, 1827, Appendix A; Report of the American Commissioner on Article 7, December 24, 1827, pp. 4–10—all in NB/NARG 76. See also note 36, below.

10 Here and the following four paragraphs, see Journal of Proceedings for October 23, 1826, attached to Delafield to Clay, November 15, 1826, in Letters Received from the U.S. Agent, NB/NARG 76;

Moore, *International Arbitrations*, 1:176–188. On the "Old Road" between the Kaministikwia River and Lac la Croix, see Delafield, *Unfortified Boundary*, 436–449; Kane *et al.*, eds., *Long Expeditions*, 218–228. Both Delafield and Long traveled the route from Lac la Croix to Fort William. Chapeau Island, which appeared on the Article 7 maps as a single island, is actually a cluster now called Gull Islands. The names of lakes and rivers used here to trace the proposed boundary lines are those found on modern maps.

¹¹ Delafield to Adams, November 17, 1824, in Letters Received from the U.S. Agent, NB/NARG 76.

¹² Hale's claim and argument, October 5, 1826, in Letters Received from the U.S. Agent, NB/NARG 76; Barclay to Planta, October 28, 1826, in FO/5, vol. 215, pp. 218–225.

¹³ Journal of Proceedings for October 23, 1826, in Letters Received from the U.S. Agent, NB/NARG 76.

¹⁴ Porter to Clay, November 2, 1826, in Letters Received from the U.S. Commissioner, NB/NARG 76.

¹⁵ Porter to Clay, October 18, August 28, 1826, in Letters Received from the U.S. Commissioner, NB/NARG 76; Clay to Porter, September 25, 1826, in Domestic Letters, vol. 21, p. 390, NARG 59.

¹⁶ Here and below, see Barclay to Planta, October 31, 1826, in FO/5, vol. 215, pp. 226, 233; Porter to Clay, October 18, 1826, in Letters Received from the U.S. Commissioner, NB/NARG 76; Clay to Porter, October 22, 1826, in Domestic Letters, vol. 21, p. 406, NARG 59. For Long's published report, see William H. Keating, *Narrative of an Expedition to the Source of St. Peter's River . . . under the Command of Stephen H. Long*, 2:230 (Philadelphia, 1824).

¹⁷ Barclay to Planta, October 28, 1826, in FO/5, vol. 215, pp. 218–225; Vaughan to Clay, October 23, 1826, in Porter Papers, 7B–0037–0039.

¹⁸ Journal of Proceedings for November 10, 1826, attached to Delafield to Clay, November 15, 1826, in Letters Received from the U.S. Agent, NB/NARG 76.

¹⁹ Clay to Porter, October 27, 1826, in Domestic Letters, vol. 21, p. 412, NARG 59; Porter to Clay, October 31, November 2, 1826, Ferguson to Porter, November 1, 1826—all in Letters Received from the U.S. Commissioner, NB/NARG 76; Porter to Clay, November 7, 1826, in Porter Papers, 7B–0066.

²⁰ Clay to Vaughan, November 15, 1826, in Porter Papers, 7B–0077–0081.

²¹ Porter to Clay, November 2, 1826, in Letters Received from the U.S. Commissioner, NB/NARG 76; Clay to Porter, November 13, 1826, in Domestic Letters, vol. 21, p. 422, NARG 59.

²² Porter to Clay, December 23, 1826, in Letters Received from the U.S. Commissioner, NB/NARG 76.

²³ Bird to Porter, October 22, 1826, in Porter Papers, 7B–0032.

²⁴ Walters, *Gallatin*, 330–333.

²⁵ Walters, *Gallatin*, 333–335; Frederick Merk, *Albert Gallatin and the Oregon Problem: A Study in Anglo-American Diplomacy*, 55–57 (Cambridge, Mass., 1950).

²⁶ Clay to Porter, November 10, 1826, in Domestic Letters, vol. 21, p. 419, NARG 59.

²⁷ Barclay to Planta, May 8, 1827, in FO/5, vol. 240, pp. 125–131.

²⁸ Barclay to Planta, October 28, 1826, Planta to Barclay, January 8, 1827, both in FO/5, vol. 215, pp. 218–225, vol. 240, pp. 29–32; Delafield to Clay, April 6, 1827, in Letters Received from the U.S. Agent, Porter to Clay, February 27, April 20, 1827, in Letters Received from the U.S. Commissioner, both in NB/NARG 76.

²⁹ Planta to Barclay, January 8, 1827, Barclay to Planta, April 4, 1827, both in FO/5, vol. 240, pp. 29–32, 115–118.

³⁰ Barclay to Planta, May 8, 1827, John Backhouse to Barclay, July 5, 1827, both in FO/5, vol. 240, pp. 47, 125–131.

³¹ Porter discharged Whistler on November 1, 1826, and Ferguson on November 15, 1826, but he rehired Ferguson for three months in 1827 to complete some maps. Barclay terminated Hale on April 5, 1827, and Samuel Thompson on July 5, 1827. Proceedings of the New York meeting of the boundary commissioners, October 22–27, 1827, attached to Delafield to Clay, November 6, 1827, in Letters Received from the U.S. Agent, NB/NARG 76. See also Barclay to Porter, September 13, 25, 1827, Porter to Barclay, September 19,

October 21, 1827—all in FO/5, vol. 240, pp. 186, 188, 190–197; Porter to Clay, October 30, 1827, in Letters Received from the U.S Commissioner, NB/NARG 76.

³² For the treaties signed in 1827, see Miller, ed., *Treaties*, 3:309, 319–323; see also Merk, *Albert Gallatin and the Oregon Problem*, 66–73; Walters, *Gallatin*, 335–341.

³³ Proceedings of the New York meeting of the boundary commissioners, October 22–27, 1827, attached to Delafield to Clay, November 6, 1827, in Letters Received from the U.S. Agent, NB/NARG 76; Barclay to Viscount Dudley, October 27, 1827, in FO/5, vol. 240, p. 182.

³⁴ For a list of the maps, see *British and Foreign State Papers*, 57:817–819; see also Moore, *International Arbitrations*, vol. 6, maps no. 26–61.

³⁵ Here and below, see Proceedings of the New York meeting of the boundary commissioners, October 22–27, 1827, attached to Delafield to Clay, November 6, 1827, in Letters Received from the U.S. Agent, NB/NARG 76; Barclay to Planta, January 6, 1827, in FO/5, vol. 240, pp. 54–58; Porter to Clay, October 30, 1827, in Letters Received from the U.S. Commissioner, NB/NARG 76.

³⁶ The manuscript reports, described here and below, are in NB/NARG 76. Verbatim versions were published in 25 Congress, 2 session, *House Executive Documents*, no. 451, pp. 7–10, Appendix A, 117–119.

³⁷ Report of the British Commissioner on Article 7, October 25, 1827, sections 11, 94, 98, 101, 105, 108, 110–113, 122, 123, 143, 158, 175, 183, Appendixes B, I, J, K, in NB/NARG 76.

³⁸ Here and below, see Report of the U.S. Commissioner on Article 7, December 12, 1827, pp. 3–10, 39–44, 46, in NB/NARG 76. Copies of the maps appended by Porter, plus "An accurate Map of the United States of America according to the Treaty of Peace 1783" from the "Atlas for Winterbothams America, 1796," and "Map Exhibiting the new discoveries the interior part of North America . . . ," by Aaron Arrowsmith, 1796, are published with the commissioners' reports in 25 Congress, 2 session, *House Executive Documents*, no. 451.

³⁹ Delafield sent the American and British reports to Clay on February 26, 1828. See Delafield to Clay, December 26, 1827, February 26, 1828, to Brent, March 31, 1828—all in Letters Received from the U.S Agent, NB/NARG 76.

CHAPTER 7.

THE WEBSTER-ASHBURTON TREATY—
Pages 63 to 71.

¹ The 1842 treaty between the United States and Great Britain was known as the Treaty of Washington from the time it was negotiated until 1871, when it was renamed the Webster-Ashburton Treaty to distinguish it from the Treaty of Washington completed between the two countries that year. Miller, ed., *Treaties*, 4:377.

² Miller, ed., *Treaties*, 4:381.

³ J. R. Baldwin, "The Webster-Ashburton Boundary Settlement," in *Canadian Historical Association Report*, 1938, p. 129 (Toronto, 1938); Julius W. Pratt, *A History of United States Foreign Policy*, 92 (3rd ed., Englewood Cliffs, N.J., 1972).

⁴ Pratt, *United States Foreign Policy*, 92, 95; Moore, *International Arbitrations*, 1:103–117.

⁵ The verbatim text of King William's award is published in Moore, *International Arbitrations*, 1:127–136, and "Paper Relative to the Disputed Boundary between New Brunswick and the United States," 7–12, in *British Parliamentary Papers, Colonies: Canadian Boundary* (Irish University Press Series, vol. 1—Shannon, Ireland, 1969). See also Howard Jones, *To the Webster-Ashburton Treaty: A Study in Anglo-American Relations, 1783–1843*, 15 (Chapel Hill, N.C., 1977).

⁶ Here and below, see *Dictionary of American Biography*, 15:184 (1935); Preble to Baron Verstolk de Soelen, Netherlands minister for foreign affairs, January 12, 1831, in "Correspondence Relating to the North American Boundary," 1–3, in *British Parliamentary Papers, Colonies: Canadian Boundary* (IUP Series, vol. 1); McInnis,

Unguarded Frontier, 161; Moore, *International Arbitrations,* 1:137–140; Charles E. Clark, *Maine: A Bicentennial History,* 83 (New York, 1977).

7 Moore, *International Arbitrations,* 1:140. On Cushing, here and below, see *Congressional Globe,* 25 Congress, 2 session, vol. 6, p. 415, and *House Journal,* 973 (serial 320).

8 For the House publication of the final reports, see 25 Congress, 2 session, *House Executive Documents,* no. 451.

9 On Forsyth's role in the northeastern boundary dispute, see Alvin L. Duckett, *John Forsyth, Political Tactician,* 203–212 (Athens, Ga., 1962); Forsyth to Fox, April 27, 1838, to Andrew Stevenson, U.S. minister to Great Britain, May 4, 1838, Stevenson to Forsyth, May 28, 1838—all in Manning, ed., *Diplomatic Correspondence,* 3:53, 54, 467. See also Moore, *International Arbitrations,* 1:141, 144.

10 On the so-called Aroostook War and sectional problems here and below, see Thomas Le Duc, "The Maine Frontier and the Northeastern Boundary Controversy," in *American Historical Review,* 53:30, 40 (October, 1947); Samuel F. Bemis, *A Diplomatic History of the United States,* 226, 257, 265 (4th ed., New York, 1955); Thomas A. Bailey, *A Diplomatic History of the American People,* 215, 221–223, 242–245 (8th ed., New York, 1969).

11 Bailey, *Diplomatic History,* 198–200; Wayne S. Cole, *An Interpretive History of American Foreign Relations,* 122 (Rev. ed., Homewood, Ill., 1974).

12 Pratt, *United States Foreign Policy,* 98; Wilbur D. Jones, *Lord Aberdeen and the Americas,* 2 (Athens, Ga., 1958); Albert C. Corey, "Public Opinion and the McLeod Case," in *Canadian Historical Association Report,* 1936, pp. 53–64 (Toronto, 1936).

13 Cole, *American Foreign Relations,* 123.

14 *Dictionary of American Biography,* 19:585–592 (1936).

15 Claude M. Fuess, *Daniel Webster,* 2:72–77 (Reprint ed., Hamden, Conn., 1963); Bemis, *Diplomatic History of the United States,* 261.

16 Jones, *Lord Aberdeen,* 1, 10; Baldwin, in *Canadian Historical Association Report,* 1938, p. 124.

17 J. W. McIntyre, ed., *The Writings and Speeches of Daniel Webster,* 11:270 (National ed., Boston, 1903), hereafter cited as Webster, *Writings and Speeches;* biographical sketch of Ashburton in *Dictionary of National Biography,* 1:1110; Baldwin, in *Canadian Historical Association Report,* 1938, p. 122; extracts from Everett to Webster, December 31, 1841, Webster to Everett, January 29, 1842, both in Hugh T. Gordon, *The Treaty of Washington, Concluded August 9, 1842, by Daniel Webster and Lord Ashburton,* 62–64 (Berkeley, Calif., 1908).

18 Aberdeen to Ashburton, February 8, 1842, in FO/5, vol. 378, pp. 1, 4; Wilbur D. Jones, "Lord Ashburton and the Maine Boundary Negotiations," in *Mississippi Valley Historical Review,* 40:479 (December, 1953).

19 On the Oregon and Article 7 matters. here and below, see Aberdeen to Ashburton, February 8, 1842, in FO/5, vol. 378, pp. 11–20. Aberdeen did not mention that Barclay and Porter had agreed on the boundary from the head of Rainy Lake to the northwest point of Lake of the Woods, but his familiarity with other sections of the boundary west of Lake Huron indicates that he was undoubtedly aware of it.

20 Aberdeen to Ashburton, February 8, 1842, List of Papers for Mission to the United States, both in FO/5, vol. 378, pp. 21–34.

21 Aberdeen to Ashburton, March 31, 1842, in FO/5, vol. 378, pp. 47–52; Jones, in *Mississippi Valley Historical Review,* 40:480.

22 Aberdeen to Ashburton, March 31, 1842, in FO/5, vol. 378, pp. 50–52; Moore, *International Arbitrations,* 1:106, 112, 119, 135.

23 Ashburton to Aberdeen, April 8, 1842, in FO/5, vol. 379, p. 1; Wilbur D. Jones, *The American Problem in British Diplomacy, 1841–1861,* 20 (London, 1974); *Dictionary of National Biography,* 1:1110; *Dictionary of American Biography,* 19:585, 587; Ephraim D. Adams, "Lord Ashburton and the Treaty of Washington," in *American Historical Review,* 17:770, 779–781 (July, 1912).

24 Webster to Everett, April 25, May 16, 1842, in Charles M. Wiltse, ed., *Microfilm Edition of the Papers of Daniel Webster,* roll 17, frames 22246–22252, 22460–22463 (Ann Arbor, 1971); Ashburton to Aberdeen, May 29, June 14, 1842, in FO/5, vol. 379, pp. 119–122, 148–154.

25 Ashburton to Aberdeen, April 25, 1842, Aberdeen to Ashburton, May 26, 1842, both in FO/5, vol. 378, pp. 55–65, vol. 379, pp. 3–19; Adams, in *American Historical Review,* 17:772.

26 Ashburton to Aberdeen, June 29, 1842, in FO/5, vol. 379, p. 172.

27 Ashburton to Webster, June 21, 1842, in FO/5, vol. 379, pp. 177, 187–190. For the American response, see Webster to Ashburton, July 8, 1842, in FO/5, vol. 380, pp. 6–26. Nowhere in the formally exchanged propositions was it indicated that an agreement on one section of the boundary was conditional on an accord concerning another section.

28 Johansen and Gates, *Empire on the Columbia,* 199; Frederick Merk, "The Oregon Question in the Webster-Ashburton Negotiations," in *Mississippi Valley Historical Review,* 43:400 (December, 1956); Ashburton to Aberdeen, June 29, 1842, in FO/5, vol. 379, p. 175.

29 Ashburton to Aberdeen, July 13, 1842, in FO/5, vol. 380, pp. 1–5; Miller, ed., *Treaties,* 4:368, 390, 404; Fuess, *Daniel Webster,* 2:107–111; Moore, *International Arbitrations,* 1:150, 154. For additional details on the red-line map, see Martin and Bemis, in *New England Quarterly,* 10:105–111. The United States agreed to pay Maine and Massachusetts $150,000 each. The Netherlands award granted the United States 7,908 square miles and Great Britain 4,119 square miles, whereas the 1842 treaty granted them 7,015 and 5,012 square miles, respectively.

30 For coverage of Ashburton's and Webster's discussions on nonboundary matters, see, for example, Ashburton to Aberdeen, April 25, June 14, 1842, both in FO/5, vol. 379, pp. 3–19, 148–154. Miller, ed., *Treaties,* 4:389, stated that July 14 is "almost certainly the exact date" that Ashburton and Webster reached their agreement on the northeast boundary. See also Ashburton to Webster, July 16, 1842, in FO/5, vol. 380, p. 150.

31 Ashburton to Aberdeen, July 28, August 9, 1842, in FO/5, vol. 380, pp. 86, 126–128. Ashburton's dispatches to Aberdeen were numbered serially beginning with No. 1 of April 8, 1842, and ending with No. 24 of August 31, 1842. That of August 9 is No. 17. All of these dispatches are in the FO/5 records; many are also in the Aberdeen Papers, British Museum, London. The author has a microfilm copy of those for the period April 1–September 30, 1842.

32 Robert Stuart to Webster, July 7, 1842, in *Congressional Globe,* 27 Congress, 3 session, 21. Here and below, see Ashburton to Aberdeen, August 9, 1842, in FO/5, vol. 380, p. 126.

33 Ashburton to Webster, July 16, 1842, in FO/5, vol. 380, p. 152.

34 Stuart to Webster, July 7, 1842, in *Congressional Globe,* 27 Congress, 3 session, 21; Delafield to Fraser, July 20, 1842, Webster to Ferguson and Ferguson's reply, both dated July 25, 1842—all in 27 Congress, 3 session, *Senate Documents,* no. 1, pp. 102–106 (serial 413).

35 Webster to Ashburton, July 27, 1842, in Webster, *Writings and Speeches,* 11:286.

36 Here and two paragraphs below, see Ashburton to Webster, July 29, 1842, in FO/5, vol. 380, pp. 158, 159. On the route of the boundary, see Miller, ed., *Treaties,* 4:366. The Convention of 1818 established the line to the Rocky Mountains.

37 For the text of the treaty and Ashburton's statement on the "Caroline" affair, see Miller, ed., *Treaties,* 4:363–370, 451–454.

38 For descriptions of Webster's efforts to influence public opinion, see Richard N. Current, "Webster's Propaganda and the Ashburton Treaty," in *Mississippi Valley Historical Review,* 34:187–200 (September, 1947); Frederick Merk, *Fruits of Propaganda in the Tyler Administration,* 8–10, 63–68 (Cambridge, Mass., 1971).

39 Here and below, see "Message from the President of the United States, Transmitting a Treaty with Great Britain, &c.," in 27 Congress, 3 session, *Senate Documents,* no. 1, pp. 19–25; George T. Curtis, *Life of Daniel Webster,* 2:133–137 (New York, 1870).

40 For examples of the assumption by historians that Ashburton claimed and then conceded the land between the St. Louis and Pigeon rivers, see Bailey, *Diplomatic History,* 214; Merk, *Fruits of Propaganda,* 75; Pratt, *United States Foreign Policy,* 96. Neither Ashburton's dispatches cited in note 31, above, nor Wiltse, ed., *Microfilm Edition,* the authoritative collection of Webster's papers and correspondence compiled from the resources of numerous repositories, contain any substantiation of Webster's later effort to imply

that he and Ashburton had a major disagreement over the northwest boundary. Both men wrote extensively during the period of the negotiations. Surely if it had been necessary for Webster to wrest northeastern Minnesota from a demanding Ashburton, this fact would have been a major topic in their letters and dispatches.

41 27 Congress, 3 session, *Senate Documents*, no. 1, pp. 19–25.

42 For examples of historians who asserted or inferred that northeastern Minnesota was known to be a valuable mineral region at the time of the Webster-Ashburton Treaty, see Walter Van Brunt, ed., *Duluth and St. Louis County Minnesota*, 1:341 (Chicago, 1921); Fremont P. Wirth, *The Discovery and Exploitation of the Minnesota Iron Lands*, 11 (Cedar Rapids, Ia., 1937); Albert B. Corey, *The Crisis of 1830–1842 in Canadian-American Relations*, 168 (New Haven, Conn., 1941). To add to the confusion, Corey, Merk, *Fruits of Propaganda*, 75, and Bailey, *Diplomatic History*, 214, also imply that the area Britain wanted but Webster secured included the ore-rich Mesabi Range; but Barclay's most extreme claim in Minnesota embraced the relatively small triangle of land bounded on the south and west by the St. Louis, Embarrass, Pike, and Vermilion rivers—comprising only the Vermilion Range and the eastern tip of the Mesabi. For a refutation of this myth, see Thomas Le Duc, "The Webster-Ashburton Treaty and the Minnesota Iron Ranges," in *Journal of American History*, 51:476–481 (December, 1964).

On the Franklin story, see Henry M. Rice, "Mineral Regions of Lake Superior," in *Minnesota Historical Collections*, 2:177 (Reprint ed., St. Paul, 1889); Soule, in *Michigan Pioneer and Historical Collections*, 26:610; Henry O. Evans, *Iron Pioneer: Henry W. Oliver, 1840–1904*, 176–179 (New York, 1942). The present writer was unable to verify the assertion that knowledge of minerals in Minnesota was extant in 1783, despite a search of Franklin biographies, his correspondence and writings, and related works. That the tale is a legend of later invention is supported by this research and by correspondence with William B. Willcox, editor of the Benjamin Franklin Papers, Yale University, May 4, 1979, and Richard B. Morris, editor of the John Jay Papers, Columbia University, May 1, 1979. See also James C. Starbuck, "Ben Franklin and Isle Royale," in *Michigan History*, 46:157–166 (June, 1962).

43 For a review of early knowledge and exploitation of minerals in the Lake Superior region, see David A. Walker, *Iron Frontier: The Discovery and Early Development of Minnesota's Three Ranges*, 1–8, 16–18 (St. Paul, 1979). On the 1826 and 1842 treaties, see Kappler, *Indian Treaties*, 2:269, 542; Alice E. Smith, *The History of Wisconsin, Volume I: From Exploration to Statehood*, 148 (Madison, 1973).

44 Walker, *Iron Frontier*, 16–38.

45 Benton's attacks on the treaty occurred in speeches of August 18, 1842, and February 2, 1843. See *Congressional Globe*, 27 Congress, 3 session, appendix, 1–3, 132–138.

46 Miller, ed., *Treaties*, 4:363; Gordon, *Treaty of Washington*, 44–51.

CHAPTER 8.
MINNESOTA EXPANSIONISM
AND THE UNMARKED BOUNDARY—
Pages 72 to 80.

1 For a brief description of the survey and marking of the northeast boundary, see IBC, *Joint Report upon the Survey and Demarcation of the Boundary between the United States and Canada from the Source of the St. Croix River to the St. Lawrence River*, 322–336 (Washington, D.C., 1925). On the land survey from the Strait of Georgia to the continental divide, as well as the San Juan Islands dispute, here and below, see John E. Parsons, *West on the 49th Parallel: Red River to the Rockies, 1872–1876*, 7–12 (New York, 1963); Classen, *Thrust and Counterthrust*, 210–283. For the broad diplomatic context of the island controversy, see Bailey, *Diplomatic History*, 383–389.

2 *Congressional Globe*, 36 Congress, 1 session, 2:1350.

3 For the early history of the Red River Colony, here and below, see Jackson, *History of Manitoba*, 32–70; W. L. Morton, *Manitoba:*

A History, 44–93 (2nd ed., Toronto, 1967); John P. Pritchett, *The Red River Valley 1811–1849: A Regional Study* (New Haven, Conn., 1942); Alexander Ross, *The Red River Settlement* (Reprint ed., Minneapolis, 1957). See also Rhoda R. Gilman, Carolyn Gilman, and Deborah M. Stultz, *The Red River Trails: Oxcart Routes between St. Paul and the Selkirk Settlement, 1820–1870*, 1–10 (St. Paul, 1979).

4 Folwell, *History of Minnesota*, 1:132–134 (Rev. ed., St. Paul, 1956). On Fort Snelling, now completely reconstructed and operated as a public historic site, see Holmquist and Brookins, *Minnesota's Major Historic Sites*, 1–8.

5 On the early American frontier in Minnesota to 1858, see Theodore C. Blegen, *Minnesota: A History of the State*, 143–211 (Rev. ed., Minneapolis, 1975); Folwell, *History of Minnesota*, vol. 1.

6 Rhoda R. Gilman, "The Last Days of the Upper Mississippi Fur Trade," in *Minnesota History*, 42:129–132 (Winter, 1970); Gilman, *et al.*, *Red River Trails*, 8–10; Clarence W. Rife, "Norman W. Kittson, A Fur-Trader at Pembina," in *Minnesota History*, 6:225–229, 249–251 (September, 1925).

7 Morton, *Manitoba*, 73; Pritchett, *Red River Valley*, 105–108; Alvin C. Gluek, Jr., *Minnesota and the Manifest Destiny of the Canadian Northwest: A Study in Canadian-American Relations*, 15, 91, 95 (Toronto, 1965).

8 Gilman *et al.*, *Red River Trails*, especially pp. 8, 9, 12, 43–54, 55–80; Morton, *Manitoba*, 75; Gluek, *Minnesota and Manifest Destiny*, 50; Rife, in *Minnesota History*, 6:230, 249. In 1856 the Hudson's Bay Company again asked for troops at Fort Garry, ostensibly to "serve as a counterpoise to the growing influence of the United States in the North West Territory," but actually to support the company's deteriorating political authority over Rupert's Land. A contingent of Royal Canadian Rifles arrived in 1857 and remained until 1861. Gluek, *Minnesota and Manifest Destiny*, 120–125.

9 William E. Lass, *Minnesota: A Bicentennial History*, 76–84 (New York, 1977).

10 Folwell, *History of Minnesota*, 1:266.

11 "Report of Major Wood, relative to his expedition to Pembina Settlement, and the condition of affairs on the North-Western frontier of the Territory of Minnesota," in 31 Congress, 1 session, *House Executive Documents*, no. 51, pp. 2–9 (serial 577). For an earlier attempt by the U.S. to discourage the British company and métis hunters from their activities south of the border, see Gluek, *Minnesota and Manifest Destiny*, 62–65.

12 31 Congress, 1 session, *House Executive Documents*, no. 51, p. 1.

13 Here and below, see 31 Congress, 1 session, *House Executive Documents*, no. 51, pp. 19, 27; Gluek, *Minnesota and Manifest Destiny*, 106; James M. Reardon, *George Anthony Belcourt: Pioneer Missionary of the Northwest, 1803–1874*, 90, 99 (St. Paul, 1955).

14 31 Congress, 1 session, *House Executive Documents*, no. 51, p. 19.

15 "The report of an exploration of the Territory of Minnesota, by Brevet Captain Pope," in 31 Congress, 1 session, *Senate Executive Documents*, no. 42, pp. 28–30, 53–55 (serial 558), and *House Executive Documents*, no. 51, p. 32.

16 Russell W. Fridley, "When Minnesota Coveted Canada," in *Minnesota History*, 41:76 (Summer, 1968); Gluek, *Minnesota and Manifest Destiny*, 105; 31 Congress, 1 session, *House Executive Documents*, no. 51, p. 41.

17 Rife, in *Minnesota History*, 6:245; Folwell, *History of Minnesota*, 1:288; Gluek, *Minnesota and Manifest Destiny*, 107. For an account of Ramsey's journey, see Willoughby M. Babcock, "With Ramsey to Pembina: A Treaty-Making Trip in 1851," in *Minnesota History*, 38:1–10 (March, 1962).

18 Folwell, *History of Minnesota*, 1:288–291. The Ojibway eventually gave up their Minnesota lands by treaties completed in 1854, 1855, 1863 (included cession of lands along the Red River from the 49th parallel southward), 1864, and 1866. Folwell, 4:190–192.

19 Gluek, *Minnesota and Manifest Destiny*, 111–116; Folwell, *History of Minnesota*, 1:354, 359, 390, 392, 393. The Minnesota Enabling Act was approved on February 26, 1857.

20 Folwell, *History of Minnesota*, 1:393, 405–411.

21 On Taylor, see Hartwell Bowsfield, *The James Wickes Taylor Correspondence, 1859–1870*, xiii–xxvi (Manitoba Record Society,

Publications, vol. 3—Altona, Man., 1968); Theodore C. Blegen, "James Wickes Taylor: A Biographical Sketch," in *Minnesota History Bulletin*, 1:155–161 (November, 1915); Gluek, *Minnesota and Manifest Destiny*, 132.

22 On speculative activity in Minnesota Territory from 1855 to 1857, see Folwell, *History of Minnesota*, 1:361–364; Minnesota Territory, *Laws*, 1857, extra session, 4, 34–48, 203, 332. St. Vincent was the site of a North West Company fur post as early as the 1790s. Later, Selkirkers settled in the community along with missionaries. The railroad reached there in 1878 and the town flourished. Grace Lee Nute, "Posts in the Minnesota Fur-Trading Area, 1660–1855," in *Minnesota History*, 11:366 (December, 1930); Kittson County Enterprise, *Encyclopedia and Historical Record of Past and Present Events*, 23, 48, 49 (Hallock, 1935); *Our Northwest Corner: Histories of Kittson County, Minnesota*, 532 (Dallas, Tex., 1976); *History of the Red River Valley*, 2:943 (Chicago, 1909).

The plat maps of St. Vincent and Pembina are in the Alfred J. Hill Papers, MHS Division of Archives and Manuscripts. On the preemption of unsurveyed lands, see Paul W. Gates, *History of Public Land Law Development*, 244 (Washington, D.C., 1968); Minnesota Territory, *Laws*, 1857, extra session, 46.

23 Gluek, *Minnesota and Manifest Destiny*, 133–136; Morton, *Manitoba*, 94–100; Palliser, *Papers Relative to the Exploration . . . of British North America* (London, 1859); Hind, *North-West Territory, Reports of Progress*. On the Fraser River gold rush, see Alexander Begg, *History of British Columbia*, 263–270 (Toronto, 1894); Margaret A. Ormsby, *British Columbia: A History*, 135–163 (Vancouver, 1958); "To Red River and Beyond," in *Harper's New Monthly Magazine*, 21:289–311, 581–606 (August, October, 1860).

24 Blegen, in *Minnesota History Bulletin*, 1:166–168. For extensive reports on the four meetings of the Fraser River Convention, see *St. Paul Pioneer and Democrat*, July 9, 11, 12, 14, 18, 25, 27, 30, 31, 1858; Minnesota, *Senate Journal*, 1857, appendixes, pp. 1–98.

25 Harold E. Briggs, "Pioneer River Transportation in Dakota," in *North Dakota Historical Quarterly*, 3:173 (April, 1929).

26 Blegen, in *Minnesota History Bulletin*, 1:171, 172, 175. Taylor retained the appointment until 1869. His reports were published in *Relations between the United States and Northwest British America*, 37 Congress, 2 session, *House Executive Documents*, no. 146 (serial 1138).

27 Alan Artibise, "The Crucial Decade: Red River at the Outbreak of the American Civil War," in *Historical and Scientific Society of Manitoba Papers*, 3rd series, 23:59, 64 (1966–67); Gluek, *Minnesota and Manifest Destiny*, 160.

28 Gluek, *Minnesota and Manifest Destiny*, 160; Reginald G. Trotter, "Some American Influences upon the Canadian Federation Movement," in *Canadian Historical Review*, 5:220–222 (September, 1924).

29 Gluek, *Minnesota and Manifest Destiny*, 183–191, 204. On the reciprocity issue, see Lester B. Shippee, *Canadian-American Relations 1849–1874*, 159–179 (New Haven, Conn., 1939).

30 Theodore C. Blegen, "A Plan for the Union of British North America and the United States, 1866," in *Mississippi Valley Historical Review*, 4:472–475 (March, 1918); Gluek, *Minnesota and Manifest Destiny*, 204–210. See also Beckles Willson, *The Life of Lord Strathcona and Mount Royal*, 1:432 (Boston and New York, 1915); George F. Stanley, *The Birth of Western Canada: A History of the Riel Rebellion*, 35–37 (New York, 1936).

31 Blegen, in *Mississippi Valley Historical Review*, 4:480n; Donald F. Warner, *The Idea of Continental Union: Agitation for the Annexation of Canada to the United States 1849–1893*, 110 (Lexington, Ky., 1960); Shippee, *Canadian-American Relations*, 201.

32 Bowsfield, *Taylor Correspondence*, 53n; Gluek, *Minnesota and Manifest Destiny*, 214–217; "Resolutions of the legislature of Minnesota, in relation to the purchase of Alaska and the transfer of territories between Minnesota and Alaska to the dominion of Canada," in 40 Congress, 2 session, *Senate Miscellaneous Documents*, no. 68 (serial 1319); Blegen, in *Mississippi Valley Historical Review*, 4:480.

33 Taylor to William H. Seward, November 18, 1868, in Bowsfield, *Taylor Correspondence*, 57.

34 Warner, *Idea of Continental Union*, 94, 96–98, 106; Shippee, *Canadian-American Relations*, 204. For more on the "Alabama," see Joe Patterson Smith, "American Republican Leadership and the Movement for the Annexation of Canada in the Eighteen-Sixties," in *Canadian Historical Association, Report*, 1935, p. 74 (Toronto, 1935).

35 Morton, *Manitoba*, 115–123.

36 Morton, *Manitoba*, 118–145; Gluek, *Minnesota and Manifest Destiny*, 249, 251, 262–294. The Dawson Road, a combined water-land route linking Fort William (Thunder Bay) and Fort Garry (Winnipeg), was named for Simon J. Dawson, the engineer who first suggested its construction in 1858. See also pp. 85, 98, below. For more on Riel and the rebellion he led, see Stanley, *Birth of Western Canada*, 44–174.

37 Blegen, in *Minnesota History Bulletin*, 1:193; Warner, *Idea of Continental Union*, 107, 109, 112; Ruth E. Sanborn, "The United States and the British Northwest, 1865–1870," in *North Dakota Historical Quarterly*, 6:36 (October, 1931); Gluek, *Minnesota and Manifest Destiny*, 218, 274.

38 Morton, *Manitoba*, 142–144. Lieutenant-Governor Adams G. Archibald was delayed en route and arrived at Fort Garry on September 2.

39 For detailed accounts of the O'Donoghue affair, here and below, see Roy P. Johnson, "The Fenian 'Invasion' of 1871," in *Historical and Scientific Society of Manitoba Papers*, 3rd series, 7:30–39 (1952); John P. Pritchett, "The Origin of the So-Called Fenian Raid on Manitoba in 1871," in *Canadian Historical Review*, 10:23–42 (March, 1929); *St. Paul Pioneer*, October 8, 11, 12, 17, November 9, 10, 1871; *St. Paul Daily Pioneer*, October 11, 1871. Both the Hudson's Bay Company post and the new American military installation near the boundary were called Fort Pembina.

40 Taylor's lingering hopes for a union of the United States and Canada finally died in 1885 with Canada's suppression of Louis Riel's second rebellion, his arrest, trial, and execution, and the completion of the transcontinental Canadian Pacific Railway. The latter helped bind the West closer to the Dominion, both practically and symbolically, and was a factor in undercutting a modest annexationist movement in British Columbia as well as in the prairie regions of Manitoba and Saskatchewan. French resentment over Riel's execution briefly rekindled annexationist desires in Quebec and eastern Ontario. Bailey, *Diplomatic History*, 374; Blegen, in *Minnesota History Bulletin*, 1:195–204; Warner, *Idea of Continental Union*, 193–195.

41 Stafford Northcote, Hudson's Bay Company, to Sir F. Rogers, November 15, 1870, in FO/5, vol. 1475, pp. 90–93; Irene M. Spry, ed., *The Papers of the Palliser Expedition, 1857–1860*, cxxiv, 98–101 (Toronto, 1968). On p. 12 of his 1859 book (see note 23, above), Palliser attributed the Long-Woods marker to "Mr. Nicolay," apparently referring to Joseph N. Nicollet, the famous French cartographer whose travels never took him to the boundary area.

42 Thornton to [J. C. B.] Davis, November 4, 1870, in *Papers Relating to the Foreign Relations of the United States, 1870*, 403 (Washington, D.C., 1870); Secretary of Interior, *Reports*, 1868, pp. 298–301 (serial 1366); Moses K. Armstrong, *The Early Empire Builders of the Great West*, 174–182 (St. Paul, 1901); Adams G. Archibald to secretary of state for the provinces, September 29, 1870, in FO/5, vol. 1475, pp. 66–68; Dennis to William McDougall, September 28, 1869, in Adams G. Archibald Papers (dispatch #9), Manitoba Provincial Library and Archives, Winnipeg. Dennis and Canadian and U.S. officials attributed the Long-Woods marker to Pope, whom they had heard of because of his Civil War fame. In a sketch of Armstrong published while he was still alive, he was said to have "discovered an error in the old international boundary post near Pembina, and by its correction added several thousand acres of land to the American domain, including the Hudson's Bay Trading Post"; *Memorial Record of the Counties of Faribault, Martin, Watonwan and Jackson, Minnesota*, 29 (Chicago, 1895).

43 Here and below, see Heap to Hancock, July 9, 1870, in *Foreign Relations of the United States, 1870*, 400.

44 Stoever to secretary of the treasury, June 23, 1870, in *Foreign Relations of the United States, 1870*, 401. Variations of the customs

collector's name include Stover and Storer; the spelling used here is from *Register of Officers and Agents . . . in the Service of the United States, 1869,* 119 (Washington, D.C., 1870).

⁴⁵ Boutwell to Fish, July 19, 1870, J. C. B. Davis to "Mr. Richardson," August 13, 1870, both in *Foreign Relations of the United States, 1870,* 401. See also p. 84, below.

⁴⁶ Thornton to Sir John Young, governor-general of Canada, July 21, 1870, to Lord Granville, secretary of state for foreign affairs, August 1, 1870, Archibald to secretary of state for the provinces, September 29, 1870—all in FO/5, vol. 1475, pp. 1–6, 66–68.

⁴⁷ Humphreys to W. W. Belknap, secretary of war, November 23, 1870, in *Foreign Relations of the United States, 1870,* 406.

⁴⁸ *Foreign Relations of the United States, 1870,* 9; "Northwestern Boundary Commission," in 42 Congress, 1 session, *House Executive Documents,* no. 12 (serial 1471); Thornton to Granville, February 21, April 18, 1871, in FO/5, vol. 1475, pp. 175, 187.

⁴⁹ "Boundary Between the United States and British Possessions," in 42 Congress, 2 session, *House Reports,* no. 1 (serial 1528); Thornton to Granville, January 22, 1872, in FO/5, vol. 1476, p. 14; United States, *Statutes at Large,* vol. 17, p. 43.

CHAPTER 9.
THE RED RIVER—
LAKE OF THE WOODS SURVEY—
Pages 81 to 94.

¹ J. Stansfeld, Treasury Chambers, to F. Rogers, Foreign Office, January 2, 1871, Foreign Office to Colonial Office, May 4, 1871, both in FO/5, vol. 1475, pp. 120, 189–191.

² Hawkins' report, in FO/5, vol. 1475, p. 171.

³ Lord Lisgar to Earl of Kimberley, December 28, 1871, in FO/5, vol. 1476, pp. 3–7.

⁴ Foreign Office to Colonial Office, May 4, 1871, H. Holland, undersecretary of state for colonial affairs, to E. Hammond, undersecretary of state for foreign affairs, October 23, 1871, both in FO/5, vol. 1475, pp. 189–191, 199–201.

⁵ Parsons, *West on the 49th Parallel,* 18; [Sir James] Lindsay to [Granville?], April 22, 1871, in FO/5, vol. 1475, p. 185.

⁶ Lindsay to [Granville?], April 22, 1871, Foreign Office to Colonial Office, May 4, 1871, both in FO/5, vol. 1475, pp. 185, 189–191; Holland to Cameron, February 23, 1872, in FO/5, vol. 1476, p. 43.

⁷ Foreign Office to War Office, April 13, 1872, War Office to undersecretary of state, May 14, 1872, Foreign Office to Cameron, June 6, 1872—all in FO/5, vol. 1476, pp. 69–73, 103–105, 124.

⁸ Parsons, *West on the 49th Parallel,* 19, 21, 30, 36; Cameron to Granville, March 30, 1872, Featherstonhaugh to Granville, April 27, 1872, Foreign Office to War Office, April 27, 1872, War Office to undersecretary of state, May 14, 1872—all in FO/5, vol. 1476, pp. 55–57, 77–80, 103–105; William E. Lass, "Introduction," in George W. Featherstonhaugh, *A Canoe Voyage up the Minnay Sotor,* 1:xv–lxiii (Reprint ed., St. Paul, 1970).

⁹ Foreign Office to War Office, July 11, 1872, Cameron to secretary of state of Canada, July 26, 1872, both in FO/5, vol. 1476, p. 213, vol. 1477, pp. 18–20.

¹⁰ Foreign Office to Cameron, June 6, 1872, Granville to Cameron, June 14, 1872, both in FO/5, vol. 1476, pp. 124, 130–135.

¹¹ George W. Cullum, *Biographical Register of the Officers and Graduates of the U.S. Military Academy,* 1:610 (3rd ed., Boston, 1891); Heitman, *Historical Register and Dictionary of the United States Army,* 1:276; Edward Thornton to Foreign Office, May 11, 23, 1872, in FO/5, vol. 1476, pp. 85, 94; Charles Hale, acting secretary of state, to Campbell, June 12, 1872, in Letters Received by the U.S. Commissioner, NB/NARG 76.

¹² Cullum, *Biographical Register of the U.S. Military Academy,* 2:812, 868, 3:38, 143; Heitman, *Historical Register and Dictionary of the United States Army,* 1:414, 474, 477, 976; *Dictionary of American Biography,* 7:565, 566, 569.

¹³ Here and below, see Granville to Cameron, June 29, 1872, Cameron to Granville, July 25, August 5, 1872—all in FO/5, vol. 1476, pp. 181, 232–234, 250–263.

¹⁴ Lisgar to Kimberley, December 28, 1871, in FO/5, vol. 1476, pp. 3–7.

¹⁵ Dominion Lands Office, Department of the Secretary of State, to Cameron, July 26, August 31, 1872; Cameron to secretary of state of Canada, July 20 [30?], 1872—all in FO/5, vol. 1477, pp. 18–20, 24–28, 37–39.

¹⁶ "List of appointments forming contingent furnished by Canada to staff of International Boundary Commission," August 31, 1872, in FO/5, vol. 1477, p. 38. King served in 1908–16 as commissioner on the joint Canada-United States boundary commission; see p. 103, below. Alexander L. Russell should not be confused with his first cousin Lindsay A. Russell, who was the deputy surveyor general of Canada when the boundary commission was organized. The former was a regular surveyor for the commission, whereas the latter was never a commission member. For biographical information on the Russells, see H. K. Wicksteed, "Alexander Lord Russell," in *The Thunder Bay Historical Society Fifteenth Annual Report,* 25–28 (1924).

¹⁷ Cameron to Granville, July 6, 1872, in FO/5, vol. 1476, p. 205.

¹⁸ Anderson to E. Hammond, August 19, 1872, in FO/5, vol. 1476, p. 246; S[amuel] Anderson, "The North-American Boundary from the Lake of the Woods to the Rocky Mountains," in *Journal of the Royal Geographical Society,* 46:230 (1876); [Albany] Featherstonhaugh, *Narrative of the Operations of the British North American Boundary Commission, 1872–1876,* 26 (Reprint ed., Woolwich, England, 1876); Cameron, final report, February 8, 1876, in FO/5, vol. 1667, p. 35.

¹⁹ Campbell to Fish, June 24, August 24, 1872, to Charles Hale, U.S. acting secretary of state, June 26, July 6, 1872, to Brig. Gen. M. C. Meigs, quartermaster general, U.S. Army, July 22, 1872—all in Letters Sent by the U.S. Commissioner, NB/NARG 76; Hale to Campbell, June 25, 1872, Fish to Campbell, July 16, 1872, M. B. Busler, Rock Island Arsenal, to Campbell, July 23, 1872—all in Letters Received by the U.S. Commissioner, NB/NARG 76.

²⁰ U.S. Dept. of State, *Reports upon the Survey of the Boundary between the Territory of the United States and the Possessions of Great Britain from the Lake of the Woods to the Summit of the Rocky Mountains,* 332 (Washington, D.C., 1878). Fort Abercrombie was built by the federal government in 1857 on the west bank of the Red River, about 12 miles north of Breckenridge. It has been reconstructed.

²¹ On Pembina here and two paragraphs below, see printed copy of Special Orders No. 115, Headquarters, Dept. of Dakota, St. Paul, June 15, 1872, in Letters Received by the U.S. Commissioner, and James F. Gregory, 1872 journal, in Survey Journals, 1872–74, both in NB/NARG 76; Featherstonhaugh, *Narrative of the British North American Boundary Commission,* 27.

²² Cameron, final report, February 8, 1876, in FO/5, vol. 1667, pp. 35, 36.

²³ Here and below, see Cameron to Campbell, October 9, 1872, in Letters Received by the U.S. Commissioner; Campbell to Fish, October 4, 1872, in Letters Sent by the U.S. Commissioner, both in NB/NARG 76.

²⁴ Cameron to Granville, September 23, 1872, in FO/5, vol. 1476, pp. 299–301; Campbell to Fish, September 22, 1872, to Cameron, April 12, 1873, both in Letters Sent by the U.S. Commissioner, NB/NARG 76.

²⁵ Anderson, in *Journal of the Royal Geographical Society,* 46:231.

²⁶ Here and below, see U.S. Dept. of State, *Reports upon the Survey of the Boundary,* 304, 333; Anderson, in *Journal of the Royal Geographical Society,* 46:231; Featherstonhaugh, *Narrative of the British North American Boundary Commission,* 30; Campbell to Fish, October 6, 10, 1872, in Letters Sent by the U.S. Commissioner, NB/NARG 76; Russell to Cameron, September 20, 1872, in Interior Dept., North American Boundary Records, Record Group 15, Public Archives of Canada, Ottawa (hereafter abbreviations RG and PAC are used).

²⁷ Granville to Cameron, June 28, 1872, in FO/5, vol. 1476, pp. 179–181.

²⁸ Morton, *Manitoba,* 115; Don W. Thomson, *Men and Meridians: The History of Surveying and Mapping in Canada,* 2:5, 18 (Ottawa, 1967).

[29] Morton, *Manitoba,* 115; U.S. Dept. of State, *Reports upon the Survey of the Boundary,* 304.

[30] Here and two paragraphs below, see Cameron to Granville, September 23, 1872; Cameron, final report, February 8, 1876, both in FO/5, vol. 1476, pp. 294–298, vol. 1667, p. 35.

[31] Here and below, see Gregory to Farquhar, December 10, 1872, Farquhar to Campbell, December 14, 1872, both in Letters Received by the U.S. Commissioner, NB/NARG 76.

[32] U.S. Dept. of State, *Reports upon the Survey of the Boundary,* 305–307. On McKay, see Gilman *et al., Red River Trails,* 19, 20.

[33] Farquhar to Campbell, December 14, 1872, in Letters Received by the U.S. Commissioner, NB/NARG 76; undersecretary of war to undersecretary of state, April 17, 1874, in FO/5, vol. 1506, pp. 40–46.

[34] Cameron to Granville, February 4, 1874; Cameron, final report, February 8, 1876, both in FO/5, vol. 1505, pp. 137–154, vol. 1667, p. 32.

[35] Cameron to Campbell, November 8, 1872, in Letters Received by the U.S. Commissioner, NB/NARG 76.

[36] Anderson, "Report [to Cameron] of Operations during the Winter of 1872–73," May 31, 1873, in FO/5, vol. 1670, p. 25. Twining's and Galwey's measurements of the starting point at the 49th parallel on the west shore of the lake differed by 28.96 feet and they accepted the mean of the difference. See also Anderson, in *Journal of the Royal Geographical Society,* 46:234; Gregory, 1872 journal, in Survey Journals, 1872–74, NB/NARG 76.

[37] Featherstonhaugh, *Narrative of the British North American Boundary Commission,* 31; Anderson, "Report of Operations during the Winter of 1872–73," May 31, 1873, in FO/5, vol. 1670, p. 23.

[38] Campbell to Fish, September 22, October 6, 10, November 13, 1872, in Letters Sent by the U.S. Commissioner; Gregory, 1872 journal, in Survey Journals, 1872–74, both in NB/NARG 76.

[39] Cameron to Campbell, November 8, 1872, in Letters Received by the U.S. Commissioner, NB/NARG 76.

[40] Here and below, see Anderson, "Report of Operations during the Winter of 1872–73," May 31, 1873, in FO/5, vol. 1670, pp. 25, 28–34; Anderson, in *Journal of the Royal Geographical Society,* 46:235, 237; Featherstonhaugh, *Narrative of the British North American Boundary Commission,* 32. Roseau Lake, with an area of 6,650 acres, lay astride the Roseau River about midway between present Roseau and Pinecreek, Minn. It has been drained in recent times. Minnesota Conservation Dept., *An Inventory of Minnesota Lakes,* 366 (Division of Waters, Soils, and Minerals, *Bulletin no. 25*—St. Paul, 1968).

[41] Anderson, "Report of Operations during the Winter of 1872–73," May 31, 1873, in FO/5, vol. 1670, pp. 30, 33.

[42] *St. Paul Daily Press,* February 22, 1873, p. 4; Campbell to Fish, February 3, 1873, to Cameron, April 12, 1873, both in Letters Sent by the U.S. Commissioner, NB/NARG 76; U.S. Dept. of State, *Reports upon the Survey of the Boundary,* 24.

CHAPTER 10.
WEST TO THE CONTINENTAL DIVIDE—
Pages 95 to 103.

[1] On the Dakota War and its aftermath, see Kenneth Carley, *The Sioux Uprising of 1862* (Revised ed., St. Paul, 1976). See also U.S. Dept. of State, *Reports upon the Survey of the Boundary,* 69; Robert H. Jones, *The Civil War in the Northwest: Nebraska, Wisconsin, Iowa, Minnesota and the Dakotas* (Norman, Okla., 1960); James C. Olson, *Red Cloud and the Sioux Problem,* 41–95 (Lincoln, Nebr., 1965). For the commissions' encounters with Indians in 1873, see Parsons, *West on the 49th Parallel,* 73, 74, 158.

[2] Anderson, in *Journal of the Royal Geographical Society,* 46:238, 241; Cameron, final report, in FO/5, vol. 1667, p. 37; Featherstonhaugh, *Narrative of the British North American Boundary Commission,* 65; U.S. Dept. of State, *Reports upon the Survey of the Boundary,* 69, 275–278, 333; Parsons, *West on the 49th Parallel,* 66.

[3] U.S. Dept. of State, *Reports upon the Survey of the Boundary,* 69; Parsons, *West on the 49th Parallel,* 53–59, 61–67.

[4] Cameron to Campbell, July 4, 1873, in Letters Received by the U.S. Commissioner, NB/NARG 76; U.S. Dept. of State, *Reports upon the Survey of the Boundary,* 69.

[5] Campbell to Cameron, August 29, 1873, in Letters Sent by the U.S. Commissioner; Cameron to Campbell, July 4, September 14, 1873, in Letters Received by the U.S. Commissioner—all in NB/NARG 76.

[6] Cameron, "Confidential memorandum for the information of the Government of the Dominion of Canada relative to the location of the international boundary line," November 19, 1873; Cameron to Granville, February 4, 1874, both in FO/5, vol. 1505, pp. 123–129, 197–200, 220–225.

[7] Campbell to Cameron, August 29, 1873, in Letters Sent by the U.S. Commissioner; Cameron to Campbell, September 14, 1873, in Letters Received by the U.S. Commissioner, both in NB/NARG 76; Cameron to Granville, February 4, 1874, in FO/5, vol. 1505, pp. 123–129.

[8] Campbell to Fish, September 22, November 7, 1873, in Letters Sent by the U.S. Commissioner, NB/NARG 76; Anderson, in *Journal of the Royal Geographical Society,* 46:239–246; Featherstonhaugh, *Narrative of the British North American Boundary Commission,* 38.

[9] Here and below, see Campbell to Cameron, July 6, September 2, 1873, in Letters Sent by the U.S. Commissioner, NB/NARG 76; Barclay to Granville, October 22, 1872, in FO/5, vol. 1476, pp. 310–316; Cameron to Campbell, September 14, 1873, in Letters Received by the U.S. Commissioner, NB/NARG 76.

[10] Cameron to Campbell, July 24, 1873, in Letters Received by the U.S. Commissioner; Campbell to Cameron, August 10, 1873, in Letters Sent by the U.S. Commissioner, both in NB/NARG 76.

[11] Cameron to Campbell, July 4, September 13, 1873, in Letters Received by the U.S. Commissioner, NB/NARG 76.

[12] Campbell to Fish, November 7, 1873, in Letters Sent by the U.S. Commissioner, NB/NARG 76; U.S. Dept. of State, *Reports upon the Survey of the Boundary,* 72; Featherstonhaugh, *Narrative of the British North American Boundary Commission,* 40. On Greene's winter work, see Topographical Party, Journal No. 2, in Survey Journals, 1872–74, NB/NARG 76; U.S. Dept. of State, *Reports upon the Survey of the Boundary,* 371–394; Parsons, *West on the 49th Parallel,* 90.

[13] Cameron, "Confidential memorandum . . . relative to the location of the international boundary line," November 19, 1873, and "Memorandum of a verbal statement referring to the demarcation of the international boundary line," November 29, 1873; Cameron to Col. Fletcher, secretary to the governor-general, December 14, 1873—all in FO/5, vol. 1505, pp. 197–204.

[14] Here and below, see Cameron to Granville, February 4, 25, 1874; Anderson to Wilson, February 7, 1874; Report of the Privy Council committee approved by the governor-general of Canada on February 23, 1874; Anderson, "Remarks on the demarcation of the International Boundary in North America from the Lake of the Woods to the Rocky Mountains," February 10, 1874—all in FO/5, vol. 1505, pp. 108, 129, 182, 185, 187–194, 213–215.

[15] Here and the following two paragraphs, see Anderson to Wilson, February 7, 1874, in FO/5, vol. 1505, p. 108.

[16] Wilson to Lord Tenterden, March 5, 1874, in FO/5, vol. 1505, p. 105.

[17] Holland to Foreign Office, March 24, 1874, in FO/5, vol. 1505, p. 210.

[18] Foreign Office to Cameron, March 27, 1874, Dufferin to Carnarvon, March 28, 1874, both in FO/5, vol. 1505, pp. 59, 226.

[19] Airy, report of April 2, 1874, in Vernon Lushington, Lords Commissioners of the Admiralty, to undersecretary of state for foreign affairs, April 10, 1874, Foreign Office to Cameron, April 17, 1874, both in FO/5, vol. 1506, pp. 17, 35.

[20] Cameron to Earl of Derby, May 18, 1874, in FO/5, vol. 1506, p. 102.

[21] Here and below, see Anderson to Cameron, January 31, 1874, Cameron to Granville, February 4, 1874, both in FO/5, vol. 1505, pp. 137–154, 161–164.

²² Wilson, report, enclosed in undersecretary of war to undersecretary of state, April 17, 1874, in FO/5, vol. 1506, p. 40.

²³ Cameron to Derby, May 23, November 3, 1874, in FO/5, vol. 1506, pp. 108–111, 260–264.

²⁴ Cameron to Derby, June 15, 1874, in FO/5, vol. 1506, pp. 130–132.

²⁵ On the 1874 season, see Anderson, in *Journal of the Royal Geographical Society*, 46:247, 248, 250; U.S. Dept. of State, *Reports upon the Survey of the Boundary*, 62, 74–77, 279, 282, 335; Cameron, final report, in FO/5, vol. 1667, p. 38; Featherstonhaugh, *Narrative of the British North American Boundary Commission*, 42, 65; Twining to Campbell, December 1, 1874, in Letters Received by the U.S. Commissioner, NB/NARG 76; Parsons, *West on the 49th Parallel*, 93–123.

²⁶ Cameron to Campbell, August 13, 1874, in Letters Received by the U.S. Commissioner; Campbell to Cameron, August 19, 1874, in Letters Sent by the U.S. Commissioner, both in NB/NARG 76.

²⁷ Cameron to Campbell, November 8, 1872, Twining to Campbell, December 1, 1874, both in Letters Received by the U.S. Commissioner, NB/NARG 76; Cameron to Derby, November 3, 1874 (two letters), June 25, 1875—all in FO/5, vol. 1506, pp. 254–258, 260–264, vol. 1532, p. 185.

²⁸ U.S. Dept. of State, *Reports upon the Survey of the Boundary*, 285; Cameron to Campbell, April 4, 1874, in Letters Received by the U.S. Commissioner; Campbell to Cameron, April 16, 1874, in Letters Sent by the U.S. Commissioner, both in NB/NARG 76.

²⁹ U.S. Dept. of State, *Reports upon the Survey of the Boundary*, 285; D'Arcy East, report, February 4, 1875, in Interior Department, North American Boundary Records, RG 15, PAC.

³⁰ Cameron to Derby, November 3, 1874, in FO/5, vol. 1505, pp. 254–258; U.S. Dept. of State, *Reports upon the Survey of the Boundary*, 37, 40; Cameron, final report, February 8, 1876, in FO/5, vol. 1667, p. 33. On the British party's Indian scares, see Parsons, *West on the 49th Parallel*, 121, 127.

³¹ Cameron to Derby, November 3, 1874, June 10, 1875; Cameron, final report, February 8, 1876—all in FO/5, vol. 1506, pp. 254–258, vol. 1532, pp. 173–175, vol. 1667, p. 33; Twining to Campbell, December 1, 1874, in Letters Received by the U.S. Commissioner, NB/NARG 76. For Greene's description of the river trip, see Parsons, *West on the 49th Parallel*, 175–192.

³² For details of the map making, see a series of some 40 letters from Anderson to Greene dated between November, 1874, and May, 1875, in Letters Received by the U.S. Surveyor, NB/NARG 76.

³³ Marjorie Forrester, "That Northwest Angle," in *The Beaver*, Autumn, 1960, p. 38; Cameron to Derby, November 3, 1874, in FO/5, vol. 1506, pp. 254–258; Anderson, "Report of Operations during the Summer Season of 1874 and Winter 1874–75," to Cameron, April 30, 1875, in FO/5, vol. 1670, pp. 96–102; East, reports of February 4, 5, 1875, in Interior Department, North American Boundary Records, RG 15, PAC.

The buildings at Dufferin were purchased by the Canadian government for an immigration center. Surplus supplies were used by the newly formed North West Mounted Police. The camp was included in the townsite of West Lynne, developed by the Hudson's Bay Company from 1876 to 1881. Morton, *Manitoba*, 178, 201.

³⁴ Dawson, *Report on the Vicinity of the Forty-Ninth Parallel*, 273–277.

³⁵ Here and below, see East, "Report of Special Survey in the Lake of the Woods District 1873–74," February and March, 1874, in Interior Department, North American Boundary Records, RG 15, PAC.

³⁶ Cameron to Anderson, April 11, 1874, Anderson to Cameron, April 30, 1874, both in FO/5, vol. 1506, pp. 200, 205–211.

³⁷ Here and below, see Cameron to Derby, May 19, 1874, in FO/5, vol. 1506, pp. 185, 186. In 1874 the southeast and southwest corners of Manitoba were 32 and 169 miles west of Lake of the Woods, respectively. A Dominion Act of 1881 enlarged the province to the north and west; it also set the stage for a Judicial Committee of the Privy Council award in 1884 which adjusted Manitoba's eastern boundary to its present location along the meridian line. U.S. Dept. of State, *Reports upon the Survey of the Boundary*, 35, 37; Norman L. Nicholson, *The Boundaries of Canada, Its Provinces and Territories*, 63, 69, 73 (Geographical Branch, Department of Mines and Technical Surveys, Memoir 2—Ottawa, 1964).

³⁸ Laird, memorandum, July 3, 1874, report of the Privy Council of Canada, July 18, 1874, both in FO/5, vol. 1506, pp. 239, 246.

³⁹ Carnarvon to undersecretary of state for foreign affairs, September 5, 1874, in FO/5, vol. 1506, pp. 234–236.

⁴⁰ Colonial Office to undersecretary of state for foreign affairs, January 7, 1875, Derby to Thornton, January 13, 16, 1875—all in FO/5, vol. 1532, pp. 12, 15–19.

⁴¹ Thornton to Derby, February 8, 1875, in FO/5, vol. 1532, p. 130.

⁴² *Dictionary of National Biography*, 18:950 (1949–50); Thornton to Derby, February 15, 1875, in FO/5, vol. 1532, pp. 137, 138.

⁴³ Information from John Olson, forestry division, Minnesota Dept. of Natural Resources; Holmquist and Brookins, *Minnesota's Major Historic Sites*, 145; N. L. Nicholson, "The U.S. Northwest Angle: east of Manitoba," in *Canadian Geographical Journal*, 91:54–59 (February-March, 1978).

⁴⁴ Cameron to Derby, June 25, 1875, Derby to Cameron, August 11, 1875, both in FO/5, vol. 1532, pp. 185, 213; Cameron to Campbell, February 8, 1876, in Letters Received by the U.S. Commissioner, Campbell to Fish, February 23, 1876, in Letters Sent by the U.S. Commissioner, both in NB/NARG 76.

⁴⁵ Here and below, see U.S. Dept. of State, *Reports upon the Survey of the Boundary*, 35, 285–287, 309.

⁴⁶ Cameron to Derby, June 10, 1875, in FO/5, vol. 1532, pp. 173–175.

⁴⁷ U.S. Dept. of State, *Reports upon the Survey of the Boundary*, 31–33. The summary introduction to Cameron's voluminous final report was "printed for the Foreign Office," July 26, 1876, and included in FO/5, vol. 1667. The appendixes in manuscript form, which include such information as lists of astronomical instruments, details of the buildings at Dufferin, and field reports, are in FO/5, vols. 1669, 1670.

CHAPTER 11.

THE BOUNDARY MARKED, 1890–1925—
Pages 104 to 119.

¹ Here and below, see Grace Lee Nute, *Rainy River Country: A Brief History of the Region Bordering Minnesota and Ontario*, 46–50, 61 (St. Paul, 1950); Lyn Harrington, "The Dawson Route," in *Canadian Geographical Journal*, 43:136–143 (September, 1951). On the settlement of Manitoba, 1871–75, see Morton, *Manitoba*, 151–198.

² *Historic Fort William: Canada's Diamond Jubilee 1867–1927*, 10 (Fort William, 1927); Elizabeth Arthur, ed., *Thunder Bay District 1821–1892: A Collection of Documents*, 128 (Toronto, 1973); Nute, *Rainy River Country*, 51–56.

³ Grace Lee Nute, *Lake Superior*, 167–170, 314 (Indianapolis, 1944). Port Arthur and Fort William are now joined as the city of Thunder Bay, Ont.

⁴ Nute, *Lake Superior*, 316.

⁵ Here and below, see *Historic Fort William*, 12; Nute, *Rainy River Country*, 83; Brabazon, report to King, February 1, 1897, p. 1, in Report on the Minnesota-Ontario Border, 1903, NB/NARG 76; Henry V. Poor, *Manual of the Railroads of the United States, 1893*, 1127, *1899*, 892 (New York). On the opening of the Vermilion and Mesabi ranges and the Gunflint Lake district, see Walker, *Iron Frontier*, 1–117, 263 note 4; Folwell, *History of Minnesota*, 4:8–23.

⁶ Here and below, see Nute, *Rainy River Country*, 50–83; *Foreign Relations of the United States 1895*, 1:724. Rainy Lake City was located at the east side of the strait between Rainy Lake and Black Bay or Rat Root Lake. The townsite was abandoned after about 15 years. Koochiching was settled in 1894; it was incorporated as the city of International Falls in 1909. Upham, *Minnesota Geographic Names*, 283, 284.

⁷ *Foreign Relations of the United States 1895*, 1:724; O. H. Tittmann to Secretary of State William Jennings Bryan, March 6, 1915, in State Dept. Decimal File, 1910–1929, file no. 711.42151, item no. 313, NARG 59.

⁸ Here and four paragraphs below, see "Boundary Line Between the United States and Canada," in 54 Congress, 1 session, *House Reports*, no. 1310, pp. 7, 9, 12–15 (serial 3461). On Stuntz, below, see Walker, *Iron Frontier*, 22–24, 27–36, 52, 68, 69, 257; on the Venezuelan boundary settlement, see Bailey, *Diplomatic History*, 438–447.

⁹ *Foreign Relations of the United States 1895*, 1:724.

¹⁰ 54 Congress, 1 session, *House Reports*, no. 1310, pp. 2, 5, 16.

¹¹ Here and two paragraphs below, see Brabazon, report to King, February 1, 1897, pp. 1, 6–14, in Report on the Minnesota-Ontario Border, 1903, NB/NARG 76. On Brabazon, see Thomson, *Men and Meridians*, 2:198.

¹² Here and below, see Winchell, in *Minnesota Historical Collections*, 8:210, 212. On the work of Newton H. Winchell as state geologist and head of the geological and natural history surveys in Minnesota, see F. Garvin Davenport, "Newton H. Winchell, Pioneer of Science," in *Minnesota History*, 32:214–225 (December, 1951).

¹³ Here and below, see N[ewton] H. Winchell, "Another Word About the Northern Boundary of Minnesota," in *Science*, new series, 26:79–83 (July 19, 1907).

¹⁴ On the Alaskan boundary dispute, see Classen, *Thrust and Counterthrust*, 284–351; Bailey, *Diplomatic History*, 507–510. For the texts of the related Treaties of 1892 and 1903, see Charles I. Bevans, comp., *Treaties and Other International Agreements of the United States of America 1776–1949*, 12:231, 263–268 (Washington, D.C., 1974). On the joint high commission of 1898–99, see Charles C. Tansill, *Canadian-American Relations, 1875–1911*, 169–189 (New Haven, 1943); Anderson, memorandum on the "Northern Boundary," p. 11, attached to Anderson to Elihu Root, November 7, 1906, in State Dept. Numerical File, 1906–1910, case file 839, vol. 120, NARG 59.

¹⁵ Classen, *Thrust and Counterthrust*, 356; Bevans, *Treaties*, 12:276–278; IBC, *Joint Report upon the Survey and Demarcation of the International Boundary between the United States and Canada along the 141st Meridian from the Arctic Ocean to Mount St. Elias*, 15–109 ([Washington, D.C.], 1918); IBC, *Joint Report upon the Survey and Demarcation of the Boundary between the United States and Canada from the Gulf of Georgia to the Northwesternmost Point of Lake of the Woods*, 34–93 (Washington, D.C., 1937), hereafter cited as IBC, *Report of Boundary from Gulf of Georgia to Lake of the Woods*.

¹⁶ John W. Foster, "The Canadian Boundary: A Review of the Methods by Which the Line Has Been Adjusted and Marked," in *National Geographic Magazine*, 14:86, 88 (March, 1903).

¹⁷ For a biographical sketch of Anderson, see *Who Was Who in America*, vol. 1, 1897–1942, p. 22 (Chicago, 1942). On his study, see Anderson, memorandum on the "Northern Boundary," attached to Anderson to Root, November 7, 1906, in State Dept. Numerical File, 1906–1910, case file 839, vol. 120, NARG 59.

¹⁸ Here and below, see Bevans, *Treaties*, 12:297–310; Classen, *Thrust and Counterthrust*, 360. The International Waterways Commission was the forerunner of the International Joint Commissions established by the Boundary Waters Treaty of 1909. L[ouis] M. Bloomfield and Gerald F. Fitzgerald, *Boundary Waters Problems of Canada and the United States*, 10, 15 (Toronto, 1958).

¹⁹ For the names and terms of King's and Tittmann's successors to 1979, see IBC, *Annual Joint Report, 1978*, 28 ([Washington, D.C.], 1979]).

²⁰ Tittmann to Bryan, August 30, 1913; E. C. Barnard to Secretary of State Robert Lansing, September 14, 1916, both in State Dept. Decimal File, 1910–1929, file no. 711.42151, items no. 303, 323, NARG 59; IBC, *Report of Boundary from the Northwesternmost Point of Lake of the Woods to Lake Superior*, 32.

²¹ IBC, *Report of Boundary from Gulf of Georgia to Lake of the Woods*, 93–99.

²² Here and the following three paragraphs, see IBC, *Report of Boundary from Gulf of Georgia to Lake of the Woods*, 100–103, 118, 140. A cast-iron boundary monument like those set in the 1870s was donated in 1934 to the collections of the Minnesota Historical

Society; it reportedly once stood at Pembina. Another stood in front of the house at 3311 Holmes Avenue South, Minneapolis, in 1975. A similar post is said to have been found in a Minneapolis freight office about 1934. *Minneapolis Journal*, August 30, 1938, p. 11.

Marker number 925 replaced the original number 2. The original monument number 1 was a reference marker placed on the north side of Angle Inlet. U.S. Dept. of State, *Reports upon the Survey of the Boundary*, 35. See also IBC, *Report of Boundary from Gulf of Georgia to Lake of the Woods*, 103.

²³ Here and two paragraphs below, see IBC, *Report of Boundary from the Northwesternmost Point of Lake of the Woods to Lake Superior*, 23, 29–54, 81. See also an accompanying volume entitled *Triangulation and Traverse Sketches*.

²⁴ On the 1913 and 1914 seasons, see IBC, *Report of Boundary from the Northwesternmost Point of Lake of the Woods to Lake Superior*, 42–61.

²⁵ Tittmann to Bryan, July 2, 1914, in State Dept. Decimal File, 1910–1929, file no. 711.42152, item no. 9, NARG 59.

²⁶ Tittmann to Bryan, March 6, 1915, in State Dept. Decimal File, 1910–1929, file no. 711.42151, item no. 313, NARG 59.

²⁷ William E. Scott, "The Nationality of Warren Island," 1, 9–12, unpublished manuscript in MHS Division of Archives and Manuscripts.

²⁸ IBC, *Report of Boundary from the Northwesternmost Point of Lake of the Woods to Lake Superior*, 62–77.

²⁹ IBC, *Report of Boundary from the Northwesternmost Point of Lake of the Woods to Lake Superior*, 88–94, 480; the monuments are listed by number and described on pp. 357–481. The author inspected boundary markers from Gunflint Lake to South Lake, on the lower Pigeon River, and on Height of Land Portage, May 17, 1973, and at Lake of the Woods, May 23, 1972. Examples of some of the 20 types of monuments that have marked the U.S.-Canada boundary are in the Canadian Landmark Collection of the National Museum of Science and Technology in Ottawa.

³⁰ Barnard to Lansing, August 10, 14, 1917, January 5, 1920; memorandum on "Boundary between the United States and Canada east of the summit of the Rocky Mountains," November 9, 1917; Adee to Barnard, November 8, 1917; memorandum on "Demarcation of boundary," November 12, 1920—all in State Dept. Decimal File, 1910–1929, file no. 711.42151, items no. 324, 333, file no. 711.42152, item no. 70, NARG 59.

³¹ Davis to Secretary of State Bainbridge Colby, October 26, 1920, in State Dept. Decimal File, 1910–1929, file no. 711.42152, item no. 70, NARG 59.

³² Here and two paragraphs below, see Bevans, *Treaties*, 6:12 (Washington, D.C., 1971).

³³ Author's interviews with Marie A. Sheehy, administrative officer, IBC, U.S. section, Washington, D.C., March 22, 1971, and A. F. Lambert, commissioner, IBC, Canadian section, Ottawa, November 5, 1971; IBC, *Annual Joint Report, 1978*, 6, 23.

³⁴ James H. Van Wagenen, "International Boundary Commission, United States, Alaska, and Canada," in *American Foreign Service Journal*, 12:197, 222 (April, 1935); author's interview with Francis X. Popper, engineer, IBC, U.S. section, Washington, D.C., August 17, 1977; IBC, *Annual Joint Report, 1978*, 24.

³⁵ IBC, United States and Canada, "Annual Report," for the years 1960–69; Sheehy interview, March 22, 1971; IBC, *Annual Joint Report, 1978*, 10, 17. The unpublished annual reports from 1926 to date are in the IBC offices in Washington, D.C., and Ottawa.

³⁶ IBC, *Report of Boundary from Gulf of Georgia to Lake of the Woods*, 116, 120–123; "Annual Report," 1938, p. 40, 1945, p. 66; inspection by author, May 24, 1972. Small monuments erected at the border on the roads between Vita, Manitoba, and Caribou, Minnesota, and between Piney, Manitoba, and Pinecreek, Minnesota, are no longer in place.

³⁷ IBC, "Annual Report," 1966, pp. 6, 24; Sheehy interview, March 22, 1971; inspection by author, May 23, 1972.

³⁸ The 1908 proclamation was clarified in a presidential proclamation of May 3, 1912, signed by William H. Taft. IBC, *Report of Boundary from Gulf of Georgia to Lake of the Woods*, 22–24; H. George Classen, "Keepers of the Boundary," in *Canadian Geographical Journal*, 65:129 (October, 1962).

Index

THE U.S.-CANADA

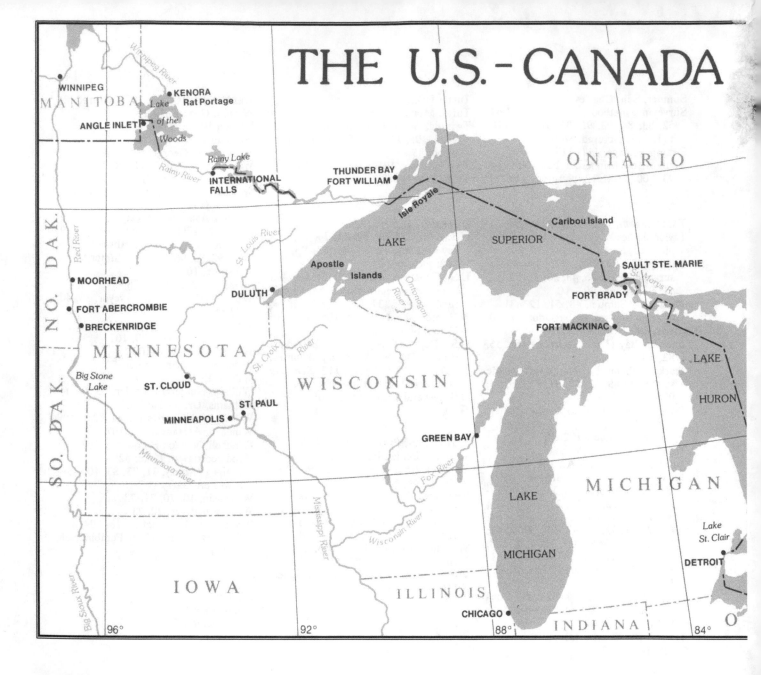

MANITOBA
WINNIPEG
KENORA Rat Portage
ANGLE INLET
Lake of the Woods
Winnipeg River
Rainy Lake
Rainy River
INTERNATIONAL FALLS
THUNDER BAY FORT WILLIAM
Isle Royale
ONTARIO
LAKE SUPERIOR
Caribou Island
SAULT STE. MARIE
St. Marys R.
FORT BRADY
NO. DAK.
Red River
MOORHEAD
FORT ABERCROMBIE
BRECKENRIDGE
SO. DAK.
Big Stone Lake
MINNESOTA
ST. CLOUD
ST. PAUL
MINNEAPOLIS
Minnesota River
Big Sioux River
St. Louis River
DULUTH
Apostle Islands
Ontonagon River
St. Croix River
WISCONSIN
FORT MACKINAC
LAKE HURON
Lake St. Clair
DETROIT
MICHIGAN
LAKE MICHIGAN
GREEN BAY
Fox River
Wisconsin River
Mississippi River
IOWA
ILLINOIS
INDIANA
CHICAGO
96° 92° 88° 84°

PACIFIC OCEAN
Vancouver Island
Vancouver
VANCOUVER
Strait of Georgia
Fraser River
Strait of Juan de Fuca
BRITISH COLUMBIA
ALBERTA
Saskatchewan River
SEATTLE
Columbia River
Rocky Mountains
Confidential Divide
WASHINGTON
ASTORIA
PORTLAND
Columbia River
Snake River
IDAHO
MONTAN
FORT BENTON
Missouri River
OREGON
124° 120° 116° 112°

BOUNDARY

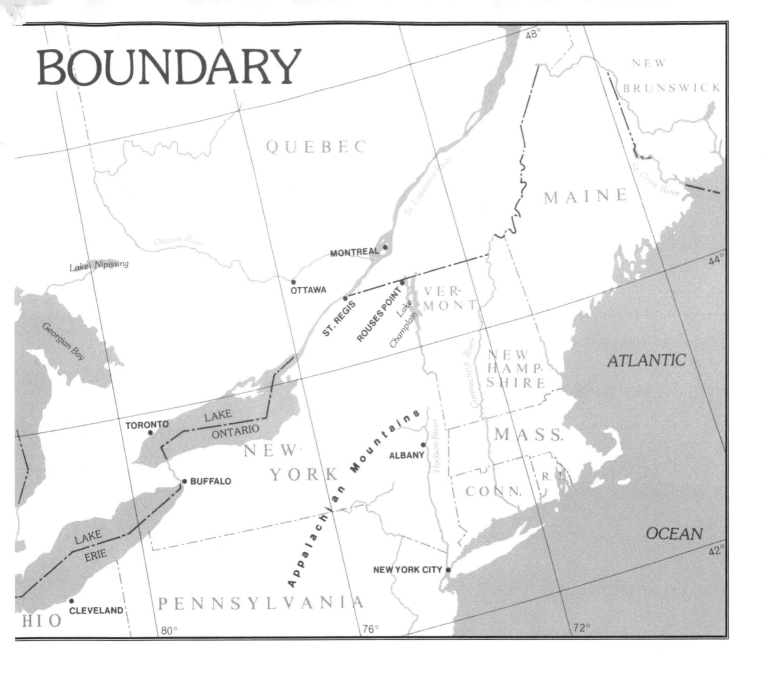

Printed in the USA
CPSIA information can be obtained
at www.ICGtesting.com
JSHW060045150824
68134JS00031B/2646